Making Welfare Work

Making Welfare Work

Reconstructing Welfare for the Millennium

Frank Field

Transaction Publishers
New Brunswick (U.S.A.) and London (U.K.)

Library of Congress Catalog Number: 99–087302
ISBN: 0–7658–0626–6
Printed in the United States of America

Library of Congress Cataloging-in-Publication Data

Field, Frank, 1942-
    Making welfare work: reconstructing welfare for the millennium / Frank Field.
      p. cm.
    Includes bibliographical references.
    ISBN 1–7658–0626–6 (pbk. : alk. paper)
    1. Public welfare--Great Britain. 2. Welfare state. 3. Great Britain—Social policy–1979- I. Title.

    HV248 .F46   2000
    361.941—dc21   99–087302

For John Grigg

Contents

List of Tables and Diagrams

Tables

Diagrams

Acknowledgements

I am very grateful to a number of the librarians in the House of Commons for helping me with material for this book. Andrew Parker obtained for me many of the publications which appear in the bibliography at the end of this volume. Nicola Chedgey, Tim Edwards and Jane Dyson gave me much of the material on the labour market, Robert Twigger on income distribution, Robert Clements on public opinion polls, Adrian Crompton, Mahmud Nawaz, Bryn Morgan and Ed MacGregor the statistics illustrating how the socio-economic changes are impacting on the social security budget. Ed MacGregor in addition prepared most of the tables and diagrams for publication. Eric James kindly read and commented on the last chapter, as did Alan Deacon. In addition, Liam Halligan checked through the entire manuscript. Jane Birkett proof read the whole manuscript and again exercised her exceptional skills in this respect.

There are in addition four special debts which I wish to record. Jill Hendey has typed and retyped various drafts over the three months of the writing of *Making Welfare Work*, and prepared the manuscript for press while accomplishing all her other extensive duties as my secretary. Without her efforts the completion of this book within such a timescale would have been impossible. Richard Cracknell has provided information on a number of the key arguments here as well as commenting on the final chapter. I wish also to record my gratitude for his ability in knowing the direction my mind is working even when I express inadequately the information I need.

Matthew Owen has read through each of the chapters and has sharpened the arguments which follow. I also owe him a debt for encouraging me to complete the book when I could all too easily have abandoned the task. Damian Leeson has read through the manuscript at least twice. But my thanks to him go beyond this task, important as it is. Over the years he has taught me that if an argument is worth stating it should be presented in a style which enhances comprehension. I trust he has been successful.

I am very grateful to all these people for the help they offered in producing *Making Welfare Work* and for doing so in such a graceful manner. None of them of course is responsible for the use to which I have put their work.

Making Welfare Work is dedicated to John Grigg as a sign of my admiration for his work as an historian and journalist as well as his contribution to public life in Britain.

About the Contributors

Jill Deurr Berrick is Associate Adjunct Professor and Director of the Center for Social Service Research at the School of Social Welfare, U.C. Berkeley.

Abraham Doron is Professor at the Paul Berwald School of Social Work at the Hebrew University of Jerusalem. His main field of research is social security policy in Israel and in cross-national comparative perspective. His recent publications include *In Defense of Universality* [(Hebrew), Magnes Press, Jerusalem].

Maurizio Ferrera is Professor of Public Policy and Administration at the University of Pavia. In 1998–99 he was co-director of the European Forum on "Recasting the Welfare State" at the European University Institute in Florence. He has written several articles in English on Italian and comparative social policy. His most recent book in Italian is *Le trappole del welfare* (Bologna, Il Mulino, 1998).

Neil Gilbert is Chernin Professor of Social Services and Social Welfare at the University of California, Berkeley and Director of the Center for Comparative Study of Family Welfare and Poverty.

Sven E. O. Hort is Senior Lecturer in Sociology at S⁻dert⁻rn University College, Stockholm, Sweden, and a visiting professor at the Department of Comparative Politics at the University of Bergen, Norway. He is a former director of the Welfare Research Center and has written extensively on social policy and comparative welfare state development. His most recent book is *Social Policy and Welfare State in Sweden* (Lund:Arkiv, 3rd ed., 1999).

Ken Judge, M.A., Ph.D is a Professor of Social Policy and Director of the PSSRU at the University of Kent at Canterbury. He was previously Director of the King's Fund Policy Institute and Visiting Professor of Social Policy at the London School of Economics & Political

Science. His current research activities include: the national evaluation of health action zones in England, a cohort study evaluating community-based services and outcomes for elderly people, and a study of poverty dynamics and health inequalities.

Peit K. Keizer is Associate Professor of Institutional Economics at the University of Maastricht. His research interests include the institutions of the labor market; the relationship between economics, psychology, and sociology; and the teaching of social sciences.

Ross Mackay is a Special Advisor in the Social Policy Agency of the New Zealand Department of Social Welfare. During 1997 he was seconded to the International Social Security Association (ISSA) in Geneva, where he had responsibilities for organizing the ISSA's Second International Research Conference on Social Security in Jerusalem, Israel. He has published papers on aspects of social security in the Social Policy Journal of New Zealand and contributed the chapter on social assistance to the ISSA's recent publication, "Developments and Trends in Social Security 1996–1998."

Introduction to the Transaction Edition*

Ideas invariably play a dominating role in politics. Sometimes they act as a gatekeeper, imprisoning political players in the past. On other occasions ideas can become a passport to a new life. *Making Welfare Work* was about helping to propel Labour into the future.

Labour's long imprisonment in opposition arose in part from an adherence to ideas which were long passed their sell-by date. The banishment from office also stemmed, more seriously, from the party, broken-backed by election defeat and intellectually bankrupt, being terrorised into mouthing ideas which were an affront to the common decencies felt by most Labour voters.

To compound matters Labour was confronted for most of its 20–year exile by an astute populist leader. Given the choice between a party espousing policies which many voters took as evidence of a severe mental breakdown, and a visionary, if demonic, leader whose assertions always contained, at the least, an element of truth, the winner came as no surprise.

Labour's long haul back to office involved rethinking its economic and social strategy. In most of the parliaments since 1979 much of my time was primarily spent challenging Labour's then current stance, and secondly proposing what an authentic Labour social policy should be. These two operations were intrinsically linked. Countering the political madness of Labour's hard left stance was essentially a holding operation, and one which attempted to offer hope to Labour's long-suffering supporters, persuading them that not all was lost for all time. But this criticism had a second purpose. Behind the first stage of this operation was an underlying set of beliefs and values which were the substructure on which an alternative approach could be built.

Confronting the policies on which Labour had fought elections in

1

1979, 1983, 1987 and 1992 was first dubbed the activity of a maverick. It was only after the 1997 election, when the Prime Minister, Tony Blair, appointed me Minister of Welfare Reform, that the media began to see our task in government as one of 'thinking the unthinkable'.

Thinking the unthinkable was never a task for government. It was, however, a central activity in Opposition. Helping the party confront what had become, for it, unthinkable (although it was only too thinkable, thank goodness, for the electorate) had also everything to do with proposing workable policies. Thinking the unthinkable became the cornerstone on which the welfare reform programme would build once the electorate had signalled its approval. Indeed, one reason why the electorate was prepared to trust Labour with the keys of office was because thinking the unthinkable on welfare had been undertaken prior to the General Election in May 1997 and, more importantly, that such thinking was believed to have been accepted by the leadership. *Making Welfare Work* played a crucial part in the New Labour project.

The Fivefold Agenda

The thinking the unthinkable amounted to a fivefold programme, which consisted of:

- confronting the size and growth of the social security budget, particularly the growth of means-tested welfare.
- accepting that welfare impacts on behaviour and thereby the character of welfare recipients.
- determining that welfare should be offered on the basis of contract as well as sometimes for altruistic reasons.
- realising that universal welfare provision would require partnership with the private sector.
- considering how welfare reform could strengthen civil society.

The Causes of Welfare Expenditure

On a number of occasions the Prime Minister has said that reforming welfare is the big issue facing the British Government. Many commentators believe that welfare is now the central issue in British politics simply because of the growth of the welfare budget during the post-war period. Yet this is only part of a whole range of reasons why the subject has moved to the centre of the political debate.

Welfare expenditure has certainly grown disproportionately in comparison with the rise in the UK's national income. Growing at twice the rate of the economy, social security payments now account for 13 per cent of GDP—up from 5 per cent less than four decades ago. But, it is not simply a matter of the size of the budget, or simply its growth, although these are not issues which should be dismissed. It is, rather, on the causes and consequences of such growth that most attention should be focused. Moreover, it was in explaining why so much of welfare expenditure had eroded life's decencies that much thinking of the unthinkable took place.

There are a number of reasons which account for welfare expenditure's eightfold increase in real terms since 1948.

- More people are eligible for welfare benefits.
- Benefits have increased in real value by two and a half times.
- New benefits, particularly for disabled people, have been introduced.
- Means-tested welfare payments have exploded.

Welfare is offered under three different sets of rules in the United Kingdom. First, there are national insurance benefits. Strict contribution conditions have to be fulfilled before benefits are paid. A second category of benefits is known as non-contributory insurance benefits. People qualify for help by being deemed to be in a particular category of need, eg a disability, and the benefits are paid irrespective of the income of the recipient. A third category of welfare is offered only after a test of income and capital, or what we call a means test. The post-war welfare settlement envisaged only a residual role for means testing.

Events turned out rather differently. The safety net national assistance scheme, which has been renamed on numerous occasions, and currently sails under the colours of income support, is now one of the major welfare players. Means-tested help is also now offered in addition to income support in the form of supplements to low wages, help with the cost of housing and meeting council tax bills, meeting the cost of eye and dental care, covering the cost of school lunches, and so on.

In 1948, when the modern British welfare state came into existence, for every one pound spent on means-tested help, over £4 went in the payment of insurance benefits. In 1992, for the first time since the

TABLE I.1
Social Security Expenditure by Benefit Category

Proportion of total spending on contributory, non-contributory non-means-tested and means-tested benefits—GB

	1948/9	**1949/50**	**1978/79**	**1997/98**
Contributory	55%	62%	67%	45%
Non Contributory/				
Non-means-tested	31%	26%	16%	20%
Means tested	13%	13%	17%	35%
Total	100%	100%	100%	100%

Source: DSS Annual Reports; DSS Abstract of Statistics 1997

establishment of a modern welfare state, less than half of the social security budget was spent on financing insurance benefits. This transformation in the ordering of the welfare state is as dramatic as it is significant for the welfare of the wider society.

While the growth of means-tested welfare was apparent throughout the post-war period, its relative importance was dramatically changed in the years following the election of the first Thatcher government in 1979. Before the Thatcher era contributory insurance payments grew in importance—from 55 per cent of the bill (at a time when a huge bill went on non-contributory war pensions which were rightly paid, but which necessarily distorted the proportions spent) up to 67 per cent in the last year of the Callaghan Government in 1978/9. By 1992 that position had so changed that only 49.5 per cent of the total budget went on insurance benefits, with 16.5 and 34 per cent respectively on non-contributory and means-tested benefits. In a little over a decade, a national insurance based system, an approach that might well have appealed to a grocer's daughter such as Mrs Thatcher, was replaced by one where most benefit payments were not linked to contributions. This is again a change that those considering Mrs Thatcher's beliefs would have thought highly improbable.

Thinking the unthinkable on the welfare budget centred on how to realign welfare's finances towards a much greater emphasis on benefits being earned. There was, however, a second reason why thinking the unthinkable concentrated attention on the dominant role means-testing was beginning to play.

Welfare and Behaviour

While it was accepted that there would always be a role for means testing, there was, I believed, before the 1997 general election, agreement on two issues. First, while means testing could not be phased out over-night, the welfare reform programme would ensure that, at the end of the process fewer, rather than more, individuals and families would be dependent upon means tested welfare. Second, welfare expenditure affected how people behaved. The reform programme aimed at a reduced role for means-testing, because this kind of welfare undermined the very behaviour that was central to the building of strong communities and the existence of a vibrant and honest society.

Means tests fly in the face of a duty-based welfare—the kind spelt out clearly in chapter eleven of the British Government's Welfare Reform Green Paper.[1] Part of thinking the unthinkable in Opposition was that a major part of Labour's reform programme would be the creation of new benefits which people would earn, and which would promote work, savings and honesty.

The reasons why post-war welfare in Britain originally laid down almost compulsory insurance coverage are disarmingly simple. With everybody included within the national scheme, risks were spread over the widest possible base. Similarly, with near universal coverage, life's free-loaders had to pay for the benefits they only too readily demanded. Moreover, the insurance principle was seen to support the normal behaviour of people wanting to work, and wishing to save, in order not to be a burden on others. The idea of providing universal flat-rate minimum benefits, determined only by the contribution conditions, was that individuals and families could work at improving their own lot, and do so in a way that added to the general prosperity of the wider society. Insurance-based welfare therefore worked with the grain of human nature.

Means tests on the other hand strike at the heart of this most basic settlement between government and people. Means tests penalise the very basis upon which a free and prosperous society depends. Means tests take account of income. They therefore impose a penal tax on working, or on working harder. Means tests take account of savings. They therefore impose a penal tax on savings. Means tests depend on answering questions about income and savings. They therefore impose a penal tax on honesty.

While any level of means-tested provision could have this impact on the actions of recipients, the concern about means tests becomes of a different order when every third pound of welfare is paid on a means-tested basis. Under the Tories the numbers of individuals living in households dependent on one or more means-tested benefits doubled from 1 in 6 to 1 in 3 of the entire population.[2]

There are a number of forces at work which account for the insidious dominance of means-tested welfare. One is that insurance benefits are paid at a lower level than means-tested entitlement. People without other income or savings have to claim means-tested benefits to bring their income up to the minimum guaranteed by the state.

Another reason was that past governments saw extending means-tested help both as the least costly option, and one which also concentrated help on the most vulnerable. Who, it was argued, could be against that dual proposition? It was when the longer-term consequences of means-tested help were factored into the equation that a much more considered answer could be provided.

An equally important and insidious reason for the growth in means-tested expenditure is that means-tested welfare teaches people the benefits of dishonesty and bad behaviour. Of course, for many people means-tested benefits are a lifeline, rightly seized after what are often long periods of low-paid employment. Many beneficiaries claim help in utterly good faith. But not all claimants are as straightforward. For many the rules are well known: do not work, and the state will look after you. Do not save, and the state will come to your rescue. Do not tell the truth, and the state will reward you with taxpayers' money. A dominance of means-tested welfare therefore undermines the very foundations of the idea of the good society, of which welfare's original idealism was a crucial part.

Moreover, once individuals are on means-tested welfare they soon realise that they are trapped. Here is one of the major reasons why this part of the welfare bill expands inexorably. Disengaging from means-tested welfare is bad for your income. Indeed, in extreme cases, individuals trying to extricate themselves from means-tested welfare can find themselves worse off. Others face marginal tax rates on their effort of 50, 60, 70, 80 or 90 per cent—all rates above what is deemed unacceptable in the UK for those paying higher rate of income tax i.e. 40 per cent. Once on means-tested welfare the pressures work to keep people there. Instead of welfare acting as a springboard to freedom it becomes a trap to long-term dependency.

Contract Welfare

The changing composition of the welfare bills—from financing the costs by way of insurance contributions to a growing reliance on taxed financed non-contributory benefits—was tracked by a transformation in the ideas the elite held about welfare. Indeed, it would have been surprising if the public language about welfare had not developed in order to justify the dramatic financial basis on which welfare is built. From a starting position that welfare was earned by way of contributions, welfare was allowed to develop into a system based on the much vaguer concept of citizenship.[3] This change in the language of welfare also reflected a fundamental shift in the nature of what welfare was perceived to be about. From the very rigorous concept of earning insurance cover, welfare developed into an altruistic act that was awarded unconditionally.

Thinking the unthinkable on this front meant asking why people needed welfare. Was it because society determined who would fail, and welfare was a compensation for failure? Or did individuals have some say in events and even some responsibility for what happened to themselves? The answers to both questions were important for they determined the nature of the welfare offered.

It is impossible to consider this aspect of the debate about thinking the unthinkable in Britain without calling into court the ideas of Richard Titmuss. Titmuss, originally an insurance clerk, became one of the most talented and creative of social policy academics. The story of how his ideas spread, largely creating a new discipline in the UK, has yet to be told adequately. Two aspects of his thinking are of importance to the challenge we are now facing.

In opening his British academic career Titmuss rallied the troops to the view that poverty should be considered, not in terms of individual failure, but in structural terms. An individual was poor because he or she lived in a society where there were not enough jobs, or the jobs paid low wages, or the earnings from those jobs prevented workers saving for their old age. Poverty was not caused by personal actions, let alone inadequacies. An individual's actions and motivations were not relevant considerations.

By themselves, such views might be considered an interesting, if eccentric part of the debate. However, when linked with another of Titmuss's premises, a very different political cocktail was being marketed. Titmuss believed that we were on the threshold of abundance: in 'an age of abundance of things, the production of consumption goods will become a subsidiary question for the West'[4]

In this age of abundance, whatever the nature of welfare had been, it would be transformed. Welfare could be delivered free of conditions and obligations. Judgements need not be made of those presenting themselves for help. Indeed, the lack of such judgements was central to Titmuss's belief about how universal welfare services could help establish a fundamental equality between individuals.

This belief in equality was the driving force in Titmuss's work. In setting this goal he followed the political tradition set by another Richard, in this case Tawney. Tawney's ideas about equality sprang from his views about the Creation. According to Christian tradition, men and women are created in God's image. Their equality stems from this most basic of facts about their existence.

But Tawney accepted in total the Christian cosmology, not just the attractive parts of it. The nature of man was the putty which the reformers might try to mould into a structure of great beauty. But that putty was stamped right through by man's fall. So while mankind had the possibility of being redeemed, and therefore of perfection, the only starting point for reformers was his fallen nature, which was his characteristic in this world.

The Christian view of mankind led reformers to promote a different view of welfare from those Centre-Left agnostics. Given the nature of man, it was unwise in most instances to provide welfare without conditions. Moreover, the age of abundance was still far off. Welfare was a scarce commodity. Given human nature, individuals were likely to respond more carefully if the benefits they were drawing had been earned and were not presented as free and without obligation.

Thinking the unthinkable on this front required placing a Christian understanding of mankind centre-stage. Understandably, though, no-one spoke in a Christian language which, far from being a purveyor of meaning, has fast become a barrier to understanding in Britain (although possibly not in the US). But the policy followed from this analysis; welfare was returned to its status of being earned, and on the basis of a contract setting out clearly the conditions which needed to be fulfilled before welfare was offered.

Similarly, the Christian view of human nature leads to a sceptical appreciation of the role altruism should play as a motive force underpinning welfare's provision. For Titmuss welfare should be organised on a basis so that the human social and biological need to help others could be expressed through national institutions. In altruism Titmuss saw a major driving force both in supporting and shaping welfare.

For the Christian apologist a comparison with love and justice is here highly relevant. Love (altruism) might be expressed within small groups such as families or within very close friendships. But it was not a motive by which the institutions of wider society could be safely governed. Here justice was the highest ideal by which human beings could operate.

This is not to say that altruism is not practised by individuals beyond the closed group. Nor that the quality of life in the public domain is not raised when it is operated on a wider platform. It clearly is. It implies, rather, that such actions will necessarily be partial and inoperative over much of society for much of the time. Thinking the unthinkable here concerned two related issues. Welfare had to return to being a good which had to be earned and was conditional on a range of qualifications being fulfilled.[5] And a clear distinction had to be made between the motive force in the most intimate of social groups, where altruism or love operated, and the more general and robust principles of justice by which welfare could operate in the wider society.

Universalism: The Goal

The fourth area where thinking the unthinkable occurred in opposition was on the means by which universal provision of benefits could be maintained. Until this point it had simply been assumed that, as night followed day, universal provision was only possible through a state-run scheme. Thinking the unthinkable involved cutting this conceptual umbilical cord which tied the form of benefit to the means of its delivery.

The British Left's response to initial attempts to see universal benefits separately from their means of delivery was one of extreme scepticism, if not outright opposition. For the Left, such a strategy was merely a clever ploy to destroy the universalism of the 1945 Labour

Government's settlement. The very opposite was, of course, the case. Only by separating the need for universal provision from a state monopoly supply would it be possible in the future to extend the universal ideal. The attempts to find new ways of delivering universalism was not an isolated policy objective. It was a crucial part in building up a strategy where social inclusion moved beyond being merely a political slogan.

To think along these lines, of course, held dangers. Politicians might simply use the first part of the analysis, that universal provision should not be equated with state provision, to cut benefits and force people into the private market. But that was not then part of thinking the unthinkable.

The reality running through much of the revisionism was an attempt to come to terms with the public's attitude to the payment of taxes and the receipt of services. In England, in particular, there was and is a resistance to the payment of taxes, yet there continues to be a demand for public services of high quality. Thinking the unthinkable was about trying to square what appeared to be two diametrically opposed circular forces.

A fundamental change had taken place in the British electorate's view of the payment of taxes. A number of factors were at work. The collapse of deference—once a pronounced British characteristic—is in part responsible. The political elite's wisdom about what was good for the masses was not now allowed to pass without rigorous questioning from voters. More important, although perhaps linked, was the impact of rising national income. The Croslandite view[6] (which I used to share) was that, as national income rose, and with it real living standards, resistance to the payment of taxes would decline.

The opposite has in fact occurred. Rising living standards have actually increased resistance to the taxation of incomes. Why? The answer is, once again, disarmingly simple. As real incomes have risen, so too have the choices open to individuals on how that income might be spent. And these are choices that individuals themselves increasingly want to make.

The idea that rising tax bills will be hidden by rising real wages has proved to be one of the great fallacies of the post-war period. Higher income now offers a growing body of voters the chance for the very first time to make major decisions about the composition of their standard of living. Unsurprisingly, such opportunities are seized with relish.

Instead of merely railing against this change, thinking the unthinkable was about accepting it as the framework within which the development of welfare should take place. The challenge for the Centre Left was how to make the provision of universal services compatible with this new set of voter preferences. New membership-run organisations would need to be offered if voters were to forgo part of their current income to meet their own future welfare liabilities.

A key area is pensions. Not only is this the largest part of the budget. So much of the successful implementation of the fruits of thinking the unthinkable rested on putting in place a successful comprehensive pensions reform.

New thinking on that subject may be said to have begun with the publication of a Fabian pamphlet by Matthew Owen and myself.[7] Its aim was to show how it was possible, with the restraint taxpayers now impose on policy makers, to achieve adequate universal provision of pensions. The means to that end was to form a partnership with the private and mutual sectors. I stress the word partnership. Thinking the unthinkable was not then about how the state could cut and run on its responsibilities. Those first ideas have since been developed. But the objective of universal funded pensions is central to the whole development.

Welfare and Democracy

The fifth area where thinking the unthinkable took place in the UK centred around the nature of civil society. This issue was not a semi-detached part of the reform agenda. It was and is intimately linked with how welfare affects behaviour and thereby character. It is crucially linked to how best to police welfare expenditure. It was equally concerned with strengthening democracy, at a time when constitutional reform is being undertaken with real vigour.

Beveridge claimed that the social security system born out of his great report[8] mysteriously grew into an adult who, in significant respects, both shocked and displeased him. Beveridge may well have been both shocked and displeased with the outcome, but the welfare system we have today is very much governed by the genes which were implanted by his 1942 report.

What was so surprising was that Beveridge seemed willing to ignore so many of the lessons he had learned over the previous 40 years, starting with forays into society from his base at Toynbee Hall.[9] Beveridge, like most of the great reformers in Britain of that period, such as the Webbs and the Bosanquets, was intrigued by the startling social advance made by so many of the skilled working class during the late Victorian and early Edwardian age. The mechanism of this success, and how it could be transmitted to other parts of the working class, was a key obsession with reformers.

Both Left and Right located the motive force of such social advance in the friendly society movement. The friendly societies were part of a self-help culture of the Victorian age and they prospered at a time when individuals genuinely believed that they could advance their own self-interest, and that of their neighbours, by joining together in voluntary associations. So why was it that Beveridge ended up making proposals which struck at the very basis of the self-help organisations in civil society?

In part, Beveridge was hoist with his own petard. His committee was established merely to conduct a tidying-up operation across the social services. It was Beveridge who galvanised that body into one which produced a great official report. But to make the case for revolutionary change—for that is what Beveridge aimed to do—he was forced to draw a picture of the unhappy state of pre-World War Two welfare. Much was then wrong. But Beveridge felt the need to exaggerate the problem with which he set about dealing.

Crucial to his argument was the inadequacy of the coverage of friendly society schemes. Above all—so the charge sheet read—they had failed to ensure universal coverage. That Beveridge underestimated the effectiveness of these schemes is now more widely appreciated. That a million fewer women had insurance coverage at the start of Beveridge's scheme in comparison with the pre-war status quo hints at a range of welfare coverage Beveridge knocked away in his bid, ironically, to provide that elusive universal provision.

Part of Beveridge's brilliance was to see the opportunity of presenting welfare reform as part of the post-war settlement, and as a prize to the British nation for enduring the hardships that the fight against Nazism necessarily entailed. To build on existing provision would have been a painstaking and slow process and it could not have been presented to a nation at war as a new beginning at the close of hostilities. So the existing structure was to be swept away and a national system of benefits paid at a minimum level introduced. As a sop to the old order Beveridge suggested that friendly societies should have a role in administering sickness benefit.

Beveridge replaced the friendly society administrator with the government official, and the voluntary organisation of welfare by a government body. He also replaced the easy policing which came from individual friendly society officers knowing personally who was claiming benefit with little, if any, checks at all by officials. The utopian belief was that people would not cheat their own schemes—as opposed to those run by private companies.

The trade unions, acting as they so often did as friendly societies, knew otherwise. Here is an example cited by Jose Harris of how tight a ship friendly societies insisted on operating.

> In cases of fraud, however trivial, unions had no hesitation in bringing benefit swindlers before the court. 'The society had no vindictive feelings', reported the AST (the Amalgamated Society of Tailors and Tailoresses) in 1910 on the occasion of the prosecution of a sick member who had altered a benefit cheque for five shillings, 'but they felt that this was a matter which should be brought forward as a warning and deterrent against the committal of similar offences.' When this particular offender was sentenced to five months imprisonment with hard labour he was expelled from the society: 'we are well rid of such characters' was the comment in the Union's monthly report.[10]

Beveridge also believed that, by proposing minimum rates of benefit, a growing body of individuals would add a second tier of benefits based on voluntary contributions. Here he was wrong twice over. The minimum soon settled in the public mind as the maximum that they needed to provide for themselves. And, more importantly, because insurance benefits were soon paid at below the value of means-tested benefits, any additional individual coverage made the saver ineligible for the extra help on offer.

It is nevertheless important not to forget in the weighing of these reforms the advantage which Beveridge's scheme provided for most contributors, and the way most contributors saw the scheme in those early days. There was considerable enthusiasm for the proposals which held out, for the very first time, the possibility of abolishing Want in the UK. But, equally, it is important not to be blind to the downside of what amounted to the nationalisation of welfare. Beveridge, the great advocate of mutuality, and of self-help as a great engine of social advance, ironically proposed reforms which cut at the very root of the self-help membership organisations. More than any person this century Beveridge laid bare a whole swathe of civil society.

The effect of this devastation is now apparent. Beveridge's welfare state has helped sap individual responsibility and initiative. It was no longer an individual's responsibility to look after himself and his family. "Once the individual had paid the necessary minimum contributions, the responsibility was seen to be transferred to the state". And then, worse still, this attitude spread to other non-insurance benefits and how they were viewed. They too became perceived as a right, even though no direct contributions had been paid to finance them.

Joined Up Policy

These five areas were not disparate initiatives. They were, in fact, part of building a new cohesive idea of welfare that would itself be part of the Government's wider objective for downsizing the state. That redefinition of the state was to be achieved by redrawing the boundary line between what should properly be undertaken by the individual and family, and which responsibilities could be safely left to the government. Thinking the unthinkable was about changing the balance between these different motive forces governing society.

The project was essentially a conservative one. It was about ensuring that the common decencies held by most people became once again the main stimulus of public policy. Thinking the unthinkable meant returning to those first principles that most of us still hold to be self-evident truths. Thinking the unthinkable involved accepting that the only sure foundation for welfare was to build on the natural impulses in most of us to look after ourselves and those we most love. This aspect joined with other elements of the project to recognise the danger means-tested provision posed to the operation of such decent impulses. Means tests undermine the foundation of an approach based on self-help and family responsibility, and makes those who behave decently feel foolish and taken for a ride by the more unscrupulous citizenry.

Thinking the unthinkable was therefore linked to ideas which pondered how best to transform the growing dominance of a means-tested welfare. Labour was to inherit a welfare state, a significant part of which acts as a ceiling over the head of most claimants, preventing them from advancing their own and their families' wellbeing by working, saving, and acting honestly. The quest was therefore for a welfare state which removed that barrier and acted as a springboard to freedom. Such a springboard could only be built if welfare provided a tier of help upon which individuals could build by their own efforts and not be penalised for so doing.

Rebuilding and repositioning civil society in the democratic life of the country also linked with other parts of the general project. The growing resistance of UK voters to ever higher tax bills led to considering in what circumstances taxpayers would more enthusiastically meet their own future welfare liabilities. The growth of membership-run organisations, helping to provide overall a universal provision, was where thinking the unthinkable inexorably led on this issue.

Equally, thinking the unthinkable was part of the great debate on constitutional change in the UK. It is impossible to conceive of a true democracy in which there is not universal suffrage. But having the vote does not alone make for a mature democracy. Both the representation of interests and the safeguarding of individual freedom require a flourishing civil society.

The rebuilding of those institutions which encompass more than individuals and families, but which are less than the state, was also part of thinking the unthinkable. Indeed, for most English voters (who constitute the vast majority of the UK electorate) the rebuilding of such defences against an all too powerful government, and the opportunities gained thereby for greater freedom, held more attraction than the seemingly endless debate on Scottish, Welsh and Northern Ireland devolution and the impending reform of the House of Lords.

How to Pay for the Future

Making Welfare Work was followed by the publication of *How to Pay for the Future*.[11] The central question posed here was whether Labour could win the new voters it needed to command a majority in the House of Commons, while at the same time maintaining its commitment to protect and promote the interests of the poor. The danger was that the poor would be forgotten in Labour's understandable desire to build a winning coalition of voters amongst the significantly expanded middle class.

How to Pay for the Future believed it was possible to achieve the dual objective of winning on an inclusive ticket, provided that three objectives were met. The first was that the significant economic and social changes, brought about by the Thatcher reign, should be largely accepted. It was not simply that they represented forces too powerful to ignore. It was rather that the move to greater freedom and choice which resulted from many, though not all, of those changes, had become inexorable and viewed as a fundamental part of the good life itself, not merely as an accidental advantage.

Second, the simple point so long ignored, that human nature underpins all practical political activities, had to become a determining force in the political debate on welfare's reconstruction. Self-interest is the great driving force within each of us. No great secular institution can fulfil the objective for which it was established unless this most basic of facts is recognised and utilised. Self-interest, a potentially positive force, is not to be confused with the negative quality of selfishness. *Making Welfare Work* and *How to Pay for the Future* sought to promote a new welfare settlement which afforded self-interest its proper place in the scheme of things. It also sought to create new institutions through which welfare could be delivered and which accepted as irreversible many of the new social and economic factors shaping Britain as it approached the Millennium.

Third, Labour required a different political strategy to that upon which it had operated in the past. The writing of *Making Welfare Work* and *How to Pay for the Future* forced me to think carefully about the process of political change in the UK. The idea that all that was required was a repositioning of the 1960s approach to reform was decisively rejected. The model I followed when working for the Child Poverty Action Group[12] was to try and harness the sharp-elbow approach of the middle classes so that as they pushed their way to the front of the queue they brought the poor along with them. Such a strategy was not absent from *Making Welfare Work*, or *How to Pay for the Future*. But a more fundamental approach in building a basis for a successful reconstruction involved grouping welfare reconstruction around that aspect of the status quo with the greatest attraction to the electorate.

Voters attach very different priorities to the disparate policies and institutions which go to make up public policy. And these priorities are clearly different in many of the member countries of the European Union. For many European member states the role of pensions and other welfare benefits is much more politically sensitive than in Great Britain. Here the re-establishment of a welfare state after World War Two played a crucial part in the post-war reconstruction of Continental Europe. They were credited with a position in public esteem which held them aloof from political attack.

It is inconceivable, given our different political culture, that a British Prime Minister should feel the need to write a personal letter to all pensioners telling them that their state pension was safe in his hands, as Chancellor Kohl did to German pensioners. Indeed, state pensions in Britain were not safe in the government's hands. That is why decisive changes were proposed to the ownership of schemes and their capital in *Making Welfare Work*. Similarly, it is unlikely that Britain would see industrial unrest erupting on the streets in protest against those welfare cuts, to the degree that Germany, France and Italy have experienced.

In Britain, in contrast, welfare's political touchstone is the National Health Service (NHS). This is one of the institutions which the majority of the electorate regard as politically sacred. Poll after poll show individuals willing to pay more for their NHS and, perhaps without expressing so directly, affirming thereby their commitment to the one area where altruism is more equally aligned with self-interest. *How to Pay for the Future*'s costings started from this point of greatest strength. It proposed that the general reform of welfare—moving to a greater degree of insurance-based and individual funding—should be seen as part of the major shift to an insurance tax base in which NHS funding is far more insurance-based than it is currently. For the first time ever, the Government Actuary[13] was employed to cost the reforms detailed in a non-government reform programme.

A basic premise of *How to Pay for the Future* was that people would be prepared to foot the bills necessary for safeguarding and improving the NHS, and other strategic parts of welfare, if they had a control over where their contributions went. The electorate are ahead of politicians in facing up to the fact that, increasingly, the state's provision of welfare will not meet their needs, and that they will have to resume greater responsibility for their family's welfare. But there is an understandable reluctance to think about meeting higher costs unless the rules of the game are radically redrafted. The schemes must be owned and run by the contributors themselves; only in this way will they become protected against the kind of raiding activity governments have launched in the past against the national insurance scheme. Such a reform was not a plea for privatisation. Rather it sought opportunities to build new individually-owned but collectively-run bodies which were independent of the state.

There was no attempt to underplay the significance of these changes. The reforms represented a decisive break with post-war paternalism. In summary, *How to Pay for the Future*:

- would accept the best of this century's social security provision as the basis on which to build the aspirations voters wished to realise in the millennium;
- would enhance the position of those in need at the expense of those claiming fraudulently;
- would build a new partnership between the state and the individual in a world where the state's role is being downsized, and the individual's wish for greater control over his or her income is increasing;
- would transform a welfare state where means tests promoted idleness, dishonesty and a lack of savings, into one which rewarded work, savings and honesty;
- would transfer the implicit individual responsibility to oneself and one's family in general taxation, making it explicit by a switch to an insurance-based contributory system;
- would transform a central state operation by new forms of collective provision which were individually owned;
- would replace the growing breakdown of joint endeavours with new organisations fostering social cohesion;
- would tackle the growing budgetary crisis by replacing Treasury control over expenditure levels with greater individual contributor control;
- would offer greater freedom to many with protection for the vulnerable.

These then were the ideas which helped put wind into its sails as Labour took possession of the ship of state on May 1 1997. Soon it will be possible to begin evaluating not only the direction of the Blair Government's welfare reform programme, but how far those reforms match the plans and aspirations set out in opposition.

January 1999

Notes

* I am grateful to John Grigg and Damian Leeson for their detailed comments on this introduction and to Jill Hendey who prepared it for publication.

1. *New ambitions for our country: A New Contract for Welfare*, London, HMSO, 1998.

2. At the time of writing this book the government stated it was unable to provide a figure on the proportion of the UK population dependent on at least one means-tested welfare benefit. The figure in the text is 1 in 3. This figure was provided by statisticians in the House of Commons Library. Once these data had been published the Government then found itself able to publish its own estimate of 1 in 6 of the entire population living in households drawing at least one means-tested benefit.

3. I agree that citizenship has a part to play in distributing welfare, as it must do in any society based on the Christian ethic. However, a national welfare system cannot exist only on the basis of responding to the definition of responsibilities to one's neighbour as set out in the parable of the Good Samaritan. It is however essential that this ethic should play a part as *one* of the underlying principles of welfare, in order to mitigate against the brutalising aspects of modern society.

4. Cited in Alan Deacon, 'Richard Titmuss: Twenty Years On', *Journal of Social Policy*, Vol 22, April 1993, 237.

5. For a study of the role of conditionality at the advent of Britain's welfare state, and its collapse, and the call for its reimposition see Frank Field and Matthew Owen, *Beyond Punishment*, London, Institute of Community Studies, 1994

6. C A R Crosland was the major revisionist post-war thinker of Labour politics, before the current round of New Labour revisionism under the Blair Government. Crosland's most influential book was *The Future of Socialism* which was published in 1956, London, Jonathan Cape.

7. Frank Field and Matthew Owen, *Private Pensions for All*, London, Fabian Society, 1993

8. *Social Insurance and Allied Services*, London, HMSO, 1942, Cmd, 6404 reprinted in 1995

9. Toynbee Hall is the most famous of the settlement houses established towards the turn of the last century as a means of bridging the gap between classes in Britain.

10. 'Victorian Values and the Founders of the Welfare State' in *Proceedings of the British Academy*, 78, 1992, p.176

11. *How to Pay for the Future: Building a Stakeholders' Welfare*, Frank Field, London, Institute of Community Studies, 1996.

12. The Child Poverty Action Group was established by a small group of Quakers in 1965 and at one time was the most influential of the campaigning social pressure groups in Britain.

13. The Government Actuary's Department (GAD) was created in 1919. The Department provides a full actuarial consultancy service to ministers and Government departments, to many public sector bodies and to some overseas Governments, covering financial and statistical matters, including pensions, insurance, social security and demography. It is staffed by over 90 Civil Servants, about half of whom are qualified Actuaries.

Introduction

Britain's welfare system is broken-backed: the number of claims escalates and so, therefore, does the welfare bill. Yet, independence is not encouraged. Already half the population lives in households drawing one of the major means-tested benefits. Means tests paralyse self-help discourage self-improvement and tax honesty while at the same time rewarding claimants for being either inactive or deceitful. Means tests are the poison within the body of the welfare state.

This introduction summarises the key points of *Making Welfare Work* which are elaborated upon in the text. The current political orthodoxy is challenged here, particularly its emphasis on the role of legislation alone in bringing about social improvement. *Making Welfare Work* argues that the impact which legislation has on character is pivotal to human advance. Any welfare reconstruction needs to address and channel the differing roles of self-interest, self-improvement, and altruism, which are among the great driving forces in human character. A successful welfare state must reflect these important forces which influence our nature. To create an imbalance between these three motive forces, the most dominant of which is self-interest, will undermine welfare's objectives.

Making Welfare Work also attempts to realign the British debate in a number of additional respects.

1. It attempts to take welfare out of the ghetto with its over-riding emphasis on tackling poverty. It refocuses the debate so that welfare is seen as underpinning living standards generally and securing improvement for the poor as part of a general advance for the whole community.
2. There is no general groundswell amongst middle-class groups for redistribution of wealth to the poor, particularly in the aftermath of the Thatcher years. Politicians who maintain otherwise are a public menace distracting from the real task. *Making Welfare Work* argues that changes

for the poor will only come about if the self-interest of the majority is mobilized in a way which also promotes the common good.

3. Similarly, defining a poverty line, or a minimum income level, is demonstrated to be a political eldorado for any welfare scheme. Nor is the aim of *Making Welfare Work* the traditional goal of raising the value of insurance benefits in order to float people off means tests. Here is the break with Beveridge. The primary goal should be to gain *comprehensive* insurance cover so that families are in a position to improve their own lot legally and by their own efforts. Welfare should create an income floor to replace the income ceiling created by means-tested welfare. The proposals here are for an insurance cover which actively promotes self-interest and self-improvement, and which will free individuals from dependence upon the state and thereby improve their own sense of worth.

4. *Making Welfare Work*'s programme aligns with the electorate's wish for a greater control over their own affairs. It sets out a series of *social* as opposed to *state* collective initiatives. The measures are collectivist in that they apply universally, but social in the sense that individuals have a decisive say over the control and ownership of the assets and entitlements which they are building up.

The public arena is increasingly a 'no go' area for agreed rules of conduct. In the vacuum created by the growing collapse of what used to be called public morality, *Making Welfare Work* seeks to establish a welfare system which affirms some of the verities—such as honesty, the importance of hard work being rewarded, and the necessity to safeguard savings, all of which are crucial to the effective functioning of a free and healthy society.

The growth of individualism is not going to be arrested by talk about rebuilding the community. Welfare has to be shaped so that individual wishes can simultaneously promote new senses of community. The stakeholder welfare scheme proposed here does precisely that. Real power is delegated to stakeholder boards governing both the new insurance scheme and the universalisation of private pension provision. Stakeholder welfare provision ushers in a period of popular or social, as opposed to state, collectivism.

Making Welfare Work fleshes out what joint public and private initiatives should mean. The traditional Left's idea of universalised provision is applied to the private sector. Already more funds are contributed each year towards private pension provision than are allocated to covering the cost of the state retirement pension. Most of British industry is now owned by pension fund trustees. This simple fact should have a profound effect on the Left's thinking in regard to its more general industrial strategy.

It is by channelling self-interest and self-improvement in a manner which enhances the common good that talents and forces in Britain's ghetto areas, and the country's burgeoning underclass, will be linked back into mainstream activities. This programme will also appeal to mainstream Britain. Here the older order of jobs for life has already passed. The uncertainty implicit in a flexible labour market needs to be countered by a certainty offered from a flexible welfare state.

The Beveridge Report reflected a broadly-based and strongly registered consensus within the wider society which does not exist today. As well as setting out alternatives, reform programmes today have an additional task: of raising hopes that reforms are not only urgent and desirable, but also practicable. In this way proposals for change will help generate their own political constituency. The aim of *Making Welfare Work* is not simply to argue how urgent the need for welfare reconstruction is, but also to show how a 20–year reform programme can operate to help mobilise the new widespread consensus for change.

Making Welfare Work's aim is to replace over this period the plethora of means-tested assistance which now catches half the population within its domain. It proposes the progressive replacement of means-tested assistance:

1. by extending coverage of a new insurance system run by a National Insurance Corporation. The corporation would be a tripartite body (employers, employees, and government representatives) which would have the power to determine the rates of contributions and benefits. The Government would retain only the power of veto.
2. by universalising private pension provision to run alongside the state scheme, which would be the task of a Private Pensions Corporation. This would be independent of the Government and would organise the task of spreading private pension provision within a framework of compulsory contributions by employees and employers.

The new insurance system would be designed to offer income security in a world of growing flexibility in the labour market. The particular reforms which would achieve this are:

1. Bringing the currently excluded part-time workers within the insurance scheme.

2. Changing the rigid contribution conditions of set years to a flexible formula.
3. Introducing earnings-related benefits for earnings-related contributions.
4. Keeping a strict link between contributions and benefits. Redistribution must not be by sleight of hand but, instead, be clear, above board and approved by the electorate. The specific Exchequer contributions would cover the lowest paid, the sick, the disabled and the unemployed, and those outside the labour market carrying on recognised and important tasks such as caring for the elderly.

Some individuals will continue to remain on income support, and this is particularly true of single parents. Income support should be transformed into a proactive opportunities agency developing career plans for all non-pensioner claimants for re-entering the labour market. Every non-pensioner claimant would be expected to draw up their career plans. Income support would act as a life raft taking people back into work rather than, as at present, as a sink into which they are dumped. All claimants—except school leavers—would be entitled to turn their income support payments into education maintenance allowances.

In addition social security fraud should be recognised as the very big business it is: operated by individual claimants, by gangs operating against the welfare state, by landlords against housing benefit and by officials within the DSS. Imaginative counter-action needs to be driven by a core of SAS-style anti-fraud officers. Benefit savings from successful anti-fraud campaigns should be ring-fenced for tax cuts and child benefit increases.

1

The New Barbarism

The effects of economic growth used to be likened to a great steamer coming into port and bringing with it a whole barrage of driftwood. The rich would get richer, but not at the expense of the poor. They, too, would benefit.

The trickle-down theory, as it is called, ceased to work in the 1980s. The rich certainly became richer, much richer. But the poorest lost ground, and not just in relative terms. Some groups experienced real cuts in their living standards at a time when the average standard of living rose by over a third.

To talk of real cuts in living standards only hints at what is happening in Britain's poorest areas. Here three important trends, economic, social and cultural, are working their way through and transforming Britain's ghettos. These forces are collectively bringing about a destruction which can only be likened to a social anthrax.

Ghetto Politics

The ghetto is fast emerging into the mainstream of British politics. Here is one of the most marked changes in Britain over the past 30 years. Three decades ago, when Harold Wilson's Government began Britain's urban programme, most poor people lived outside officially designated poor areas. That position is now totally reversed. Most poor people now live in areas which are becoming progressively poorer and more polarised at the same time.

On five criteria, living standards have worsened in the poorest areas during a decade when average living standards rose sharply. The most recent PSI *Urban Trends* (1994) shows evidence of further polarisation:

On Population

Here is one of the signs of growing polarisation not merely between poor areas and the rest of the country but within the poor areas themselves. While the proportion of people with managerial and professional jobs increased faster than the national average in nearly all the poorest areas, so did the proportion of residents from ethnic minority communities and, more significantly, the numbers of one-parent families. The proportion of one-parent families in deprived areas, already higher than the average in 1981, continued to increase 10 years later at a greater pace than in other areas.

On Unemployment

The rate in 1991 was much higher, relatively and absolutely, than in the rest of the country, compared to ten years earlier. Among young men the unemployment rate was on average one in four and rising to one in three in areas such as Hackney, Knowsley and Liverpool.

On Poverty

The proportion of families with children in poverty (defined as having no adult in work or living on income support) increased more in deprived areas than elsewhere over the 1981–1991 decade.

On Crime

Measured in 1983, 1987, and 1991, people in the poorest areas experienced more crime than people living elsewhere and were, understandably, much more concerned than were other people about this issue.

On Death

Life expectancy was shorter in the ghetto areas. The poorest areas again registered higher standards of mortality ratios than elsewhere and for two-thirds of the ghetto areas, the gap between them and the rest of the country continued to widen. Perinatal (during the first week and still births) and infant (during the first year) mortality rates show an upward rise in some of the poorest areas.

These, then, are the main changes over the past decade. How do the ghetto areas look from the inside and what lessons do they hold for the rest of Britain?

The Disinherited Male

The first and dominant force derives its strength from unemployment. Understandably the Government draws attention to its success in job creation. (Conversely, though, it is the world economy, or some other celestial force, which is responsible for redundancies.) Comparing June 1979 with September 1994 we find that not only were there fewer jobs than there had been in 1979; but the total shows a fall in the number of full-time, and a substantial rise in the number of part-time, jobs. Most of the new jobs moreover are in service industries. Most are low paid and part-time. And most have been taken by women. At the same time there has been a major haemorrhage of higher-paid manual jobs in manufacturing industry, traditionally the preserve of male workers.

During the 1979–81 recession 1.8 million manufacturing jobs were destroyed and almost the same number of people joined the dole queue. The balance of trade moved into the red for the first time since Britain pioneered the industrial revolution. The 1981 Budget, still heralded as a miraculous feat which laid the basis for a decade of prosperity, continued the process of wiping out manufacturing jobs and pushing unemployment to a record post-war high. The 1991 Census lists unemployment on a local government ward basis. The blackspots of unemployment show rates in excess of 40 per cent in the worst affected areas. Yet even these figures are an underestimate. Over two million people failed to complete, or appear on, the Census form. Overwhelmingly these are people banished from Mrs Thatcher's kingdom. Unwilling or, much more likely, unable to pay the poll tax, such people voluntarily disappeared from any official count for fear of being traced as non-payers.

Worse still, the poll tax encouraged whole armies of people to break the law for the first time. Some could not pay, like the mentally handicapped pensioners dragged through the courts for non-payment of this now abandoned tax. For these people the poll tax is still a living nightmare. Others have been much more adept at avoiding officialdom. Such fast footwork has its cost. It shows that breaking the law pays. Hundreds of thousands gained their first experience of profitable law-breaking in Mrs Thatcher's tutorial group.

Nor does the Census record the length of time people in areas of mass unemployment have been in search of work. Some families have totally abandoned the idea that paid work has any relevance for them at all, such is the impossibility of finding, let alone being offered, a job.

That simple fact has the most deadly effect. What can we expect from those schoolchildren who, because no member of their family is in work, have not the slightest idea of what it means to earn one's living, of the structure which work gives to the daily round, or of the importance of saving in order to bring forward into reality those small fantasies which are such an important part of life?

Being without work permeates everything. It changes how women regard men, for example. It not only leads to crime but also affects how the probation service then deals with the criminal. What kind of hope can you build into a person's life if there is no chance of work and of therefore beginning to plan what type of life they might lead with their partner?

Destroying Self-Respect and Self-Improvement

Unemployment's evil influence is also to be seen in family life. I leave aside the near continual pain it causes families who have been blighted in this way. I similarly leave aside its corrosive influence on a person's self-worth. I have become hardened to the brave men with laughing mouths but wintry eyes who tell me that it doesn't matter that they may never work again. 'We are working the system,' they defiantly assert. Those wintry eyes, however, tell another story. For others that mask slips. I try to be equally hardened to the men who simply cry before me. Their lives are in ruins. All of the values they have believed to be true are being turned against them as if they were being condemned for adhering to such beliefs. What do you say to a father with mounting debts who will be better off if he asks his teen-age children to leave home? What does that, in turn, say for our benefits system? What does it say about our continuing belief in the importance of the family? What does it teach those children, coming as they have from a family which has always practised what love and mutual responsibility mean?

Here another equally deadly lesson is being taught. The only way to survive is to cheat. And what right do I have to caution, let alone reprimand? Some of my constituents and I share a sense of failure. But it is they who suffer the effects of an economic hurricane which has struck at poor areas.

The cheating stems from the impact of a cruel pincer movement: a dearth of jobs and means-tested welfare. Young single mothers and the young unemployed never gain the right to national insurance cover. For them, and all too often for their parents, the only help is means-tested income support. *Means tests penalise all those values which make strong, vibrant, communities.* Those with savings above a certain level do not qualify. Those who try a part-time job lose almost pound for pound from their benefit. Those who do work, or who have put a little money aside for a rainy day, can qualify, but only if they lie. And the second lie is always easier than the first. Thus the practice of deceit is encouraged by the form of welfare provision. The only cumulative impact of such lying and deceit is the further erosion of any sense of pride, respect and self-worth, which are themselves already under attack in the wake of long-term unemployment.

The New Male

I do not accept the line, fast becoming fashionable here and which, like so much of the poverty debate of the last 30 years, has been dragged across the Atlantic. The latest American wheeze is that working-class girls are faced with a hideous dilemma: all of a sudden there are apparently fewer decent men to marry. It is as though Darwin is being invited to take speed before being called upon to rewrite his *Origin of Species*.

I was first taught about what was happening when going around a tin manufacturing plant in Birkenhead (long since bulldozed as part of making British industry leaner and fitter) in 1981. A number of women workers told me that thanks to family income supplement (now replaced by family credit) and the more generous housing rebates introduced by the last Conservative Government—the one in which Mrs

Thatcher was the big spender at Education—they had got rid of the 'jerk' to whom they had been married. Here was the beginning of a trend which is changing the social position of so many mature working-class men.

Many of these women told me that they had begun their families in fairly conventional circumstances. But now, ten years or more later, they preferred to go it alone. The break-up agreement was that the men would leave, no maintenance would be demanded, but in return, the leaving had to be complete, with fathers having no continuing access to the children. All of the women I spoke to that day expressed satisfaction with the arrangement. The children were not there to ask whether they viewed events so calmly.

I have no doubt that the arrangements were in the best interests of the women. While I am more doubtful about, and less interested in, the effects on the expelled 'jerks', I have almost no doubts about the effects of these unwritten agreements on the children. In most circumstances they are harmful. Stage two of the Child Support Agency's agenda ought to be a rewriting of the rules of access. That was the topic that dared not speak its name when Parliament debated establishing the Agency.

Of course those who have shown any violence, or who are likely to be violent, will be rightly barred by the courts from intruding on their first families. But others, as they begin paying proper levels of maintenance, will probably demand access to the children they are once again supporting. Here, as in so many areas of life, less than wholesome motives can ironically give rise to beneficial results. Irritation at being obliged to contribute a proper amount, so regularly, will lead to the erosion of some mothers' monopoly of access to the children of a broken marriage.

There is a clear distinction between those families which suffer a marital breakdown and those which start out as, and remain as, single-parent families. Marital breakdown is no new phenomenon. It has always played a part in our society. It was a sad reality for my own great-grandparents. Lower life expectancy was then the major cause of limiting the length of a partnership. Offering marriage vows at a time when a marriage lasted possibly only a dozen years, was then a different prospect. Now, when life expectancy is so enhanced, marriages can last for up to 60 years. Here we need to keep a sense of proportion.

It is misleading for the BBC, for example, to keep reassuring the public that most single parents are divorced or separated. That is undeniably correct. But heresy is not the peddling of lies. It is the propagation of one truth to the exclusion of all other truths.

Here then is a modern social heresy. The single parents so described by the BBC are the largest group but only if divorced and separated parents are added together. But the fastest-growing group comprises those who have never married. The likelihood is that among this group mothers will have a number of sexual partners in succession. A series of half siblings results.

One impact of this is to be found in our inner city schools. Children with two parents are rare, and they are made to feel as though they are freaks. One friend of mine ceased to pick up his daughter at school as her classmates pressurised her over the fact that her father came to collect her. The Census data show that there is now a huge number of local government wards where two-thirds of children are being raised in single-parent households.

Unless we are the product of a non-marriage or a broken marriage we cannot appreciate the impact of that fact on the children concerned. At least my grandparents, plunged on to life's helter-skelter with stepbrothers and sisters, knew that their absent parents had not willingly absconded. They had done no more than roll over into dusty death.

The hurt and bewilderment resulting from broken marriages runs deep. A friend in Broken Rites—a support group for deserted clergy wives—told me of her son's wedding. She had always worked and prayed that the impact of a collapsing marriage on her children had been minimised. The great day arrived and there she was sitting in the front pew with her ex-husband. At the point where the registers were to be signed her son announced to the whole congregation that his mother, but not his father, was to be invited into the vestry to sign the register. That was the very first intimation she had ever had of the strength of her son's view about the marriage break-up, and of his attitude to his father. That young man's first comment came in the form of a calculated public humiliation for the man who had left him as a young child over 15 years previously.

Now imagine what it is like never to have known one's father. What does it mean for hundreds of thousands and possibly, by now, millions of young people that their mother has had a number of other partners, most of whom gave her children—their step-brothers and sisters? What message is being put across to children when much of family life is spent eating in front of a TV screen while a succession of different boyfriends occupy the seats behind them?

Permanent Adolescence

The reaction of young women and men arriving at the foothills of adulthood and living in such industrial desolation is becoming marked. Faced with the option of staying with their parents and fulfilling family duties there, many young women are moving away and starting their own families in conditions such as I have described. These young women are generally the least able of their peer group. They have the fewest basic skills and many of them are almost illiterate.

So too are their young male counterparts, but their future is even more dire. There are three main options. They can leave home and become drifters, ending up begging on the streets of one of our main cities. Alternatively they can try their hand at the drug trade and, given the high level of their native intelligence, they believe they will soon be in the big time. Or they may be eventually forced back on to their parents, also desperately poor, and into a state of permanent adolescence. When we consider these young people being stripped of their age of innocence as very young children, and then catapulted into the hazy world of apparently never-ending adolescence, it becomes more obvious why the level of aggression and violence is steadily on the increase.

The common thread of unemployment runs through all these wretched trends. It is unemployment which is the most effective recruiting sergeant for Britain's underclass.

A good case can be made against the use of this term. Bob Holman does precisely this. (*A New Deal for Social Welfare*, Lion, 1993) The phrase has pejorative connotations. When used by the Right, particularly as part of an indiscriminate campaign to cut welfare, it becomes a term of abuse. The word underclass snaps from right-wing tongues like a scourge whipping the feckless, dangerous, and even criminal poor.

I use the term to emphasise that something new is happening and, indeed, has happened. Whatever Britain was like 60, 160 or 360 years ago, the immediate post-war era saw the disappearance of the dispossessed class. Full employment, and both the Coalition and Attlee Governments' welfare reforms are responsible for that revolutionary transformation. Of the two, full employment was the more important causal factor. Its subsequent collapse has been accompanied by the re-emergence of the underclass.

But I don't want to be unfair to the Government by not giving credit where it is due. The Thatcher Government's social security reform, abolishing benefit for the under 18–year-olds, deserves a mention in this infamous roll-call. Many of the thousands of youths begging and sleeping on the streets of our cities are there as a result of these changes. Similarly, the selling off of hospital sites under the guise of a community care programme, and the dumping of long-stay patients outside hospital walls, account for many of the mentally ill who drift aimlessly around our streets. While no one is now supposed to be evicted from hospital until a community care programme is in operation, most patients were unceremoniously dumped before any such guarantee was offered.

The underclass, as I understand it, encompasses more than these two groups. It also consists of those young unmarried mothers who have almost no chance now of leading a normal life unless the welfare rules are radically changed. Likewise, the young unskilled male unemployed worker has been equally banished beyond society's pale. A life on welfare, drugs and crime throws up the most fundamental of challenges from this group.

In all this discussion the danger is that the picture I present will be one-sided; that in an eagerness to report on what is happening I will ignore all those brave souls, the majority, who continue to fight to maintain what most of us would quickly identify as decent standards. It is crucial that in describing the new barbarism which is aggressively making onslaughts in our poorest areas, we never forget those who fight against being overpowered, or simply worn down by the thuggish behaviour all around them. Life in the inner city can be unbelievably cruel. Families not accepting gang norms are quickly picked upon and pushed out or driven into mental illness. But there is a struggle. The gang's values don't command universal acknowledgement, let alone respect. Politicians have yet to begin thinking of policies which support and strengthen this beleaguered majority.

So that possibility of one-sideness must be borne in mind in any discussion about unemployed male youths, and particularly those from the inner cities, or the windswept council estates tossed so casually outside the town's borders.

Cutting the Supply Routes

It is among this young group of males that an underclass of dispossessed youth has been created. Like young women who opt to start a family, these males have been failed by our education system. As the unskilled job openings began disappearing in the late 1960s and 1970s, the school system simply failed to adjust. It kept on spurting out young males who were amply fitted, for example, for work in the docks, which were fast being closed. These lads had none of the skills necessary to win jobs in any of the new industries which were then struggling to establish bridgeheads in the British economy.

The working-class pattern—which appeared set in concrete during the prosperity of the post-war years—was for young, unskilled males, not only to find work speedily on leaving school, but also to be earning a good wage. Here were those years of relative prosperity which Seebohm Rowntree depicted in the cycle of poverty and prosperity which he drew from the first inquiry he conducted of residents in his native York at the turn of the century.

That world has been wiped away as though it never existed. The diet is now restricted to staying on at school or going on to what are kindly described as Mickey Mouse training courses. Not all training courses are poor, thank goodness. To witness some of these young men (and women too) on the best training courses attempting to add up, or being taught to read, leaves me breathless. There are very few signs of the 11 to 12 years of educational investment to which each of these young people has been subjected.

The Devil makes work for idle hands and does so very quickly. With most of the boxing clubs closed, and with no national service, some of these young men expend their excess physical energy in street fights and night-club brawls. With almost no prospect of picking up a job, let alone one with a reasonable pay packet, the temptation to commit crime is considerable. I stress in all of this the word 'temptation'. Some resist. But given that the odds are so stacked against them, the marvel is that all do not succumb.

The Drug Trade

The vacuum left when so much of manufacturing industry was killed off has been filled by a drug culture which now grips many of the areas of high unemployment. And there is nothing remotely romantic about a drug culture gaining sway in what was once a rough but proud working-class community. Hard drugs invariably destroy the life of the addict. The drug economy is policed by fear, violence and, now, ever more commonly, by murder.

Unemployment has also played a part—but only a part—in the seemingly inexorable rise of one-parent families. It is hard to over-emphasise the destructive impact of never-ending unemployment. Recently the head teachers in the poorest areas of Birkenhead delegated one of their number to see me about deteriorating social conditions. There have been outbreaks of dysentery. Some families are permanently suffering from diarrhoea. Some children are now dirty. The collapse of the school health service is good news only for headnits and lice.

At one time these children would respond eagerly to questions about what they wanted to do when they grew up. Now such questions are answered by a surly silence. When pressed about their future the children snap back that they simply want to get out.

And there is one apparently certain way of getting out. The only model of success in their island of desolation is the drug pusher. If ever there was a black economy this is it. There are jobs to be had from the junior position of a young lookout to the more advanced post of small-scale pusher. The drug economy is the only visible model of success in some of Britain's inner city areas. That statement is worth repeating. What it spells for Britain's future is difficult to exaggerate. If the present drift continues, the future will be bleak for an increasing proportion of the population: those affected directly by drugs and those affected indirectly by the crime it brings in its wake.

The line between drugs and crime is a fine one. In some respects it is non-existent. The aim may be to become a big figure and make millions. The goal is understandable. Practically all the TV news on this subject reports gangs making millions. Each drug haul is presented in units of millions of pounds.

Far from seeing examples of such success—maybe there aren't any in Birkenhead—what I do witness is the squalid sight of young people who seem possessed by drugs. Life becomes totally rewritten. Instead of achieving those imagined great business heights of organised drug trafficking, a young person is soon addicted. Everything then revolves around getting the next fix and the ephemeral satisfaction that follows. Money must be obtained—£130 a day in Birkenhead—for cocaine of varying quality.

Possibly as much as three-quarters of urban crime is drug induced. It certainly is in Birkenhead. So not only are those young people destroying their own lives, but they do so in a way which puts whole communities under attack. Nothing is safe. Break-ins are a regular occurrence in some areas. And when there is little left to steal the robbers go further afield. So middle-class areas come under attack. Their videos are as good, sometimes better, than those they have been stealing in their own neighbourhood. Middle-class children also know from school what drug pushing is all about. I cannot explain why some young people become addicted and others do not. There was a time not so long ago when the opinion leaders on the estates were very hostile to drugs. That macho culture recoiled from the despised weirdo who took drugs. Prisons helped change all that. Drug taking is rife inside. Not only is someone making a lot of money in organising such supplies, but, if controlled, drug taking, it is argued, leads to a quieter life amongst the inmates locked up for 23 hours at a time. The prison staff trafficking in drugs have been tolerated on both sides of the iron bars.

The consequences of this are now all too plain. Some of the self-same young men who were once so hostile to drugs, have themselves become addicted in prison. Once a number of them returned home after completing their sentences—sentences which were often handed down for what in retrospect now look like petty crimes—a collapse soon followed on the estates.

Inner City Apartheid

In all sorts of ways the poor are being as successfully segregated geographically as they were in Victorian towns. Housing subsidies, repair grants, and council house sales policy are all playing an important part in achieving this result.

The inner city has been changed too as whole tranches of manufacturing industry have been wiped out. Gone are those crucially important small, back-street firms. If penal interest rates and high exchange rates did not finish them off, local planning regulation renewed the onslaught on their very livelihood.

In some inner city areas nothing much now happens. There are few if any jobs. Local authority budgets have been drastically cut back. City Challenge and similar initiatives now spend what was once local government money.

Apart from endlessly repairing roads (no bad thing) these budgets go on large capital projects—like covered tennis complexes and swimming pools, which will provide few jobs and will see even fewer poor kids being able to meet the entrance charges. Worse still, if Birkenhead is anything to go by, these capital projects employ few local people in their building stages. It is a new and insidious form of imperialism, with private contractors cast in the role of missionaries. There is, however, one difference. This time the missionaries are scooping up all the taxpayers' largesse.

No wonder the normal social fabric gives every appearance of collapsing. Half the workforce is without a job. The vacuum left by the loss of traditional jobs has been quickly filled by the drug trade whose very existence is so far unknown in more affluent areas. Crime has escalated as the drug barons' domain has extended. Each fix has to be paid for one way or another. In some areas two-thirds of the children are being raised by a single parent. A totally new pattern of child rearing and of family life is therefore being established in this country. The return of mass unemployment, the growing influence of the drug culture, and the rise of single parents are all revolutionary changes.

Outside the Ghetto

I have concentrated on what is happening in the poorest areas of the country for this is itself another key change. Thirty years ago most poor people did not live in the ghetto-type areas I have been describing. Now they do. Life is qualitatively different for those poor, and for the people among whom they live, than for the very large numbers of poor who still live outside Britain's ghetto estates. Take, for example, the unemployed who live in areas of high employment. Clitheroe is 54 miles from Birkenhead. Unemployment there is 2.3 per cent. The chances of gaining a job in such circumstances are light years away from the ghetto with more than a 50 per cent unemployment rate. Similarly, single, never-married mothers also have far greater opportunities of breaking back into mainstream life if they live in areas of high employment.

Where there is a greater common denominator between life in the ghetto and the areas beyond is in respect of old people who are poor. While the elderly poor who live outside the ghetto do not face the onslaught of a gang mentality, which now results in so many lives being wrenched asunder, there is a commonality in that for the elderly poor there is no effort they can make on their own behalf which can result in any major material improvements to the shameful, dowdy existence to which many of them are condemned. Only government action offers the prospect of spending the last years of their life in greater material comfort, in greater dignity, and free from the ever constant worry of debt which cannot be repaid.

Policy Conclusions

The charge sheet described in this chapter calls for the election of a great reforming government with the strength and vision to match that shown by the 1906 and 1945 administrations. This book does not, however, aim to detail fully the range of policies which hopefully such a third great reforming government would embrace. These welfare reforms will be critical to that government's success. The macro-changes the Government makes—concerning jobs, inflation, homes, education and so on—will be undermined if the welfare system remains one which works against the grain of human nature. This is a battle which welfare cannot win.

The starting block is a willing acceptance of the fundamental role self-interest plays in human motivation. The job of a welfare reconstruction is to plan a series of benefit reforms which allow self-interest to operate in a way which simultaneously promotes the public good. The fact that the current system rewards lying, cheating and deceit is indicative of the revolutionary change which such a welfare reconstruction would bring about in this country.

Welfare reconstruction would have a major impact in the ghettos. It would begin to set the people free to build their own lives modelled on life outside the ghetto. Self-interest would be allowed, indeed encouraged, to operate within the framework of the law. The ghetto's energies would then be channelled in a way which links, rather than divides, it from the rest of Great Britain Limited.

But whereas the debate here is limited to a discussion of the principles which need to govern a welfare reconstruction, the argument is not directed exclusively at the poor. The welfare debate cannot simply address those people living on the barren outer city estates or in the decaying inner city regions. For far too long welfare has been seen exclusively in terms of combating poverty. The failure of this strategy has been abject. A totally new perspective is required. There are simply not enough votes in an old-fashioned anti-poverty strategy. Merely railing against undeniable injustice has little electoral appeal.

If a welfare reform programme is to be successfully enacted it must be seen as relevant to the majority of our society, not just the poor. This is the first and by far and away the most important lesson which radicals must learn and digest. It sets the direction as well as the tempo of change. The following chapter therefore begins the task of identifying the interest which the majority of voters themselves have in a major welfare reconstruction.

There are a number of other fundamental policy considerations arising from the present chapter, however. The first concerns the crucial importance of supporting those people on low incomes who spend so much of their time resisting the new barbarism they witness operating and destroying all around them. Without this group the fight is lost.

No political party has yet begun to listen, let alone act, to counter the fears of this group of resisters. Politicians have no idea how to rebuild community. Policies are urgently required to prevent the continuing destruction of local neighbourhoods. Given the limited police resources, how would this group like their area to be policed? Given the general failure of policing policy, why shouldn't local residents in inner city areas have a decisive say in the deployment of police skills? What are the crimes which are most destructive of the lives of the decent citizenry and how should offenders be punished? What range of jobs would improve the local environment and how can job creation programmes be tailored to meet these preferences?

The growth of a largely illiterate young underclass calls for a revolutionary change in secondary schooling. Why so many intelligent young people leave school basically illiterate and innumerate after 11 or 12 years of public investment calls for some clear answers from teachers, educationalists and politicians. The introduction of the national curriculum, while welcome, amounts to little more than a rearrangement of deckchairs on the sinking Titanic. In recasting such secondary education we need to seek ways of allowing young males and females to develop wholesome, rewarding and worthwhile roles.

We also need to confront the values which are taught by our social security system. No system of welfare can be independent of values. These values need to be brought to the fore. Is it right, for example, that young, never-married mothers, should gain additional income support premiums when few if any voters think that such behaviour is acceptable, let alone rewardable?

But while new policies have to be tailored to meet newly emerging problems, it must never be forgotten that it is not only the poor to whom attention must be addressed but also the wider market of voters and politicians. Welfare has to cease specialising in poverty alleviation and become more generally concerned with underpinning living standards. The basis for this wider spectrum is the theme of the next chapter.

2

The Winter of Our Discontent

Crisis is a much over-used word, particularly in relation to British institutions. In as much as it catches the headlines it all too often excuses the Cassandras from providing careful analysis. It would therefore be wrong to talk of the welfare state being in crisis. There is no immediate danger that the system will implode. Nor is there an immediate prospect of a taxpayers' revolt over the escalating welfare bills. But the absence of an imminent crisis should not be used as an excuse for not facing the deep unease which now surrounds the operation of the welfare state. The welfare state cannot continue as it is currently constituted. And it is again at this point that the interests of the ghetto and the wider society overlap. Welfare no longer meets the requirements laid upon it by voters, beneficiaries or politicians. This section examines the springtide of reform which is steadily lapping and rising around the foundations of Britain's welfare state.

Voters' Dismay

It Isn't Working, So Fix It.

There is more widespread unease about the way the welfare state operates than is ever picked up by opinion polls. Most polling questionnaires focus on what support there is—or is not—for increases in expenditure. Faced with generalised questions, and not wanting to disconcert the interviewer, voters recite answers they believe the interviewer expects to hear. Surveys never encourage their respondents to court the idea that there may be an alternative.

A system instigated by the 1906 Liberal Government, added to by Neville Chamberlain during the inter-war years, and then universalised by the war-time Coalition and the 1945 Attlee Government, should need a major review half a century later in any circumstances. The task of reconstruction becomes doubly urgent once the revolutionary socio-economic changes of the past few decades are taken into account. As well as expecting politicians to propose a reconstructed welfare system fit for the new millennium, voters have other anxieties which they expect Parliament to address.

Huge Bills, But More Poverty

Here is a paradox. The welfare bill is by far and away the largest of many paid by taxpayers. It is currently edging its way towards the £90bn mark. It costs working taxpayer £15 each day from their weekly wage packets. Yet, despite major cuts initiated under the direction of Mrs Thatcher, the bill grows faster than any other item in the Government's programme. Ironically, the bill has increased at a greater rate under the Thatcher Governments than it did during the 1945 Parliament's original implementation of the Beveridge Scheme. And still the numbers on very low income inexorably rise. Surveys ask taxpayers if they are prepared to fund additional pensions and improve the living standards of the unemployed. But no survey has asked voters whether they think the £90bn could be spent more effectively. There is little doubt what the response of voters would be if they were ever given the chance to answer that question.

Fraud

Nor are the opinions of voters solicited on the question of fraud. Some fraud is small scale. But it ranges from petty fraud by individuals, through more serious individual acts of fraud, to large-scale fraud organised by sophisticated gangs. Examples of welfare fraud include:

- Claimants claiming benefits while working for small sums of money which are unreported.
- Fictitious desertions of the male partner in a family, thereby claiming benefit as if the mother were alone.
- Single mothers cohabiting with boyfriends and continuing to claim ben-

efit—with the boyfriend sometimes also claiming benefit from a different address.
- Claiming to be unemployed but working full-time and drawing benefit.
- Gangs stealing blocks of order books.
- Gangs buying order books from claimants, recycling them with new covers and cashing them elsewhere in the country, while the original owners state that their order book has been lost.
- Claimants colluding with landlords to make false housing benefit claims.
- Landlords making claims on behalf of fictitious tenants.
- DSS employees registering claims on behalf of fictitious claimants

Any welfare system will be open to attack from organised gangs. But Britain's welfare is also open to attack from within. Most of Britain's welfare is offered on a basis which perversely works against self-interest. Lying, cheating and deceit are rewarded while honesty is penalised. Not surprisingly, therefore, welfare fraud probably runs into many billions of pounds each year.

Reluctance to Pay Higher Taxes

Labour believes it lost the last election due to its threat to increase taxes. Certainly the Tories campaigned during the election as though Labour's tax proposals were a vote loser. Yet none of the exit polls or survey data taken since the election supports this contention. But ever since the votes were counted Labour has not ceased to explain that the voters are in no mood to stump up for extra taxes, and that this was the root of the Party's fourth electoral defeat. So pervasive is the conviction that parties cannot win elections while promising tax increases, that the view may indeed now be held by those groups of key voters necessary to win a general election. Here then is a spindoctor's nightmare. A misreading of the voters' reactions to Labour's 1992 defeat and a communication of that misreading may now have resulted in educating the very same voters into believing the doctrine that higher taxes automatically results in electoral failure.

A Breakdown of Contract

A further cause of the present discontent about welfare is that voters feel that the benefit system can no longer be viewed as part of a range of duties and rights which societies have to operate if they are to survive. What is happening on the welfare front is only part of a much wider concern. All societies require a shared ideology, containing an agreed moral framework, if they are to function effectively over long periods of time. In the modern world these public ideologies have invariably stemmed from religious beliefs. As the agreed ideology breaks down, major institutions of that society appear to crumble and ordinary people become uncertain and nervous about the future. Trust, the cement binding societies together, ceases to operate. Yet societies cannot function properly without a high degree of trust. Trust stems from a confidence that society's rules are agreed and will be upheld: I play my part because I know you will be acting similarly in the same circumstances.

One of the most obvious areas where trust is ceasing to operate is welfare. Others cheat, so why shouldn't I? The benefits I receive bear no relationship to what I pay. Speeding up this whole process has been the Government's switch in emphasis, away from national insurance benefits—which are paid on a contributory record only—to means-tested benefits which are not based on direct contributions.

The 1945 Model Doesn't Fit Today's Mood

While the American entry into the Second World War was crucial to its outcome, for a long time Britain stood alone against the Axis powers. The country's mobilisation to a full war economy was buttressed by a fair shares policy. That emphasis continued into peace time. This was an era when there was a major overlap between very large sections of the working class and the poor. Living standards were uniformly low for the vast majority of the population. Most food was rationed throughout the early post-war years. Beveridge's scheme of universal benefits—paid at modest levels so that the low-paid could meet their contributions—was part and parcel of the age. Beveridge hoped that large numbers of people would make additional contributions, particularly towards their retirement. Here Beveridge was not to be disappointed, although his hope that such provision might be through organisations such as the friendly society movement was not realised. Company pension schemes expanded in a very significant manner. Different forms of private insurance also continued to play a significant and indeed growing role. Today more is contributed to private pension provision schemes than goes towards covering the cost of state pensions. Even if politicians thought the Beveridge model was one to which we could return, the electorate, by its actions, has shown that it has moved on.

The Changed Socio-Economic Landscape

Six fundamental changes have occurred in British society since the Beveridge welfare state was adopted and these will be developed more fully in chapter 6. Briefly, the main changes are:

1. A flexible labour market

Britain has been transformed steadily over the post-war years, but much more markedly of late. The phrase 'flexible labour market' is used in a number of different ways. One use is to denote the new world order where most workers will expect to hold many jobs over their working lives, to have perhaps an equal number of different employers, to be hired on a contract basis for a set period only, or to be self-employed for all or part of their working lives. A welfare state built around the job-for-life principle is clearly going to fail to deliver the social security such workers and their dependants will require. This is just one of the lessons we need to consider when reconstituting welfare.

2. Dishonesty

We have already mentioned the growth of social security fraud but this is part of the much wider phenomenon of declining honesty. In the last thirty years we have witnessed a revolutionary change in attitude. While Beveridge saw the need to police the benefit system, he would be shocked by the extent to which fraud is committed. This change in attitude, reflected throughout society from boardroom to benefit office, has also to be taken into account when devising the new welfare state. The welfare rules must make it easier for people to remain honest and not provide incentives to become dishonest. Moreover, the assumption now underpinning welfare's rules has to be that people will not necessarily behave honestly. That a growing number of citizens will lie if they thereby gain additional income from the state has, sadly, to be an assumption built into the sound operation of welfare distribution. Here then is the next lesson which must be part of any serious consideration of welfare's reconstruction.

3. Single-parent families

The largest group of families with children dependent on benefit are single parents, and it is the never-married single parents who are now the largest group of single parents. This group will soon form the majority of single parents on benefit and, because of their rate of increase, they will, by the turn of the century, constitute two-thirds of all single parents. The inexorable rise of single parents on welfare, and the predominance of never-married mothers within this group, is light years away from where Beveridge thought we would be as we approached the millennium. He envisaged a world in which widows would be by far and away the most common form of single parenthood. The lesson for reconstructing welfare is that we therefore need to devise for the new welfare state, rules which do not penalise the nuclear family, a term which I consider covers those who are married and those who are living together in stable relationships.

4. Inequality on the march

Income inequality in Britain today is probably larger than at any time over the past hundred years. Growing inequality has been caused by the Tory Government's tax changes, and changes in the labour market, with a growing division between two-wage and no-wage households. All of these factors have contributed to a record degree of inequality in income. But behind these figures there is also a growing dispersion of earnings. One of Beveridge's many hidden assumptions was that in the post-war period the growing equality in income and earnings experienced during the war would continue into peace time. This trend will be considered in greater detail later (chapter 6) when we examine how this change throws new stresses on the welfare system.

5. Britain is now part of the European Union

The Beveridge Report was published days after the first most significant Allied victory of the war, occurring as it did in the North African desert by troops of the British Eighth Army. Beveridge's report was implemented as most of mainland Europe collapsed into near chaos. The ingenuity of the British and the lead Beveridge's plan would give us in the post-war world, was a familiar message in the welfare state's introduction. Now, as Britain faces the millennium, we are firmly part of the Single Market and tied under European law to the judgements of the European Court which will become an increasing force in the shaping of welfare provision in this country.

6. The age revolution

Old age pensions were first introduced for a limited number of people aged 70 or over in 1909. In that year life expectancy for men was 45 years. When Beveridge's national insurance benefit became operative those old people who survived to retirement did so against the odds and for only a short number of years. No longer is this the case. We are now fast moving from a situation where the vast majority of people's living standards were determined directly by the amount they earned on a weekly basis, as the working life constituted the major time span of human activity, to one where a growing number of individuals is spending more time outside rather than within the labour market, not only because of changing patterns of employment, but also because of increased longevity. Spreading an individual's earnings from work over a whole lifespan becomes a much more important element of redistribution than reallocation from rich to poor.

The Poor's Response

Discontent with the welfare system expressed by voters is matched by those who are welfare's beneficiaries. Here four considerations predominate.

Inadequate Benefits

The Beveridge scheme was based on the convoy principle. In an attempt to prevent ships being picked off one by one by German U-boats, convoys of ships were formed and, wherever possible, protected by the Royal Navy. But for convoys to work requires that all ships limit their speed to that of the slowest ship—otherwise the convoy fragments. The word insurance was rigorously interpreted by Beveridge both in respect of what causes could be genuinely covered by insurance and similarly by what constituted an equal insurance cover. The convoy principle was thereby applied to the national insurance contributory system.

This insistence on operating the insurance principle as though the state were running a private sector scheme fundamentally shaped the welfare state. The low-paid could only afford low contributions. And low contributions could only produce low-level benefits. This did not worry Beveridge. His primary aim was to abolish Want, not to lessen inequality. Significant modifications have since been made to the contribution levels, moving away from a simple poll tax when a set sum from all earnings, irrespective of their size, was replaced by a percentage contribution over a limited range of income. The lower level of income was called the lower earnings level and the cut-off point for percentage contributions was the higher earnings level. Above this level contributions did not increase at all. Below the lower earnings level no contributions were extracted. While a whole series of changes have been made to the contributory basis of the scheme, the tax of employees still only operates over a set band of income.

Beveridge accepted that the benefit levels based on a poll tax principle, which included the low-paid, would have themselves to be low. He argued that they should nevertheless be adequate for subsistence (see the discussion in chapter 3). At first, benefit levels were rarely reviewed and it was only when inflation accelerated that annual reviews became the norm. Even so it was only in 1974 that what were called the longer-term national insurance benefits—the principal one being pensions—had to be uprated in line with rising living standards or prices, taking the most favourable calculation from the beneficiaries' point of view. That link between prices or earnings was abandoned in 1980 (since when benefits have been increased only in line with prices). The net result of these changes has been the payment of only modest national insurance benefits. Their modesty is particularly remarkable if benefits are measured against average earnings—to take one of the measurements currently used. To make substantial increases in the payment of benefits paid to beneficiaries irrespective of their income level is usually very expensive. The numbers currently claiming the main benefits paid without a means test are listed in table 2.1.

Table 2.1 shows why Labour's 1992 election pledge on pensions and child benefit would have been so costly. Labour promised a £5 and £8 increase in retirement pension for all single and married pensioners. The cost of this promise alone was estimated at £3.9bn gross. A second, equally important promise, was an across-the-board increase of £5 a week in child benefit. The cost of this reform was estimated at £0.72bn gross. In the event it appears these promises made no noticeable difference to the voting intentions of pensioners and families.

TABLE 2.1
Numbers Claiming Non-Means Tested Benefits

Benefit	Claimants total thousands	Date of enquiry
Non-means tested benefits		
Attendance Allowance	996	March 1994
Child Benefit	5,883	November 1994
Child's Special Allowance	99	December 1993
Disability Living Allowance	1,400	August 1994
Guardians Allowance	1,977	December 1993
Invalid Care Allowance	261	September 1994
Industrial Death Benefit	22	September 1994
Industrial Injuries Disablement Benefit	209	April 1993
Invalidity Benefit	1,580	April 1993
Maternity Allowance	40	April 1992
Non Contributory Retirement Pension	28	March 1994
One Parent Benefit	902	November 1994
Other Industrial Injuries Benefits	1	March 1994
Reduced Earnings Allowance/Retirement Allowance	155	April 1993
Retirement Pension	10,090	March 1994
Sickness Benefit	147	April 1993
Severe Disablement Allowance	316	April 1993
Unemployment Benefit	541	May 1994
Widows Benefit	330	March 1994
War Pension	306	September 1994

Source: HC Deb 7 December 1994 c246–7w

Perhaps the voters did not believe the promises would be delivered, or considered that they were in any event simply undeliverable. So here is yet another paradox. The vast majority of the main beneficiaries believe that the benefits they claim are inadequate. And yet they are politically unmoved when offered an opportunity to gain a substantial improvement.

It is at this point that the debate opens up into one about the role of universal and selected provision. It is one to which the discussion must return in the final chapter.

Benefit Traps

We have already touched on the massive changes in the distribution of income over the past 15 to 20 years and a more detailed discussion is given in chapter 6. All that it is necessary to note here is the shape

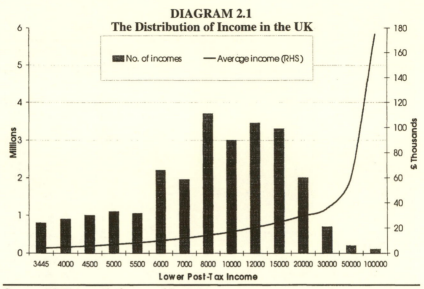

DIAGRAM 2.1
The Distribution of Income in the UK

Source: BZW Annual Abstract of Statistics

of the income distribution in this country. The average point (i.e., the total income divided by the population) is below what is called the mean income (i.e., the person who is exactly in the middle point of the distribution). This difference between the average and the mean draws attention to one of the salient characteristics of income distribution in this country. There are vastly more people on very low incomes than on very high incomes (diagram 2.1).

This simple fact underlines just how important additional income from welfare is to the majority of the population and its similarly profound impact on the working of our social security system. Due to circumstances which are explained in the following chapter, the Beveridge ideal of insurance benefits paid at a level above the means-tested safety net has not been achieved. Almost half of all households draw one of the major means-tested benefits (for details see chapter 5). Poverty, or its contemporary label, benefit dependency, is no longer a fringe pursuit.

The information does not distinguish between those people who are legitimately making a number of claims and those committing fraud (this issue is explored further in chapter 5). It does, though, show a claimant population which is continually at risk of losing their benefit entitlement as their income from other sources rises. So pensioners, for example, lose income support as their occupational pensions are increased. They suffer similar adjustments to housing benefit to which they may be entitled. There are strict rules about how many hours each week income support claimants can work and remain eligible for benefit. Once the 16–hour-a-week threshold is crossed an income support claimant is transferred to family credit, which is the benefit paid to workers earning low wages. But family credit is only paid for claimants with children (although experiments allowing single people to claim this benefit are to be introduced). If an income support claimant works over 16 hours and has no children, then that person will lose entitlement to an income support benefit and, as if to add insult to injury, the housing benefit is reduced to the point where, as the claimant's income rises, it is totally withdrawn.

These disincentives operate generally for those in work. As wages increase, housing benefit and family credit are reduced. At one time families faced a loss of benefits sometimes greater than the increase in income which triggered off the benefit losses. It was to describe this situation that David Piachaud and I coined the phrase 'the poverty trap' (Frank Field, *Poverty and Politics*, Heinemann, 1982). Since then the Government maintains that no claimant is faced with more than a 100 per cent benefit and tax rate, although large numbers of claimants face tax and benefit withdrawal rates combined of over 80 per cent.

Given how means tests work, there are considerable penalties placed on claimants who are resourceful and who honestly declare their changes in financial circumstances.

Working the System

Welfare must be designed so that the innate intelligence and inventiveness of the nation is turned to positive and productive use, rather than being confined to working the welfare system to an individual's maximum immediate financial advantage. Working the system, as it is called, is not new. It is only now a major concern because it is more openly recognised. But it is not only individuals who work the system; institutions do so as well.

Beveridge was fully aware of how institutions adapted their practices to the prevailing rules. In viewing voluntary action during the nineteenth century he commented on the conduct of the Prudential which went against the strict wishes of Parliament. Parliament's intention was that the selling of funeral policies should be the exclusive domain of the friendly societies. The privilege was, however, assumed without authority by joint stock companies, especially the Prudential. Friendly societies had an apparent advantage in being exempt from government stamp duty on any policies issued by them for funeral cover. As the Prudential secretary at the time, Mr Hudson, was anxious to point out to the Commissioners on Friendly Societies (1871–4) the Prudential had no wish for a similar concession. It willingly paid the stamp duty. Their secretary told the Royal Commission that people 'imagine that if the policy has a government stamp upon it, it has some particular guarantee about it'.

The complexity of welfare provision has led not only to a mushrooming of welfare rights agencies, but also of individuals who of their own volition work out how best they can maximise their income. This would not have surprised Beveridge. His views were quite clear. Men and women were economic creatures and maximising income was such an obvious outcome of our natures that it was hardly worth commenting upon. The likelihood is that he would have been disconcerted, however, by the extent to which welfare eligibility rules currently present a different aspect to man's economic nature.

Knowledge of changes in the rules and regulations spreads like bushfire amongst a large proportion of claimants. The whole of the claimant's effort is not put into finding a job, but into maximising his or her income on benefits. Self-interest clearly (and properly) operates. But the public interest is not served. Indeed the opposite occurs as the numbers on long-term benefit continue to grow. Here then is the next lesson we need to record when we begin the task of reconstituting welfare. Remodelling welfare must begin with a clear appreciation of human nature. *Self-interest is too powerful a motive to ignore. Politicians who do so are a public menace. The task must be to harness this aspect of our nature in a way in which the common good is also enhanced. The welfare rules must be constituted in such a way as to maximise the number of exit routes from welfare and not to build up unnecessary long-term dependence.*

Incentive to Fraud

Claimants of working age on means test are faced with three choices. In the first instance they can attempt to improve their lot and increase their income. However, as means-tested help is reduced, they will see their net income change little if at all. For a married wage earner with two children, moving off benefit on to a low-wage job of, say, £60 a week, will, with means-tested benefit help, see net family income rise to £125 per week (after housing costs). Increasing earnings from work will have little effect on the family's income. To add £10 per week net to family income would require gross earnings to increase by around £140 per week—a rise of around 235%. To double net income would require earnings to rise by over six times. Claimants may therefore take the second choice and decide to sit tight, and do nothing, with no consequent net change in benefit. Or claimants may choose to take the third route and undertake work and not declare it. This option would do most to increase their income.

Their partners may also work, and because these earnings are part of a household income, they are taken into account when computing family eligibility for means-tested benefits. The temptation for claimants on income support (paid to those out of work) and family credit (paid to those on very low wages) is therefore not to declare any additional income.

This is the charge against means testing. The Government claims that it is the most effective way of concentrating help on those with lowest income and at least cost. In one sense this is true. Giving benefit only to the poorest, rather than to whole groups of the population, is the cheaper option. But there is a price, which becomes clearer as time marches on. It is not merely that means tests feed fraud. That is bad enough. But most of the fraud committed constitutes a criminal offence. Welfare is therefore having the opposite effect than that for which it was originally devised. The welfare state was constructed as a means of extending full citizenship to the entire population, many of whom might otherwise remain outside civil society. Welfare fraud now acts as an expelling agent encouraging numbers of people into criminal activity.

Here then is one of the most important lessons we have to learn from what has gone before. When we consider the human motivation which underlies so many of our actions we must accept the way self-interest and self-improvement operate. Self-interest is too powerful a motive to be ignored. Indeed it is highly irresponsible for politicians to do so. Self-interest is closely linked to self-improvement, but it is not identical. *The aim of politicians must be to channel self-interest so that it leads to a collective self-improvement, beneficial to society as a whole, and not exclusively of value to the individual alone.*

Politicians' Dismay

Politicians too have major concerns about the operation of the welfare state. Three issues dominate their agenda.

Deep Unease about Its Effectiveness

One of the many advantages flowing from single member seats is that it allows MPs the opportunity to become well informed about what happens in their constituencies. Welfare features as part of this ongoing seminar of constituents teaching their MP about the facts of political life. The first impression MPs gain on this issue is that the welfare state they have helped create is now a legal jungle. Neither MPs, nor their constituents, understand it. Such Byzantine regulations have helped to build up an aura of mystique around the subject and have fostered the belief that it should therefore be left to the so-called experts. But welfare is no different from any other part of the Government's agenda. It is no more or less complicated than the operation of sterling in the currency market, the role of the bond market, the financing of major capital projects like the Channel Tunnel or attempts to make sense of whether, and if so, to what extent, the national health service budget is growing in real terms. Yet politicians shy away from understanding the largest item in the Government's spending programme. This has a major impact on the debate. MPs know that something is rotten in the state of Denmark, but are unable to articulate clearly what might be done to put it right.

MPs see two dimensions to just how complicated the welfare rules are. The first set of complications derives from trying to find out what help may be available and from whom. There are twenty-five benefits administered by the DSS, which include housing benefit for which the DoE is responsible. Even if we are able to establish the 'right' to benefit, a new dimension of complications then tumbles into place. A six-page means-test application form must be completed. And this is invariably followed by questioning in the local DSS office. What part of income is disregarded or ignored for the purposes of calculation, what if any part of a claimant's partner's income is so treated, and how are savings brought into the equation? Is there a tariff income which, it is alleged, claimants gain from their savings? How does this change from benefit to benefit, and at what level do savings disqualify claimants from benefit? Should possible help be forthcoming from a national insurance benefit, then the issue of the claimant's contributory record arises: yet female partners of male contributors may qualify for benefit on their husband's record. It is not surprising that baffled claimants regularly turn to their MPs who have little choice but to turn to the high priests of such arcane mysteries in the DSS.

Aside from the confusion of our 'reformed', 'streamlined' benefit system, MPs are well aware of the blatant inequity of the system. They also gain numerous examples of how many welfare state rules penalise those who have responded to the Government's rhetoric down the ages to provide for themselves. The rules for means-tested help penalise those who have built up a small nest egg of savings, are buying their own house, or are working beyond the usual retirement age to gain an additional pension.

Self-improvement is one of the great liberating human forces and its nurturing should be at the centre, not at the periphery, of the welfare state's role. In fact too many of the welfare state's rules operate against this cardinal principle.

MPs are also aware that while the welfare bill is by far and away the largest part of the Government's programme, the expenditure of £90bn a year still leaves whole armies of people without a roof over their head, ill-clad and poorly nourished children, and pathetically poor old age pensioners.

Locked into Past Budgets

Like all other parts of the Government's budget, today's social security expenditure is governed by the decisions of politicians long since dead. At the current time well over five-sixths of the money spent on social security has been decided, not by the present government, but by legislation either inherited from or implemented by the Attlee Government during the 1945–51 period (Richard Rose and Phillip

L Davies, *Inheritance in Public Policy*, Yale University Press, 1994).
Of course the rates of benefits paid have been changed, and sometimes
the groups eligible extended. But unemployment pay, widow's benefit, the retirement pension, and child benefit, to mention only a few
such benefits, have their origin in the period before World War I or in
the programme the Attlee Government put on the statute book. Fifty
years on all the key players of these reforms have long since died, but
the dead hand of past politicians restrains a government's ability to
match resources to current needs.

In fact, changing the social security budget can be compared to
navigating a great oil tanker. The captain of the oil tanker knows that,
once the decision is taken, it is a full three miles before any further
impact can be made on the direction of the ship. Similarly, because
past government legislation established a range of rights and expectations to benefit, a Social Security Secretary finds it more difficult to
change the priorities of the social security budget, let alone implement
a raft of new priorities, than does the captain guiding the oil tanker.
Politicians may attempt to slow down the rate by which benefit payments are increased, hand them over to the private sector to pay, or
even move to deny eligibility to groups yet to register their right to
benefit. But no Social Security Secretary, however radical, has felt
politically strong enough to deny groups of voters the benefit to which
they were previously entitled. The only example of wiping out a right
to benefit was the Thatcher Government's decision to raise the eligibility for income support from 16 to 18 years and, noticeably, this
group was one which did not and still does not have the vote.

Here then is another rule which should govern the reform of welfare. *A radical reconstruction would take two or more decades. The
framework for that reform has to be spelt out and immediate moves set
in hand to achieve that objective.*

Creating a Class of Outcasts

Tory policies have achieved the twin objectives of creating both a
class of outcasts as well as an underclass. The Tudor Poor Law aimed
to deal with the hordes of beggars then moving around the country.
Magistrates had the power to compel vagrants to move back to their
parish of origin. Beggars, often the result of the expulsion of peasants
as the land enclosure movement gained pace, became a constant fea-

ture of English life over the next four centuries. One of the achievements of the 1945 Attlee Government was the disappearance of beggars from British streets. Their disappearance came about not from coercive measures, but as a consequence of the successful running of the British economy, together with universalisation of the welfare benefits initiated by the 1906 Liberal Government and added to by Tory Governments of the inter-war period. The sixteen years of Conservative Government since 1979 have seen beggars return to British streets in large numbers. It is now impossible to go into the capital, or to any of the major cities in the kingdom, and not see people begging once again for their livelihood. No doubt some of these people who think the public are a soft touch and that a good income can be gained thereby. But it is obvious from the condition of most of those on the streets that their actions there are a last resort.

Students make up the second group of Britain's new outcasts. The legislation stripping the right to income support from young people aged between 16 and 18 is the first ever measure this century to take away from a whole group an entitlement to benefit. The Government maintained that young people should either be at home supported by their parents, and attending school, or that they should be in work, or undertaking a training scheme for which an allowance was payable. The Government guaranteed all students not attending school, or not in work, a place on a training scheme. This guarantee has not been fulfilled and Barnardos and Youthaid estimate that each year something like 90,000 students are cut loose with no training place and are thereby denied an income (Ianthe Maclagen, *Four Year's Serve Hardship*, Youthaid and Barnardos, 1993). This 90,000 total in any one year of course excludes those students for whom a training place has been found, but for whom the training place is not suitable either because of the student's preferred career or known skills, i.e., students wishing to learn the skills of a bricklayer being directed to become hairdressers. Denied any social security help it should come as no surprise that Britain's beggars wear a predominantly young face.

The third group of the new class of political outcast are those who have been unwilling or unable to pay the poll tax and who have thereby disappeared from the electoral roll. The reason why such individuals have taken their names off the electoral roll is that they were concerned that their whereabouts could be traced from this source of information. The size of the electoral register shrank by half a million at the time of the poll tax registration. But in order to slip the poll tax net people felt it necessary to disappear in other ways from mainstream society. Those in full-time work paying national insurance contributions could have easily been traced. It is therefore thought that large numbers of people not only refuse to register themselves for the poll tax, but at the same time cut themselves free from other ways by which their whereabouts might be discovered. The implementation of the poll tax also taught large numbers of people for the first time how easy it was to break the law. The actions of this Tory Government have therefore brought to a shuddering halt the whole movement which, over the last four centuries, has been about incorporating people into civic society. The seventeenth century was concerned with limiting the arbitrary power of the monarch; the eigthteenth century in gaining equal rights before the law. The nineteenth century established the right to vote and the twentieth century focused on gaining economic and welfare rights. Four centuries of English politics dominated by extending the comprehensiveness of civil society have now been fractured.

Similarly, the economic changes of the last fifteen or so years, together with a near revolutionary change in attitudes, have laid the foundations for a British underclass. An overvalued pound, and the fiscal policy of the 1979 Thatcher Government, resulted in 1.8 million manufacturing jobs being wiped out and 1.7 million people joining the dole queue. Unemployment rose towards the 3 million mark and has stayed there ever since. This radical transformation of job opportunities, working against those who are least skilled, has resulted in a whole group of young people leaving school, completing training courses, and having no prospect of work at all. Part of this group is on benefits and working on the side. Others have given up any pretence of claiming benefit and have carved out a life for themselves on the fringes of the criminal fraternity. A link between both these groups has been the drug trade.

Allied to the growth of a young underclass who have found no work has been the growth of the very young single parent. We noted earlier not only the massive rise in the numbers of single parents but also a change in the composition of this group. Over a 40-year period single parenthood, which began as one largely composed of widows, is now made up of never-married mothers. Within this group very young single mothers are becoming a dominant concern. These are mothers who are themselves less skilled than their peers who have not had children, and who show all the likelihood of being trapped on benefit for very long periods of time.

A little over 50 years ago the Beveridge Report was published. It was acclaimed as a blueprint for a new society—one in which social insecurity would be abolished. It held out the prospect of abolishing Want. Why have events turned out so differently? The answers, and the lessons we need to draw, are sketched out in the following two chapters.

Policy Conclusions

What main policy recommendations stem from this necessarily brief overview of voters, claimants and politicians and today's welfare state? Of those themes not developed in other chapters four major consider-ations cry out for attention.

First, and of paramount importance, is the need for politicians when reviewing the scope and nature of welfare reform not to ignore, as they have for the last 30 years or more, the importance of how human character is going to respond to any welfare system. Our characters are not passive elements in the process, but the most vibrant and powerful of players. Both Left and Right fail to strike the correct balance on this issue. Successful politics owes more to getting the balance right between conflicting forces than any other consideration. The Right stresses too much the corruption of mankind. The Left makes a similar mistake in ignoring the darker side of our characters. Self-interest is the most powerful of our motive forces. The role of the politician is to accept this simple but profound point as a starting point for policy. Reform measures need to be shaped by resolving how self-interest can be rewarded in a manner which simultaneously allows the enhancement of the public good. This is a theme which underpins all the policy considerations in this book.

Second, any reconstruction of welfare is bound to raise the old argument about universal and selective provision. That is an important consideration. But to leave the discussion here gives a somewhat back-ward-looking feel to the debate. The discussion around the universal/selected axis is important but only if it is extended to encompass the role of both public and private provision. With resistance from taxpay-ers to vote increases in government expenditure it is incumbent on reformers to meet simultaneously two objectives: to consider how best to spend the existing £90bn social security budget, and, when considering how best to re-establish the national minimum, the principle of universalisation can be applied to the private sector. Up until now it has been considered a concept relevant to the public domain only.

Third, the changing ratio between work and non-work, and in particular the growth of dependency during our non-working lives, has to be part of the evolving agenda. The long dependency years in childhood are now being matched by a simultaneously long period towards life's end. This change throws up two major challenges for any social security system. The first concerns pensions. How can adequate pensions be funded when the life of many people in retirement will be almost as long as their period spent in work? The second consideration is how to pay the escalating bills associated with residential and nursing care for what is, for many individuals, a period of up to ten years, and for some even longer. The need to redistribute earnings into an income over a much more extended lifespan is developed in the last chapter.

Fourth, reforming welfare is like steering a great oil tanker. It is massively difficult to change direction, and impossible to do so in the short term. Any sensible reconstruction will therefore set out clearly a 20–year plan which at the same time details the first crucial moves which will help steer the welfare ship towards those long-term objectives. Equally important is the need to resist quick political fixes which may be judged popular in the short run but which not only send out conflicting or wrong messages on the standards of behaviour required of all citizens but also make the achieving of a long-term reconstruction of welfare even more difficult.

3

The Flawed Vision

Welfare's Fault-Lines

The first moves to establish a national insurance scheme began in 1911. Other measures followed, but they offered only an inadequate patchwork of coverage. At the outbreak of World War II the Poor Law still flourished, offering outdoor relief to the old and able-bodied alike. It fell to the Coalition Government to establish a committee to review social security provision. But many saw this activity as a tidying-up operation. Beveridge, however, had other ideas. He argued for a war against the five great giants of Disease, Ignorance, Squalor, Idleness and Want.

Today most people would talk of poverty rather than Want. This chapter seeks to explain why Beveridge was unsuccessful in burying the Poor Law tradition of providing maintenance to those out of work and not covered by the insurance scheme. In particular we consider the lessons which we should draw from the Beveridge initiative and ask to what extent people are today dependent upon means-tested benefit because of:

- fault-lines in his original scheme?
- changes which politicians made to his design? or
- socio-economic changes which Beveridge could not have foreseen?

In recalling what went wrong with Beveridge's vision we are drawn into the role which accident and personality play both in providing political opportunities and in underscoring failure. We also draw a number of crucial conclusions which need to be taken into account when reconstructing welfare for the next millennium.

Poverty Studies

It is widely believed that Charles Booth was responsible for the first attempt in this country to provide a scientific measurement of the numbers of people living on low incomes (see the next chapter for a fuller debate on this point). Booth typified the prized Victorian characteristic of hard work.

Toiling away during the day running a major shipping line, Booth worked on his massive survey of *London Life and Labour of the People of London*, only in his spare time. Seebohm Rowntree, likewise an industrialist, carried out a more limited survey of the extent of poverty in York in 1899.

These pioneering researchers were followed by a series of similar studies throughout the inter-war years. Reviewing their findings Beveridge commented:

> From each of these [inter-war] social surveys the same broad result emerges. Of all the Want shown from the surveys, from three-quarters to five-sixths, according to the precise standard chosen for Want, was due to interruption or loss of earning powers. Practically the whole of the remaining one-quarter to one-sixth was due to failure to relate earnings to size of family. (*Social Insurance and Allied Services*, Report by Sir William Beveridge, Cmd 6404, HMSO, 1942, para 11.)

Beveridge's Second Coming

We shall return to this point later to demonstrate that Beveridge's interpretation of the results of these studies was wrong. In order not to break the chronological order of our discussion we need first to centre our attention on Beveridge's career, for it illustrates vividly the role of character and chance in politics.

Beveridge's first experience of government came before the First World War. On leaving Balliol, Beveridge, along with a whole generation of serious-minded students, was challenged by the then Master of the College, Edward Caird, 'to go and discover why, with so much wealth in Britain, there continues to be so much poverty, and how poverty can be cured'. Working from the spring of 1903 from Toynbee Hall, the premier settlement house in London's East End, Beveridge soon came to question the causes of joblessness (in 1909 that great tome entitled *Unemployment: A Problem of Industry* was produced) and became a leading activist in what was then known as the Central (Unemployed) Body. Here Beveridge won his spurs, advocating major reforms to the labour market including the introduction of labour exchanges. It was only a short step from his role as political activist and lobbyist to what today would be viewed as a political adviser to Winston Churchill when the latter was appointed by Asquith to be President of the Board of Trade. The Board of Trade was then the department responsible for employment matters. Beveridge's rise was swift and, after being called back into the civil service during World War I, he had, by 1919, gained a permanent secretarialship.

When Britain was again at war in 1939 Beveridge expected the same treatment a second time around. Along with a number of other academics who had gained top administrative posts during the 1914–18 period, he waited to be catapulted back to the pinnacles of the civil service once the British Army moved against Hitler. Beveridge was to be disappointed. His efforts to gain the pivotal position as Director-General of Manpower were countered. As a consolation prize he was asked to conduct a survey on skilled manpower in the armed services.

His boss was Ernest Bevin, the towering Transport and General Workers Union leader, who had joined the Coalition Government in 1940. Beveridge quickly crossed his new chief and repeatedly did so. But here the downside of his character gained Beveridge a crucial opening as a great administrative and social reformer. When discussions started about the establishment of an inter-departmental committee to operate a tidying-up operation for welfare services, Bevin was none too enthusiastic, until Beveridge's name was suggested. Once that name was in the frame Bevin immediately jumped at the opportunity to dump this prickly figure outside his department. Beveridge's appointment as chairman of the committee was duly announced in June 1941.

The 'tidying-up operation' may have been all that was originally envisaged for the working party. That, certainly, was how some politicians and officials viewed the exercise. It was not, however, Beveridge's intention. He was soon announcing to all who cared to listen that a radically new blueprint was what was called for, and that was precisely what he intended to provide. Why politicians did not act swiftly at this stage to curb Beveridge's aspirations and ego has not yet been satisfactorily accounted for. The figure of Attlee, in effect Prime Minister on the home front during the Coalition Government, perhaps explains a great deal. Attlee, ever one to appreciate the advantages of doing nothing, was probably more than content to let Beveridge charge around, demote the members of the inquiry to the role of assessors, and raise expectations that an earth-shattering report was on the way. This time the peace as well as the war would be won, and Attlee's beady eye was ever on the approaching peace.

At first Beveridge did very little. He was busy trying to complete his inquiry into the manpower of the armed services and devising for Hugh Dalton an abortive plan for fuel rationing. Indeed throughout the autumn of 1941 the Beveridge Committee, as it was called, met infrequently, and Beveridge did not fully turn his mind to the issue of transforming the welfare state until the very end of 1941. Between December of that year and February 1942 he drafted two papers for consideration by the other civil servants who comprised the committee. The main ideas of the Beveridge Report were contained in these two major submissions, although it was not until May 1942 that he gave his undivided attention to reforming social insurance (Josie Harris, *William Beveridge*, Oxford, 1977, 377).

At the beginning of his report, *Social Insurance and Allied Services*, Beveridge clearly demonstrated his approach of building on existing provision, rather than attempting to design a new social security system from scratch. The near impossibility of pursuing any other approach is discussed in the final chapter. In reviewing the causes of pre-war Want or poverty Beveridge commented:

> All the principal causes of interruption or loss of earnings are now the subject of schemes of social insurance. If, in spite of these schemes, so many persons unemployed or sick, or old or widowed are found without adequate income, this means that the benefits amount to less than subsistence. To prevent interruption or destruction of earning power from leading to Want, it is necessary to improve the present schemes of social insurance in three directions: by extending the scope to cover persons now excluded, by extension of purposes to cover risks now excluded, and by raising the rate of benefit. (*Social Insurance and Allied Services*, para. 12)

Furthermore, 'abolition of Want requires adjustment of incomes, in periods of earning as well as interruption of earnings, to family needs, that is to say, in one form or another it requires allowances for children' (*Social Insurance and Allied Services*, para. 13). Here we see that Beveridge had a clear conception of how finally to bury the Poor Law approach of offering help on a test of means. So, what went wrong with Beveridge's design and what lessons should we draw from the Beveridge experiment?

First Thoughts

In his first major paper on the reform of social security, *Basic Problems of Social Security with Heads of the Scheme*, Beveridge wrote that the success of the scheme was dependent upon the implementation of three other major reforms. The first of these was the introduction of the National Health Service; the second the payment of children's allowances; while the third major policy was the maintenance of full employment. The Beveridge scheme itself was built on a number of key principles, four of which are important to our discussion. These are:

- the need for a universal flat-rate benefit;
- that benefits should themselves be paid at an adequate subsistence level;
- that the range of benefits should cover all types of Want;
- that benefit should be paid as long as Want lasted.

Beveridge's preliminary papers for the committee show that in three very important aspects the scheme failed to meet all the key principles Beveridge himself laid down. In respect of women, Beveridge failed to extend comprehensive coverage; a similar failure occurred in meeting the needs of non-industrial disabled people; and in his treatment of the question of rent, Beveridge failed to design a scheme which gave adequate subsistence benefits.

Excluding Women

In respect of the rights of women Josie Harris has observed that Beveridge was 'determined to give each category of woman a foothold in social insurance' (Harris, 1977, 402). That Beveridge had radical views on women probably owes much to Mrs Mair, the wife of a colleague with whom today's press would have said Beveridge enjoyed a 'close relationship'. They married in December 1942.

In *Basic Problems of Social Security with Heads of the Scheme*,

Beveridge considered the rights that should be given to what he had termed 'unmarried wives'. In one of his great understatements, he observed that this issue 'involves acute differences of opinion and principle. The state has already gone so far in recognising the marriage in relation without marriage— that it hardly seems possible to take a strict line— that the unlawful marriage relation should not be recognised in the social security scheme at all.'

However, when Beveridge came to listing the groups to be helped by his scheme he proposed five insurance coverages for women:

1. Single women would contribute, like men, for a comprehensive insurance coverage.
2. Married women would be entitled to a special housewives' policy based on the insurance record of their husbands.
3. Employed married women would have the choice of relying on their husbands' insurance record or to contribute to the scheme themselves.
4. Unmarried wives would be entitled to the coverage given to married women except that they would be denied a furnishing grant or widow's pension.
5. Domestic spinsters—women working at home often caring for an aged relative—would be classified as an occupied person contributing solely in order to gain an old age pension.

Once Beveridge opened up discussion on these proposals he ran into considerable difficulties. Women's organisations argued that he had not gone far enough. Others—the TUC and friendly societies in particular—argued against undermining the insurance nature of the scheme. Here it is important to recall just how fundamental the insurance principle was to the whole of Beveridge's proposals. *An over-legalistic interpretation by Beveridge of the idea of national insurance holds an important lesson when we come on to a programme of reconstruction.*

Slowly, but inevitably, the logic flowing from the turgid way Beveridge defined national insurance began to undermine the scope of welfare provision for women which he had originally proposed. Indeed, two months after the first complete draft of his report, Beveridge had come to the conclusion that the giving of a separation benefit as part of the cover for married women in an insurance scheme was impracticable. He recommended instead that a deserted wife should have the right to means-tested public assistance and that that body would pursue through the courts the right to maintenance from her husband.

Similarly, Beveridge began to change his mind about the correctness of proposing a separation allowance. As Josie Harris has acutely observed, this question 'placed Beveridge on the horns of a dilemma and brought into conflict two of his most deeply held beliefs about social insurance' (Harris, 1977, 407). On the one side was the problem of paying benefit to a 'guilty wife', for the scheme would be underwriting an event which was under the control of the individual. On the other side, if a benefit as a right was not paid, the wife would then be subjected to a means test.

By September 1942 Beveridge envisaged that such a benefit could only be paid in the case of divorce or legal separation. In his final report he proposed a Housewife's Policy to cover what he saw as the six marriage needs of a woman. In cases of separation, benefit would be paid to the woman whom the husband had failed to maintain after a legal separation or if the husband's desertion was publicly established. Here Beveridge proposed an adaptation of the widow's benefit, together with a separation benefit, a guardian's benefit and a training benefit (*Social Insurance and Allied Services*, para. 311). In 1942 unmarried mothers hardly registered as an issue.

Excluding the Disabled

The second group which failed to gain a foothold in the social security system was the non-industrially disabled. That Beveridge was only concerned with industrial injury when considering the problems of disability can be seen from his preliminary paper *Basic Problems of Social Security with Heads of the Scheme*. The discussion of disability in this document is exclusively concerned with industrial injury and the compensation which should arise from death resulting from industrial injuries. Beveridge proposed that the larger invalidity benefit for permanent incapacity and death benefit should be given, not according to the cause of incapacity but according to the industry in which the man was engaged, with compensation for engaging in dangerous but necessary work. Again the limited legalistic view Beveridge had of insurance widens the fault-lines in his scheme.

There are two reasons why Beveridge made no distinction on behalf of the needs of the congenitally disabled. First, the issue was a much less important one then than it is today. One of the major benefits of medical advance is to keep alive more people who would have previously died as a result of their disability at, or shortly after, birth. The second reason stems from Beveridge's insistence on an insurance scheme. How could people who had paid no contributions benefit from an insurance-based scheme? The problem was not insuperable, for Beveridge could have argued that the right to benefit existed by way of the insurance record of their parents.

Renting a Failure

How a non-means-tested benefit should cover a claimant's rent was another issue which faulted the Beveridge scheme from the outset. The next chapter details the debate on attempts to define subsistence income. As this level of income is meant to cover all the necessary expenditures of a claimant, rent is obviously a key element in this calculation.

Rowntree was one of a group of unofficial assessors Beveridge used for his ideas as they quickly took shape. Yet, true to form, Beveridge was far better at asking for advice than taking it. Rowntree pointed out immediately this fatal flaw in the Beveridge approach. Rent levels across the country varied greatly. As any calculation of subsistence income had to cover the rent a household paid, how could this be achieved? Either each individual insurance payment would have to take account of the claimant's rent—causing administrative delay and probably chaos. Or a standard rent allowance could be added. Those with lower rents would be net gainers. Those claimants with above-average rents would not merely be losers, but would also have an income below the defined subsistence level. In the end Beveridge rejected the idea of a variable rent payment and opted instead for a flat-rate payment.

Most of the arguments about subsistence level income were, and are, bogus. This is a crucial point and we shall consider it in the following chapter which examines the British debate on this key issue. But with the scheme he was devising, Beveridge's decision on rent undermined his goal of lifting the population free of means tests. This flaw was exploited by those opposing the Beveridge scheme once the author entered into discussion with the Treasury prior to its publication, and again after the report was published and civil servants began work on the details of the Government's response.

Extending the Fault-Lines

From conception, there were three fundamental fault-lines in Beveridge's scheme:

- The needs of women were not adequately covered.
- The needs of all the disabled were not met.
- The benefits paid to all claimants were not adequate as some claimants' rent payments would not be covered in full.

Once Beveridge had completed his draft report, pressures were brought upon him to modify it in other important respects. Ironically, Beveridge was initially encouraged to review his plans and expand their costs (see Josie Harris, 'The social thought of William Beveridge', a paper given at the seminar on the Beveridge Report, University of Edinburgh, 1982, for just how ambitious Beveridge was for post-war reconstruction). It was not long, however, before Beveridge began a series of discussions with Maynard Keynes, then an economic adviser to the Treasury, and later with other Treasury officials, on ways of limiting the scheme's budget. By August 1942 Beveridge conceded further fundamental modifications to his scheme. In a paper entitled The *Problem of Pensions*, Beveridge moved from a target of adequate pensions from the start to making this an ultimate goal to be achieved over a 16–year period. (See *Power and Influence*, Hodder & Stoughton, 1953, for Beveridge's reasoning.)

The other fundamental change which Beveridge made, prior to the publication, concerns support for children through family allowances. Originally, Beveridge envisaged a family allowance payment of 5 shillings per child. The scheme envisaged a payment to every child, including the first. But in his report Beveridge observed that a careful analysis of the studies of working-class incomes during the inter-war period showed that even the poorest wage-earners had an income adequate for the support of a family with one child.

The evidence of these studies proved nothing of the kind (Frank Field, *What Price a Child?* Policy Studies Institute, 1985, 20). Moreover, those studies conducted during the early years of the 1930s found, not surprisingly, that the most important cause of family poverty was unemployment. But as Britain slowly pulled out of the inter-war recession, low wages again became the key cause of poverty among families with children. Beveridge's final report contained a proposal that family allowances should not be paid to the first child in the family and until war-time inflation had been taken into account, the new suggested rate looked more generous than the original proposals.

Government Cuts

At first the Government hoped it would be able to publish the Beveridge Report without attracting widespread publicity. They held up the publication for this very reason. This was not their only misjudgement in handling the report. *Social Insurance and Allied Services* was launched on 1 December 1942—only nineteen months after Beveridge was first given the commission to begin work. The timing could not have been more advantageous, from Beveridge's point of view. Victories by Montgomery's soldiers at Alamein hinted that, at long last, the balance of power had decisively shifted, and it was now only a matter of time before the Allies emerged victorious. Lord Longford, acting as Beveridge's assistant, proved his skills in what today would be called spindoctoring. Newspapers carrying details of the Beveridge Report were quickly sold out; so, too, were the Stationery Office supplies of the report.

It was not only the solitary Tory backbencher complaining that it was not the done thing for the chairman of the committee to go thumping up and down the country selling his report who was disconcerted by the reception given to Beveridge's ideas. The noses of senior politicians were also firmly put out of joint. Attlee crisply observed that it was always a mistake for someone to think that they were more important than they actually were. More importantly, the Coalition Government appeared to be thrown off balance by its own failure to respond to the report. This only served to increase the hostility which senior politicians felt towards Beveridge. At one point the Coalition Government feared that the three-day parliamentary debate to receive the report would end with a vote against the Government and the fall of the Coalition.

Despite this threat, the Government was successful in amending the scheme in three significant ways which flawed the Beveridge plan still further. In replying to the debate Herbert Morrison, then Home Secretary, announced that the Government rejected the idea of paying benefits generous enough to guarantee a subsistence-level income, while adding that the aim was to 'fix a benefit for unemployment and ill-health on the same basis as nearly as possible' (*Hansard*, 18 February 1943, col. 2038–9)

Turning to the question of pensions, Morrison cleverly presented the Government's climb-down as an improvement on what Beveridge was proposing. The plan advocated a phasing-in of subsistence pensions with full pensions being paid in 1956. Morrison reported that 'the government...may...be able to better the Beveridge proposals at the beginning' (col. 2042). Pensions were to be paid at a higher level at the introduction of the scheme than was advocated by Beveridge 'even if we had to make an adjustment the other way at the end' (cols 2042–3).

The third major modification to the scheme centred on the provision of family allowances. Beveridge had already modified his proposals before publication in order to limit the cost of the scheme. The universal benefit of 5 shillings per child was replaced by an allowance of 8 shillings for all children except the first child of the family. The Government's immediate response was to reduce this sum to 5 shillings a week for each eligible child.

The White Paper Chase

It is at this point that Beveridge's personality began impacting on the politics of reform in a wholly negative manner. Once the Coalition Government had secured its vote in the House the detailed work began about how best to implement the report. From this crucial process Beveridge was excluded. The report was therefore delivered into the hands of politicians and officials, some of whom were openly hostile to the author and opposed to the objectives of the report.

A number of writers assert that the White Paper, *Social Insurance*, 'followed Beveridge remarkably closely' (A Marwick, *Britain in the Century of Total War*, Bodley Head, 1968, 315, and A Bullock, *Bevin*, vol. 2, Heinemann, 1967, 325). A perusal of the White Paper suggests otherwise. The three major modifications to the scheme which the Government announced in early 1943 were reaffirmed in the White Paper. And here officials seized on Beveridge's insistence on flat-rate benefits to put a ceiling on the level of benefits paid. The White Paper observed that benefits must be paid for, and a high level of benefits would mean a high level of contributions. 'The Government therefore concluded that the right objective is a rate of benefit which provides a reasonable insurance against Want', in other words, set at a level which, given people's savings and other forms of income, would prevent the mass of claimants from becoming poor (*Social Insurance*, Cmd 6550). This approach—known as 'the convoy principle' (see chapter 2) contains a second lesson we must take on board when reconstructing welfare. *Benefits must be related to the size of the contributions paid and graduated contributions should lead to graduated benefits.*

The White Paper, in addition, contained two further major modifications to the scheme. One of the principles underlying the Beveridge Report was the right to draw benefit so long as need lasted. The Government replied that it would be 'prudent' to limit both sickness and unemployment benefits; the White Papers failed to clarify to whom the prudence was supposed to apply.

The White Paper also made major changes to the provisions for women claimants. The report recommended a marriage allowance and, more importantly, a separation allowance. The Government rejected the first proposal on grounds of cost and the second on grounds of morality. The cost of underwriting a marriage allowance was such that 'the government do not consider the benefit attractive enough to justify…[the] charge'. On the separation allowance the Government willingly allowed itself to be bogged down on the question of blame. 'The government feel that the question whether loss of maintenance is the fault of the wife is not one which should be determined by a department responsible for administrating the social insurance scheme. The wife must seek other remedies open to her to secure maintenance' (*Social Insurance*, 29).

One good proposal which did emerge from the White Paper was to pay a higher relative benefit for sickness and unemployment benefit— even if for a limited duration.

Yet More Cuts

The final modifications to the Beveridge proposals occurred at the introduction of the scheme itself. In introducing the National Insurance Bill the Minister for National Insurance confirmed the Government's rejection of subsistence-level benefits. However, it was accepted that the initial level of benefits should be revised in line with

rising prices. The index which the Government used for this calculation was one drawn up in 1914 and included items like calico and
candles, on which working-class families spent little or no income at
all. On the other hand, it excluded most of the goods on which people
did spend their money, apart from a small range of basic necessities.
Thus the increase calculated by this bogus index was inadequate to
match price rises recorded in this bizarre manner.

The second change which occurred at this stage concerned the relative value of allowances paid to children. In calculating the needs of
children Beveridge advocated a flat-rate benefit for children which
would be paid to parents drawing the main national insurance benefits
as well as those in work. Beveridge's work on the National Insurance
Advisory Committee had convinced him of the danger of paying higher
allowances to the children of the unemployed than to the children of
men and women who were in work. The Coalition Government deval-
ued the family allowance rates. Further modifications were made to
the children's rates when the Attlee Government came to determine
the new national insurance rate.

Policy Conclusions

There are five major lessons for reformers to draw from Beveridge's
attempt to make a decisive break with the Poor Law tradition of segregated relief for the poorest. The first is that while it is intellectually
possible to devise a social security system which guarantees everyone
freedom from means-tested assistance, it is impossible to do so if an
over-legalistic interpretation is placed on the definition of insurance.
Balance here is important. Individuals must feel that their benefits are
related to their contributions. For this to be a reality, and not simply a
political con trick, it is crucial that any redistribution brought about
through the operation of national insurance schemes is overt. The
redistributory element should be paid for by the general body of taxpayers. It should be openly detailed and voted upon by Parliament.

The second lesson to be drawn from Beveridge's heroic efforts is
that to devise a welfare strategy does not by itself guarantee success.
The Treasury has a duty to protect public funds and will rebut any
major attempts to ratchet upwards public expenditure. This resistance
will come from a group whose primary interest will be the *level* of
public expenditure, and thereby the *level* of taxation and borrowing,

rather than the *objectives* on which the money is to be spent. The need to plan reform over a very long period is therefore crucial if resistance from this source is to be minimised. Equally crucial to success is the winning of the Prime Minister's and Chancellor's support, particularly important to the self-employed who would be brought into the scheme properly for the first time.

A third lesson follows directly from this need to build up both a coalition of support in the country (about which this book is primarily concerned) and in the top echelons of government. Big bang theories of welfare reform may be good news for headline writers. They often spell political disaster. We need only to consider the poll tax fiasco to see that the more ambitious the reform the greater the danger of a political disaster. The poll tax not only cost £13bn in forms of sweeteners (House of Commons Library, 14 February 1995) but brought millions of people for the first time not only to break the law but to learn that the chances of being caught are quite slim. Similarly, the fiasco of initiating the Child Support Agency, making it retrospective as well as dealing with new cases, has resulted in the Government offering an amnesty to those parents colluding with each other to cheat taxpayers. Both reforms have done more to undermine law-abiding citizenry than any other government initiative—except possibly for the Thatcher Government's careless destruction of Britain's industrial manufacturing base. An opposite strategy to the big bang approach is offered here. The aim is to build upon the existing structure of benefits so that, over a 20–year period, the welfare state is transformed.

The fourth lesson is that the best-laid schemes of mice and men, to paraphrase Robbie Burns, will be knocked off course by events almost impossible to predict. No one foresaw the big rise in single-parent families, let alone the burgeoning groups of never-married mothers. Beveridge would probably have viewed this trend as a collapse into social anarchy. Welfare state proposals set in tablets of stone are likely to fail very quickly to produce the desired effects. The case for a body charged with the responsibility to seek out and report on emerging social trends and their likely impact on the welfare budget is crucial.

The fifth lesson according to Beveridge is that his scheme was inherently flawed from the start. On his own rules of comprehensiveness it failed. It also failed, more understandably, in not foreseeing the gigantic rise in unmarried single parents. But attitudes have changed on this score and on another which is equally important for our studies. Here lies the sixth lesson.

For totally understandable reasons after the recession of the 1930s, Beveridge was concerned with abolishing Want. His emphasis was to define a poverty line and then attempt to guarantee everybody an income above it. With national income almost three times as high, and with a widespread wish in the country for greater personal autonomy, efforts to transform Britain's social provision need to move away from this obsession with subsistence rates and the perennial approach of equating the drawing of income support with being in poverty. The full argument for doing so is given in the next chapter. The need is to measure means-tested dependency and to adopt a strategy for its reduction which thereby finally slays the renaissance of the Poor Law tradition in Britain's welfare.

4

Minimum Income Levels

It has been a deliberate policy of the Government to increase the numbers of people on means-tested benefits. It must be conceded that a doubling of welfare dependency in a 15-year period is no mean achievement. The larger part of this army draws income support in order to get by. It is this income support level which is often referred to as an official poverty line (the remainder of those drawing a major means-tested benefit are largely dependent upon housing benefit). In the early post-war period the Labour Party was unmoved by the fact that being eligible for insurance benefits did not automatically lift claimants free from means-tested support. Yet, for the reasons given in the previous chapter, freeing people from means-tested dependency has to be a major objective of a reconstructed welfare state. What the income support rate actually represents is therefore crucial to the development of our argument. Does it represent a carefully drawn poverty line above which the national insurance level should be set, or has there always been something rather 'rough and ready' about the calculations which have determined the rates of benefit? And if the latter, what impact should this have on our thinking about how best to reconstruct welfare?

A National Minimum

During the Boer War the failure of the recruitment campaign alarmed the informed public. Perhaps as many as 45 per cent of young men presenting themselves for arms were found unfit to serve. Such a large proportion of those wishing to fight in South Africa being turned down as physically inadequate helped concentrate the public debate on securing a national minimum. War has often been a great precursor of reform, at least in this country. A string of defeats at the hands of the Boers did not herald the end of imperialism as some historians have alleged (G M Young, *Portrait of an Age*, Oxford, 1977, 183). Rather the war and its aftermath turned the force of imperialism in on this country: the white man's burden could not be carried on impoverished shoulders. The quest for national efficiency therefore gained new and widespread political support. 'Imperialism and the condition of the people question became linked' (Bentley Gilbert, *The Evolution of National Insurance in Great Britain*, Michael Joseph, 1966, 60–1) and by skilful political footwork by the Webbs, to the idea of establishing a national minimum in respect of living standards.

Many other forces were at work too, including the intellectual shift which Beatrice Webb described. Fighting insomnia by scribbling in her journal, she recorded that the origin of this ferment

> is to be discovered in a new consciousness of sin amongst men of intellect and men of property . . . The consciousness of sin was a collective or class consciousness; a growing uneasiness, amounting to conviction, that the industrial organisation, which had yielded rent, interest from profits on a stupendous scale, had failed to provide a decent livelihood and tolerable living conditions for the majority of inhabitants of Great Britain. (Beatrice Webb, *My Apprenticeship*, Longmans, Green, 1942, 154–5)

Much of this 'consciousness of sin' was also channelled into the practical political task of how best to establish a national minimum. The home programme of the 1905 Liberal Government was in every sense an attempt to legislate in this field. But how was a national minimum underpinning the whole of society to be defined? Enter Charles Booth and Seebohm Rowntree, part industrialists, part social reformers and part social scientists.

Charles Booth

Of Booth's contribution to the social sciences, his biographers, the Simeys, have written that his

> most striking innovation was his invention of the Poverty line and his exploration of the methods whereby this might be established— His definition of poverty was perhaps the first operational definition in the social sciences, 'operational' in the

sense that it provided the means whereby the truth or falsehood of his provisional hypothesis could be tested experimentally. (T S & M B Simey, *Charles Booth*, Oxford, 1960, 184)

In fact Booth only used the term 'a line of poverty' and his main concern was to distinguish between those who may be poor and those who were in want. He set out his definition of poverty, however, in the second paper he presented to the Royal Statistical Society in 1887, a paper which also contained the preliminary results of his London surveys. He informed his audience that

> by the word 'poor', I mean to describe those who have a fairly regular though bare income, such as 18 shillings or 20 shillings per week, for a moderate family, and by 'very poor', those who fall below this standard, whether from chronic irregularity of work, sickness, or a large number of young children. I do not here introduce any moral question: whatever the cause, those whose means prove to be barely sufficient, or quite insufficient for decent independent life, are counted as 'poor' or 'very poor' respectively: and as it is not always possible to ascertain the exact income, classification is also based on the appearance of the home. (C Booth, 'The inhabitants of the Tower Hamlet School Board Division', *Journal of the Royal Statistical Society*, vol. L, 1887, 328)

The Simeys understandably observed that 'Booth never achieved a clear definition of "poverty" ' (Simey, 1960, 178). Indeed, in a paper to the Society in the following year, Booth made it plain that he was not seeking a 'scientific' definition of poverty. The classification of those who were poor and very poor was determined by popular opinion as expressed by his interviewers who had the job of classifying the families surveyed.

Booth's findings on this score have usually been misread, partly because of the way he presented them. Booth classified 30.7 per cent of London's residents as in poverty or in want. Four classes, A to D, made up this total. Of classes C and D, Booth observed, 'Though they would be much the better for more of everything [they] are not "in want". They are not ill-nourished or ill clad, according to any standard that can reasonably be used' (E P Hennock, 'Poverty and social thought in England', *Social History*, January 1976, 73). So not only was Booth not the originator of the term poverty line, but he defined people as poor although they were not necessarily in 'want'. And he did not ascribe to these people what we would today regard as the characteristics of poverty.

The purpose of Booth's survey was not to refute, as so many assert, the Social Democratic Federation's claim that a quarter of the metropolis was living in poverty (Hennock, 1976, 70). Its aim was first to enumerate and then describe the conditions in London. Was the issue of poverty one which could be tackled or was society to be overwhelmed by a new class of barbarian (Class A)? By showing how relatively small this group was, making the distinction between it and the very poor, on the one hand, and the 'true working classes' on the other, Booth was in fact arguing that remedial action was well within the capabilities of late Victorian society. Indeed, it allowed Booth to concentrate the public's mind on the greatest cause of poverty in London, which stemmed from casual and irregular employment. Booth also had ideas about how poverty from these causes could be combated. So, as Hennock concludes, 'it was the categorising as much as the enumerating that brought the reassurance, for the totals were the result of a method of investigation that put the emphases on subdividing rather than aggregating phenomena' (E P Hennock, 'Concepts of poverty in the British Social Surveys from Charles Booth to Arthur Bowley', *The Social Survey in Historical Perspective 1880–1940*, ed. Martin Bulmer, Kevin Bayles and Catherine Cishsklar, CUP, 1991, 196). Seebohm Rowntree's achievement was rather different.

Seebohm Rowntree

The source of the belief that poverty could be defined almost independently of the society in which the investigation was being carried out is to be found in Rowntree's work. Because Rowntree's calculations played such a dominant role in defining the parameters of the poverty debate in this country, and impacted thereby on the mainstream of politics, we need to spend a little time examining how he went about his work.

'Before we can arrive at an estimate of the number of those who are living in "primary" poverty in York,' wrote Rowntree at the beginning of his first report, 'we must ascertain what income is required by families of different sizes to provide the minimum food, clothing and shelter needful for the maintenance of mere physical health.' He went on to add:

> Expenditure needful for the maintenance of the mental, moral and social sides of human nature will not be taken into account at this stage of the enquiry. Nor in

thus estimating the poverty line would any account be taken of the expenditure for sick clubs or social insurance. We confine our attention at present strictly to an estimate of minimum necessary expenditure for the maintenance of merely physical health. (B S Rowntree, *Poverty: A Study of Town Life*, Macmillan, 1902, 87)

There were three components in Rowntree's poverty line: food, rent and household sundries. Of these, food was by far and away the most important item of expenditure and Rowntree calculated a person's minimum food needs in four stages: by looking at the functions of food in the body, the quantity necessary to fulfil these functions, its kind and its cost.

To help answer the technical side of the question, Rowntree relied heavily on the work of Professor W O Atwater, who worked in the United States Department of Agriculture. Commenting on this choice, Rowntree's biographer, Asa Briggs, has written that 'it was a good one, for Atwater, whose research on energy and nutrition marked a landmark in the history of nutritional science, had carried his studies to the point where they could be directly related to social investigation' (A Briggs, *Seebohm Rowntree*, Longmans, Green, 1961, 32). Rowntree also relied on Atwater's work when calculating the dietary requirements of people of different ages and sexes. These differences were expressed as a fraction of the food required by an adult man.

Rowntree's next decision concerned the kind of food which would fulfil the dietary requirements. 'To this end,' he observed, 'valuable suggestions may be obtained from the diets provided to able-bodied paupers in the workhouses, as the object of the institutions is to provide a diet containing the necessary nutrients at the lowest cost comparable with a certain amount of variety' (Rowntree, 1902, 98). New guidelines on standard diets for the workhouse came into force in March 1901. In making selections from these guidelines the guardians were given certain instructions: for example, they were to provide not fewer than two boiled or roast meat dinners a week. Rowntree selected a diet from the rations specified in the new regulations, 'but the cheapest rations only have been chosen, and on this account no butcher's meat is included in the diet sheet. The standard adopted here is therefore less generous than that which would be required by the Local Government Board' which was responsible for running the workhouses (Rowntree, 1902, 99). Rowntree costed his diet on the average prices paid for food by a sample of working-class families in York, ignoring their findings only when prices were lower at the Co-operative Store.

Rowntree then turned his attention to calculating minimum rent and household sundry costs. In estimating the necessary minimum expenditure for rent, he said he would have 'preferred to take some reliable standard of the accommodation required to maintain families of different sizes in health, and then to take as the minimum expenditure the average costs in York for such accommodation'. But he was forced to conclude that 'this course would, however, have assumed that every family could obtain the needful minimum accommodation, which is far from the case'. In all his minimum income calculations Rowntree therefore took the actual rents paid 'as the necessary minimum rent expenditure' (Rowntree, 1902, 106).

As regards household sundries, the principal items of which were boots, clothes and fuel, his estimate of the minimum expenditure on these was based upon information gathered 'from a large number of working people'. Families were asked:

> What in your opinion is the very lowest sum on which a man can keep himself in clothing for a year? The clothing must be adequate to keep the man in health, and should not be so shabby as to injure his chances of obtaining respectable employment. Apart from these two conditions the clothing to be the most economical available. (Rowntree, 1902, 107–108)

Information on the amount of clothing and fuel was collected without great difficulty. The data on the average sums required on other household necessities 'proved very difficult to obtain'. Rowntree recalled how 'enquiries about this were usually answered by some such remark as, "if we have to buy anything extra, such as pots or pans, we have to spend less on food, that's all" '. In response, he added, 'It will not be overstating the fact if we allow twopence a head to cover all household sundries other than cloths and fuel' (Rowntree, 1902, 109).

By bringing together all these calculations Rowntree was able to establish a minimum income level and from this it was possible to work out the costs which had to be covered to ensure that each member of the family reached minimum income levels. (For criticism of Rowntree's relativities between different members of the family see Frank Field, *What Price a Child?* Policy Studies Institute, 1985.) This then was the basis of Rowntree's minimum income which was consistent with 'merely physical efficiency'.

Most of the criticism of this approach has been centred on the belief that the expenditure patterns Rowntree claimed were consistent with gaining physical efficiency from a poverty line income were unrelated to the lifestyle of most working-class families. Ironically this criticism is true, but in the opposite way to what it implies. Rowntree's attempt to produce a subsistence definition of poverty resulted in minimum income levels substantially above those obtained in reality by many working-class families. The only person to notice this was the statistician A L Bowley (*The Nature and Purpose of the Measurement of Social Phenomena*, P. S. King & Son, 1923, 170–1).

Much more detailed criticisms were made by Helen Bosanquet. In a lengthy correspondence *in The Times* (16 September and 4 October 1902) and in an article in the *Charity Organisation Review* (January–June 1903), the journal of the Charity Organisation Society, she registered four reservations about Rowntree's approach. First, Rowntree had not collected income data for the families being surveyed. He estimated the earnings of many workers. For skilled workers he assumed average wage rates of the trades in that area. Next, whether a family was in poverty was determined partly by the nature ascribed to the family together with the observations of Rowntree's interviewers. Helen Bosanquet was quick to point out that the seven months' survey would have required 62 visits every working day from the investigator: 'the impression obtained from such flying visits must be almost worthless' (*Charity Organisation Review*, 13). Rowntree's relative costs of different members of the family were challenged as was his averaging out of these costs. For good measure Mrs Bosanquet questioned what general conclusions could be drawn from the science of dietetics. Rowntree was apparently unperturbed by this onslaught and spent regular parts of the next half-century revising his poverty line.

These criticisms by Helen Bosanquet, and others, including newspaper reporters, showed they had read Rowntree as he wished to be understood; that he had defined a poverty line income and then calculated the numbers of people living below this level. Yet, amazingly, the income figures devised for defining poverty were not used for measuring the extent of poverty in York (John Veit Wilson, 'Paradigms of poverty: a rehabilitation of B S Rowntree', *Journal of Social Policy*, 1986, Hennock, 1991, 194). Rowntree wished to test Booth's findings. He had not made the mistake that so many have made over the past hundred years in thinking that Booth had a precise money definition of poverty which had been applied against detailed earnings data. Accordingly:

Although Rowntree had taken great pains to obtain information on family income which he regarded as reasonably reliable, he reached his conclusion on the total amount of poverty in York by ignoring it. He chose instead to judge by the appearance of the household and occasionally checked on this by talking to neighbours. (Hennock, 1991, 194)

The Poverty Line's Political Impact

Rowntree impacted on the political debate in three important respects. By defining a mere physical efficiency income line he brought his poverty study immediately into the mainstream of political debate as it erupted over the issue of national degeneration in the aftermath of the Boer War. 'The highest commercial success will be impossible so long as large numbers even of the most sober and industrial of the labouring classes receive about three-quarters of the necessary amount of food' (Rowntree, 1902, 256). It was for maximum effect that Campbell Bannerman—the Liberal Opposition Leader at the time—and Lloyd George, would cite Rowntree's findings in the long run-up to the 1906 general election.

In addition, Rowntree impacted on the political debate by his application of the idea of a life-cycle's income. This imaginative adaptation of a concept used by Booth moves the debate from looking at snapshots of poverty towards a dynamic approach, i.e., one not only concerned with who is poor now, but also with who would be poor in the future.

Equally important was the impact of his distinction between primary and secondary poverty. In a way which Rowntree never intended, part of the poverty debate which was about to open was now cast for the whole of the century. By mismanagement (secondary poverty) the poor had brought their misery upon themselves (Veit Wilson, 1986), or so the critics maintained.

After the publication of his study, Rowntree's definition of poverty played a part in the evolving minimum wage debate. Yet when it came to the crunch about how his poverty definition could be translated into policy the difficulties became insurmountable, at least for Rowntree. The 1899 definition of poverty had been devised for measuring the numbers falling above or below the line (although, as we have seen, it was somewhat ironically not used for this purpose by Rowntree himself). Its arbitrary nature made it a deeply inflexible tool when it came to devising actual policies, a fate which, as we shall see, also befell

Beveridge's attempt in this area. 'In 1913 Rowntree drew attention to the difference between the income envisaged for the purpose of the primary poverty line and the notion of a reasonable living wage, but had to confess that he knew no generally acceptable way of proceeding from one to the other (Hennock, 1991, 204–5).

The work of the academic and the policy maker had begun to diverge, although the major participants seemed unaware of this fact. The lack of appreciation of this turn of events, and the increasingly arbitrary and unreal definition which was to be attached to the idea of poverty, particularly through the work of A L Bowley, added a lasting confusion to the debate about what benefit levels actually represented. (The most sustained study of Rowntree's work in this area comes from John Veit Wilson, 1986.)

As we leave the examination of Rowntree's first attempts to define poverty, two issues particularly require emphasis. First, Rowntree's minimum income level guaranteed a standard of living in excess of that enjoyed by many working-class families. Second, at this time the poor and very large parts of the working class were interchangeable groups. The political significance of this last point will be commented upon later.

From Theory to Practice

Rowntree's studies directly influenced policy in two ways. Rowntree was on Beveridge's panel of advisers, helping him to define minimum income levels. Earlier, however, Rowntree's influence had been felt during the discussions of the newly established Unemployment Assistance Board (UAB) which in 1934 had the task of setting benefit rates for the unemployed. What was Rowntree's influence in these two crucial areas?

It is to Tony Lynes that we need to turn to find a review of the influences at work within the UAB, and the political pressures applied from without when, in 1934, the Board came to set the scale rates of benefit (T Lynes, 'Making of the Unemployment Assistance Scale', in *Low Incomes*, Supplementary Benefit Administration Paper 6, HMSO, 1977). Lynes lists six influences on the Board's deliberations at this time. These were:

- The level of payment made to the unemployed under the national insurance scheme.

- The level of payment being made by the Public Assistance Committees whose powers were being assumed by the Board.
- The level of wages paid to those in work.
- The level of expenditure restraints within which the government intended the Board to work.

Two final influences on the Board are of particular importance to our discussion on the extent to which benefit levels reflected minimum income requirements. The first of these influences was the debate on the level of income with which working-class families could manage without being pushed into destitution. Lynes records how judgements about where this line should be drawn underlie not only the official memoranda drawn up for the Board by its officials, but also many of the discussions which took place among Board members themselves. If considerable numbers of families were found to be living at a given level of income without there being too many obvious signs of hardship, and some such evidence was produced for the Board's consideration, those members advocating scale rates at a higher level found their task particularly difficult. Such arguments on this score tended to work against those lobbying for more generous benefit levels.

The second factor was the work of social scientists in calculating minimum income levels. This was also a topic on which the Board set out its views when it published its annual report in 1935. It stated that 'it was concerned with such primary needs as those of food, shelter, fuel, clothing and the like', but that it 'took account of authoritative opinion' on the cost of living which was to be found in the British Medical Association's Report on Nutrition, the Report of the Ministry of Health's Advisory Committee on Nutrition and the social surveys recently carried out in London and Liverpool (Lynes, 1977, 33).

Attempts to foster a debate on what constituted an adequate minimum were vetoed by the Board's secretary. At an early stage in their deliberations Board members were informed that 'there is no absolute criterion or scientific basis of need...any "minimum standard" must be determined largely by time and place' (Lynes, 1977, 43). A UAB minute reads that, in respect of determining the level of benefit payments, the Board had 'proceeded on the principle of less-eligibility' (quoted in John Veit Wilson, 'Condemned to deprivation?' in *Beveridge and Social Security*, ed. John Hills, John Ditch and Howard Glennerster, Oxford, 1994, 101).

This review of the background to the UAB's decision on benefit levels bears directly in one important respect on the wider question we are considering. Not only were the UAB rates the first official national minimum income levels but also, because the Board's papers have been made public, it has been possible to examine those arguments which weighed most heavily with the Board's members when they made their decision on the scale rates. The prevailing level of wages for the unskilled and semi-skilled worker, together with the widely held view that those out of work should not be more favourably treated than those earning low wages, were far more important in determining the level of UAB benefits than the work done by social scientists. Does that conclusion still hold when we consider how Beveridge went about his task in setting a minimum income adequate to prevent Want?

The Beveridge Report

In *Social Insurance and Allied Services* Beveridge argued that the primary poverty scale Rowntree had allegedly drawn up for his first study of poverty in York would 'be rejected decisively by public opinion today'. What he did not say was that he also rejected the more generous definition of income needs which Rowntree had devised for his 1936 study of poverty in York. Beveridge asserted that insurance benefits would have to guarantee a minimum standard of living related to Rowntree's human needs scale.

Beveridge's aim was to provide a system of insurance benefits which would prevent Want. To do this, a claimant's individual minimum needs would have to be met in full, including the payment of his rent. Rowntree argued with Beveridge that if Want were to be abolished, one condition of doing so would be to pay claimants their actual rent in full. But, as Josie Harris observes: 'Beveridge...was for once swayed by his official advisers—especially by the suggestion that a variable rent allowance would invest social insurance with the taint of a means-test.' Beveridge therefore proposed a flat-rate benefit which included a notional 10 shillings for weekly rent and, as a result, 'he allowed himself to be stuck with the paradoxical position that benefits should be based on subsistence needs and yet should be uniform in all parts of the country' (Josie Harris, *William Beveridge*, Oxford, 1977, 399).

It is at this initial stage of the discussion about benefit rates that

Beveridge's ideas confronted reality. It is a relatively simple exercise for social scientists to devise minimum income levels for their survey work, and even to influence official bodies with their findings. But the task of devising an accurate minimum income level on which a workable benefit system could be based was as impossible then as it is now. However, if Beveridge comprehended this crucial point he kept it to himself. For, after falling at the first hurdle called rent, he picked himself up as though nothing had happened, and continued to discuss the basis for calculating a minimum income adequate to ensure the abolition of Want.

Apart from rent, Beveridge's subsistence level of income comprised six parts: food, clothing, fuel, light and sundries, together with a small allowance which he called the 'margin'. To calculate the food requirement Beveridge turned to the 1936 and 1938 reports of the Technical Commission on Nutrition by the League of Nations. He used data on actual expenditure levels from the Ministry of Labour's family budgets to calculate the cost of clothing and of fuel, light, and sundries. In addition Beveridge allowed 'some margin—for inefficiency in purchasing [of food] and also for the certainty that people in receipt of minimum income required for subsistence would, in fact, spend some of it on things not absolutely necessary'.

One event had occurred before Beveridge had begun any serious thinking about his report and which undermined the political attractiveness of a subsistence level national insurance benefit scheme. In 1941 the Determination of Needs Act was passed. This heralded a change in policy towards the poor in more than one significant respect. First and foremost it brought to an end the hated household means test. Up until that Act, individuals seeking assistance were means-tested on their household's entire income. Not only was the income of the husband or wife taken into account, but also that of any other member of the household, whether an aged relative or, much more likely, the earnings of unmarried sons and daughters who were still living at home. The household means-test was understandably loathed. Children resented the assumption that the whole of their income would be put at the disposal of their parents when a decision was being made by the Public Assistance Board about their parents' needs. The parents similarly loathed children being placed in this position. Much family distress resulted and many families broke up as a consequence.

The 1941 Determination of Needs Act had a very important impact on the attitude of Labour MPs. Most politicians, including senior figures like Aneurin Bevan, believed that, with this Act, the main campaign against the means test was won. Alan Deacon quotes Bevan years later remarking: 'I have spent many years of my life in fighting the means-test. Now we have practically ended it. In future only the resources of men and dependent children...will be taken into account in determining their needs'. (Alan Deacon, 'An end to the means-test?', *Journal of Social Policy*, 1982, 291–2).

Two other forces were at work in the immediate aftermath of the publication of the Beveridge Report which helped shape the views of most of those MPs interested and knowledgeable in this area. The Assistance Board had moved from being the target of widespread criticism to one which, as a result of the effective way it dealt with families made destitute by German bombing, benefited from a more relaxed attitude. Then, in 1943, the assistance scales were raised appreciably. Those politicians who thought about the issue accepted that assistance payments were now above subsistence level.

This was the background to the setting up of the national insurance and national assistance rates in 1948. But, beginning with the 1943 assistance rates, the unchallenged assumption at the time was that the assistance scales did not constitute a poverty line.

Parliament debated the principles in the Beveridge Report on a number of occasions. The first full-scale parliamentary expression of views on the report occurred during a general debate on receiving the report and, naturally enough given the circumstances, most Members who spoke were concerned about the apparent lack of commitment to the report from the Coalition Government. (For details of this and subsequent debates see Frank Field and Matthew Owen, *Beyond Punishment*, ICS, 1994.) In this and in the main debate on the National Insurance Bill itself only two Members saw clearly the direction in which the country was heading. Graham White, the Liberal Member of Parliament for Birkenhead East up until the 1945 election, spelt out where the Coalition Government's approach would lead. And in the 1945 Parliament it was a newcomer of eight months' standing, Barbara Castle, Member for Blackburn, who repeatedly put her finger on the weakness of the Attlee Government's proposals.

Most Members expressed little interest in the issue that Barbara Castle raised, namely, the relationship between the level of national insurance and national assistance rates. Deacon records the minister, Thomas Steele, telling the Commons that the new rates in 1948 ensured 'an appreciable margin over bare subsistence' (Deacon, 1982, 303). Deacon concludes:

> The new scale rates were widely regarded as generous, and few commented upon the extension of means-testing which they implied. Indeed, the issue seems to have lost its former significance following the dramatic drop in unemployment and the removal of the household means-test. (Deacon, 1982, 302)

It was the work of Peter Townsend, more than anyone, who raised the spectre of poverty in the post-war welfare state. An early tract published at Political and Economic Planning was followed by a joint work with Brian Abel Smith (*The Poor and the Poorest*, Bell & Sons, 1965). These two authors examined the Family Expenditure Survey data to determine the numbers of people living at or below the then national assistance scales. This began the debate in earnest, not only about the numbers on low income, but also about equating poverty with the rates of benefits approved by Parliament for the welfare state's safety net which was, then, national assistance.

Peter Townsend's work renewed interest amongst a number of researchers in the whole area of benefits and particularly their real value. (See T Lynes, *National Assistance and National Prosperity*, Codicote Press, 1962, for example.) Indeed, the more ambitious of this group raised the extent to which the differentials in the benefit rates took inadequate account of the cost of children. This work by Margaret Wynn led first to Sir Keith Joseph (Social Services Secretary during the 1970–4 Government) and subsequently Norman Fowler and Tony Newton, as Secretaries of State in the late 1980s, to increase the relative value of the rates paid to children. This is an example of a book having a decisive impact on policy.

An examination of the value of national assistance/supplementary benefit/income support benefit rates since 1948 shows three trends:

- over this time scale, rates have kept ahead of inflation, although there have been periods where some groups have suffered real cuts in benefit between one uprating and another;
- the Conservative Government in the late 1950s decided that benefit levels should also reflect the growing prosperity of the country *Improvements in National Assistance*, Cmnd 782, HMSO 1959);
- this trend has continued even under the Tories since 1979 largely be-

cause their hardline supporters who call for cuts in the real value of
benefits remain ignorant of the Government's record. It is important to
stress two qualifications. This increase in the real value of benefits for
those on income support has been far less than the average increase in
living standards experienced by practically all other groups of the community. Also, some groups suffer real cuts in benefit between one
uprating and the next.

Yet there is a dilemma here. If the income support level is to be
regarded as a poverty line—official or unofficial—increases in the real
value of income support rates can paradoxically result in an increase
in the numbers of poor, despite the fact that those on income support
have gained advances in their living standards. This is an issue to
which the Social Security Select Committee has attempted to bring
some common sense. In two of its reports on the Low Income Statistics series the Committee asked the Institute of Fiscal Studies (IFS) to
calculate from FES data the number at and below the income support
level since 1979 (Social Security Committee, *Low Income Statistics*,
House of Commons Paper 359, HMSO, 1992, and *Low Income Statistics and Low Income Families 1989–92*, House of Commons Paper
254, HMSO, 1995). The Committee then requested the calculations to
be undertaken assuming that there had been no increase in the real
value of benefits. This second set of calculations gives a much more
accurate measurement of whether the numbers on low income are
increasing due to real increases in benefit levels, or to other causes.

Policy Conclusions

Rowntree set the parameters of the poverty debate in Britain this
century. Yet, as we have seen, it is one thing to attempt to define an
income sufficient to guarantee 'merely physical efficiency'; it is quite
another to translate this into benefit rates or minimum wage proposals.
*Seeking an exact definition of poverty in money terms and translating
the findings into a workable benefit system is a political eldorado. We
need to sidestep this futile exercise.*
The aim should be twofold. We have seen that the welfare state in
this country has been skewed almost exclusively to the question of
combating poverty. Such an emphasis stems directly from the impact
of the early social surveys conducted by Booth and Rowntree. In most
other European countries the debate has been cast much more widely

to address the question of how best to underpin working families' living standards. A reconstruction of Britain's welfare must bring our debate into line with that which has dominated the European agenda for most of this century.

Moving away from an exclusive debate about poverty is therefore a first priority. The long-term interests of the poor can best be served by setting their needs in the context of a much wider political agenda. The second move is to begin offering individuals a welfare income which harnesses their self-interest and wish for self-improvement so that they are motivated to leave the welfare roll, rather than, as at present, merely to maximise their income while remaining on welfare. Neither of these objectives will be achieved if income support levels are regarded as the official poverty line income.

Income support rates should simply be regarded as offering a minimum income level. To use the rates to measure the numbers of poor is perverse, given that both Booth and Rowntree used appearances rather than income to 'measure' the numbers of poor in their surveys. Moreover, as we have seen, the way the minimum benefit rates have been calculated has been, at best, arbitrary. Nobody who has any experience of living on the income support rates, or observed others doing so, has any illusion about the modest standard of living afforded by them, even for those with the most able budgetary skills. *The aim is not to define or redefine these levels with greater accuracy, but to free people from income support altogether. How can this be achieved?*

A political party must first recognise how dire the problem is, acknowledge its scale, and set out a strategy which aims to replace means-tested dependency, even though such a programme will take twenty or more years to achieve. This goal then becomes a yardstick by which to judge all welfare reforms; do they help or hinder the achievement of this objective?

Hard choices follow from this decision. The aim is to free people from means-tested dependence. Any redirected or new expenditure must go towards extending the coverage of national insurance benefits, not in raising what has been called the poverty line income itself.

Such an approach will attract a fair amount of political flak. Critics are likely to raise at least two major objections to this strategy. The first is that the living standards of those on benefit have not kept pace with the general rise in living standards, and, indeed, the living standards of the poorest 10 per cent since 1979 (the composition of this group largely comprises those on benefit) showed no increase at all before housing costs were taken into account, and fell by 17 per cent after housing costs (DSS, *Households Below Average Income: A Statistical Analysis 1979–1991/92*, HMSO, 1994).

There will be in all likelihood a campaign for raising the relative value of income support. The powerful case for raising rates in line with earnings has already been made (Jonathan Bradshaw and Tony Lynes, *Benefit Upratings: Policy and Living Standards*, SPRU, 1995).

Here the argument opens up and becomes a predominantly political one. Can such a commitment be delivered? I do not believe it can. Nor do I believe that it is in the long-term interest of most claimants for such a campaign to be successful. Its inevitable result is for means-tested welfare not merely to survive but to swell to even greater importance. *A strategy which enables people to see that their own efforts will be rewarded by increased living standards is the alternative.* Such a strategy would be open to a second line of attack. Critics will point out that a policy of building up non-means-tested coverage at the expense of raising the real value of means-tested benefits will result in the very poorest gaining no help, and any increase in income going to those above the state minimum income level.

There should be no dispute about the arguments. It is irrefutably correct to argue thus, for such an outcome is precisely what has to happen if individuals and families are to be given a real option of leaving means-tested assistance. What needs to be challenged is the political judgement of those who criticise this strategy. Unless the key decisions being outlined here are made and adhered to, there is no possibility whatsoever of reversing the growth of means-tested welfare dependency in this country other than by cutting the real value of that support. Equally important, the strategy advocated here allows the harnessing of self-interest and self-improvement to this objective. Current policies penalise these most powerful of human motivations.

5

Social Insecurity

In Britain today, seven times the number of people are wholly dependent upon means tested welfare as work in manufacturing industry. This is the appalling legacy of 16 years of Conservative Government. Hand in hand with means-tested welfare there is a new and invidious form of social insecurity. This outcome is the opposite of what war-time welfare reformers intended.

The aim of Britain's welfare state was to underpin a widespread sense of social security—that people would be full citizens, able to respond to economic and other incentives while at the same time liberated from Want. Today we would talk of means-tested welfare dependency rather than Want. For an ever-growing army of citizens the outcome has been very different from that original goal. Abolition of Want there has been, but at a cost. Today's welfare state offers claimants of working age three stark choices: of opting for a safe life on minimum benefit payments, doing nothing other than claiming benefit and sinking back into the lumpen poor; or they can respond to the opportunities to increase their income—as beneficial for the individual as it is crucial to society's wellbeing—only to find that active citizenship can all too often lead to possible loss of income and sometimes to loss of benefit entitlement itself; alternatively they can improve their lot by beginning to cheat and defraud their country.

In this chapter we are concerned with explaining the question of the form of social insecurity. We need first to consider the groups most exposed. From this analysis we will gain important pointers as to why the welfare bill is not only escalating but also channels human motives in a socially destructive direction.

95

TABLE 5.1
Number of National Assistance/Income Support
Claimants in 1950 and 1993

	(000s)			(000s)	
	1950 (a)			**1993**	
National Assistance		%	*Income Support*		%
NI Pensioners	644	50.1	Elderly (over 60)	1,736	30.8
Unemployed	73	5.7	Unemployed	1,920	34.0
NI sick/disabled	109	8.4	Sick & disabled	527	9.3
Other over pension age	167	13.0			
			Lone parents (b)	1,013	18.0
Widows	91	7.1	Widows	18 (c)	0.4 (c)
Other under pension age	201	15.6	Others	446	7.9
Total	1,285		Total (d)	5,643	

Notes: (a) Distribution estimated from live load data
       (b) Excluding those included in other groups
       (c) 1987 data: separate data was not collected after this date
       (d) Excluding 1987 data for widows
Sources: "Social Security Statistics" and Annual Reports of the Ministry of Social Security
       and National Assistance Board

Who Is Getting What?

The Beveridge model offered comprehensive insurance cover for all major categories of need. For exceptional cases there would be a safety net provided by national assistance. Few would need to resort to this form of help and for those who did there would be an element of stigma attached.

In chapter 3 we examined the development of Beveridge's thinking and how his social insurance scheme was modified in crucial respects by Keynes, by other civil servants and then by politicians. National insurance benefit rates were set below the national assistance rates. The impact of this decision, which was to push those without other resources on to means tested assistance, can be seen in table 5.1 on the number of claimants on the principal means-tested benefit in 1950 and 1993. At first there was no concern expressed by those on the Left. The assistance rates were accepted as being paid at above subsistence level. However, as the post-war years progressed, a scenario began to emerge which was very different from what had been originally planned.

Equally important is the total number of people living in households of claimants of income support. Under the social security ruling,

TABLE 5.2
Numbers Dependent on National Assistance/Income Support
in 1962 and 1993

	(000s)			*(000s)*	
	1962			**1993**	
National Assistance		*%*	*Income Support*		*%*
NI pensioners	1,340	45.0	Elderly (over 60)	2,044	20.8
Unemployed	528	17.7	Unemployed	3,315	33.8
NI sick/disabled	340	11.4	Sick & disabled	904	9.2
Other over pension age	225	7.6			
			Lone parents (a)	2,829	28.8
Widows	123	4.1	Widows	25 (b)	0.3 (b)
Other under pension age	419	14.1	Others	730	7.4
Total	2,975		Total (c)	9,822	

Notes: (a)   Excluding those included in other groups
         (b)   1987 data: separate data was not collected after this date
         (c)   Excluding 1987 data for widows
Sources: "Social Security Statistics" and Annual Reports of the Ministry of Social Security
         and National Assistance Board

the head of the household draws benefit for all of his or her dependants. Unfortunately these data were not collected on a systematic basis until 1962, an indication of how little importance was and still is attached to making a detailed study of the types of people claiming help and their reasons for so doing. And separate data on the number of single mothers, other than widows, were not collected until 1967. Table 5.2 lists the number of claimants and dependants according to the reason why the head of the household was drawing welfare.

A number of trends clearly emerges from these tables, two of which are of particular importance. The first is the sheer size of the numbers of people claiming the safety-net income support benefit. There is a dramatic increase from 1.2 million regular claimants in 1950 to 5.6 million in 1993. Far from the safety net becoming less and less important, as was originally envisaged, it now supports almost five times the number of claimants. Even more staggering is the increase in the number of people dependent upon the safety net—claimants and their families. Here the figure shows an increase from 1.8 million to 9.7 million, again between a four—and a five-fold expansion. These figures do not of course include the number who are eligible and for one reason or another refuse to claim means-tested help. The Government estimates this total at 1.1 million in 1991. In addition, there are those who are eligible for housing benefit but ineligible for income support.

A second trend which clearly emerges once the figures are presented over a longer period of time is the changing composition of those people resting on the safety net. While there are more pensioners drawing means-tested assistance than at the outset of the welfare state—up from 660,000 to 1.74 million, their proportion of the total has fallen from around a half to a third of all claimants. Their proportion falls further, to one in five, once the numbers of claimants and dependants are considered.

Single Parents and Poverty

Dependants are an important element. Table 5.1 shows that unemployment is now the major reason for pushing people down to income support income levels. But once the dependency figures are included, as they are in table 5.2, the picture is transformed. Single mothers rival the unemployed as the major reason for dependency. And once we consider the number of children of families on income support—as we do in table 5.3 below—the figures change again, with single mothers becoming the main cause of poverty or welfare dependency amongst children.

In 1988 every four children in single-parent families dependent on income support were matched by five children from the families of unemployed income support claimants. Within four years this position had been transformed. With falling unemployment the number of children dependent upon income support because their parents were unemployed has fallen to below 800,000. Although, of course, the number has been rising recently with the fallout for individuals from the Lawson boom, the number of children in single-parent families continues to increase. The total of 1.16 million children in 1988 had risen by over half a million, to 1.73 million, in a space of only five years.

The relative importance of the different kinds of single parents—never-married mothers, separated, divorced or widowed mothers—has also changed appreciably in the last few years. In 1987 there were more children in families where the parents were separated than there were children whose mothers had never married. That was the last year, however, when separation was the major cause of child poverty

TABLE 5.3
Dependent Children of Supplementary Benefit/Income Support Claimants
Great Britain (000s)

SB	Over 60 or claiming widow's benefit	Incapable of work due to sickness/disability	Lone parent	Under 60			
				Unemployed		Other	Total
1984	19.5	53.3	810.8	1,052.6	–	12.7	1,949.0

IS	Over 60	Disabled	Lone parent	Under 60			
				Unemployed	Government training	Other	Total
1988	20.3	62.7	1,167.5	782.9	9.8	48.6	2,091.8
1989	20.6	79.1	1,250.3	574.4	56.1	49.0	2,029.6
1990	21.9	96.4	1,333.3	476.8	61.2	55.3	2,044.8
1991	22.0	111.2	1,464.8	638.1	49.8	82.2	2,368.1
1992	23.5	154.9	1,617.6	755.9	55.0	96.0	2,702.9
1993	27.4	212.1	1,723.0	832.2	62.8	108.5	2,966.0

Source: IS/SB Annual Enquiries

or welfare dependency. By 1993 the number of children on income support with never-married mothers had risen to 1,189,000 children. This compares to the 970,000 children in families where parents had separated and the mother was dependent upon income support.

The major cost of single parenthood is probably borne by the children. Even so the cost to taxpayers remains very considerable. In 1979 the means-tested benefit welfare bill for single-parent families stood at £640m. By 1993–94 this total had shot up to over £6.4m. Diagram 5.1 below illustrates these figures and includes the total cost of child benefit and the addition paid to child benefit for single-parent families, the one-parent family benefit.

Poverty's Younger Face

If one considers pensioners as one group and then juxtaposes the number of claimants below pensionable age, it is apparent that, during the last 45 years, welfare dependency has increasingly been wearing a younger face. The numbers of non-pensioners rose from 37 per cent of all claimants in 1948 to 69 per cent in 1993. The younger face is even more marked if dependency figures are used: up from 47 per cent to 79 per cent of the total over the 1962–1993 period.

The increase in the proportion of younger claimants has not occurred at that part of the age distribution we might have expected. The 'voluntary' retirements among 50–year-olds has had an impact on the figures, as diagram 5.2 shows. But the growth in welfare dependency amongst this group has been massively overshadowed by the truly staggering jump in the numbers of younger people on benefit. The 20–29–year-olds, who formed 4 per cent of claimants in 1950, now account for a quarter of all those claiming income support in 1993. The next largest group, those aged between 30 and 39 years old, have grown from 5.8 per cent to 18 per cent of all claimants. Combining these two groups, 20–39–year-olds already comprise over 44 per cent of all income support claimants. If we add the 'depressed', the 16–19–year-olds who are despondent because the Government has all but denied them benefit rights, the total is in excess of 50 per cent. Expressed another way, over half of all income support welfare dependency is concentrated within a 20–year age group of 19–39–year-olds. And once again these figures underestimate the number of people living with claimants in this age group. The data unfortunately only

DIAGRAM 5.1
Social Security Benefits for Lone Parents 1978–9 and 1993–4

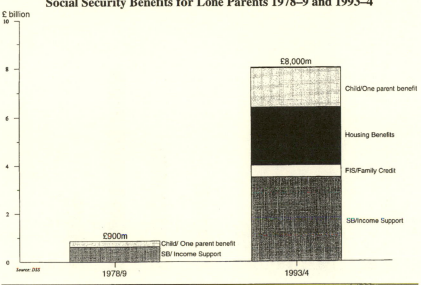

record the number of claimants and do not include their dependants. It is, however, this younger age group which features so heavily in the ghetto areas which are being created in Britain's inner cities and on the outer city council estates. Over half of all men, however, will be without work with almost no chance of their prospects changing unless the limits for a market-led job regeneration are reflected in changes in policy.

Poor Law Revival

Here then is the full extent of the survival of the Poor Law in Britain—nearly 40 years after Labour politicians boasted that it had been finally laid to rest. Today almost one in five of the population are caught on income support—a proportion many times larger than was ever achieved under the Poor Law itself. Why, when Labour was committed to abolishing the hated mean test, did the Party not foresee this outcome? This question will be considered in the following chapter.

Income support is paid only to those outside the labour market. That, at least, is the theory. As we have seen, Beveridge's subsistence income included the payment of rent. Income support claimants have

DIAGRAM 5.2
Age Composition of Income Support Claimants

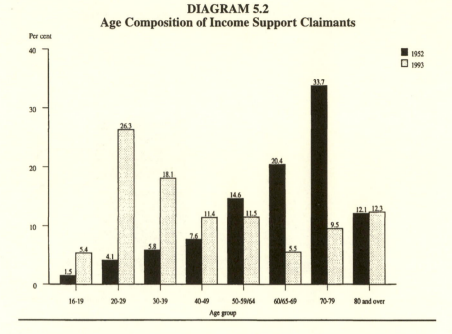

their rent paid in full and also, generally, the interest on mortgage repayments. The scheme of rent rebates and allowances (rebates for public housing and allowances for the private sector), which was previously run by local councils, was unified into a national scheme in 1972. In that year 1.8 million rebates were paid (if supplementary benefit claimants in local authority housing who claim their rent payments automatically are included) together with 48,000 allowances. By May 1994 the data show a surge in the number of claimants—up to 2.57 million for rent rebates with the number of rent allowance payments to private landlords up to 1.6 million. These increases naturally show up in the budget. The cost of housing benefit had risen in 1976–7 from £730m in today's prices to a staggering £8.7bn in 1983–4.

A national rate rebate scheme became operative in 1966 and in the following year 896,000 rebates were paid in England and Wales. By May 1993 4.7 million people were in receipt of council tax rebates. The cost of this benefit has risen to £1.8bn.

Housing benefit and council tax rebates are paid automatically to those registering for income support. Payments may also be made to people in work on low incomes. At this point the means-test net spreads

TABLE 5.4
Composition of Housing Benefit and Council Tax Benefit Recipients
May 1993

	000s	% of total
Housing benefit recipients	4,529	100
In receipt of income support	2,852	63
Not in receipt of income support	1,676	37
In work	*288*	*6*
Council tax benefit recipients	5,251	100
In receipt of income support	3,018	57
Not in receipt of income support	2,233	43
In work	*321*	*6*

Source: HC Deb 22 Feb 1995 c251w, Social Security Statistics 1994

out into the working population. The numbers claiming housing benefit and council tax rebate who are at work are given in table 5.4.

Apart from these two benefits paid on grounds of low earnings, there have been, since 1971, subsidised payments directed to those earning very low wages. Merely to pose the question, 'Who could be against subsidising low wages?' highlights where short-term thinking has landed welfare in this country.

In the run-up to the 1970 election the CPAG criticised the Labour Government for allowing the poor to get poorer. As the campaign between the Labour Government and the Group became more acrimonious the qualification that CPAG attached to its finding that the poor were becoming relatively poorer became lost. The Tory Opposition led by Edward Heath took up the cry and, as Alan Watkins reported at the time, no Tory rally was complete without Heath mentioning CPAG's findings to his astonished hearers. That the Group was practically unknown to the Tory faithful listening to their leader's condemnation of Labour was irrelevant. The Conservatives committed themselves to increased family allowances, as child benefit was then called, and to 'clawing' the increase back from richer taxpayers by simultaneous adjustments to child tax allowances.

Once in office the Tories realised something which had eluded CPAG. The tax threshold, the point at which individuals pay tax, was below the level of income which people could claim when not working. To increase family allowances, as CPAG campaigned, while at the same time limiting the cost by adjusting child tax allowances by a

similar amount so that the increase was clawed back from all taxpayers, would have resulted in some wage earners on very low pay losing
the whole of the family allowance increase.

The way around this difficulty, of course, would have been to raise
the tax threshold so that no one paid income tax on earnings below
what the state regarded as the official poverty line. The Conservative
Government's response was different, however. In 1971 they introduced the family income supplement (FIS), the first scheme to subsidise
low wages since the 1834 Poor Law Reform had superseded the
Spedhamland system. FIS was replaced by family credit in 1988. The
numbers show that in 1971 65,000 claimants and dependants benefited
from FIS payments. Currently over 570,000 are FIS claimants. The
numbers covered by family credit are of course much higher. Once
dependants are included the total rises to a little over 2 million. Family
credit payments also provide eligibility for housing benefit, free school
meals and free medicines.

Only low wage earners with children are currently eligible for family credit. But, on what can best be viewed as the salami principle of
welfare reform, the Government now proposes to experiment to extend eligibility to childless wage earners. Once again, if our concern is
only for the here and now, who could be against such a move? But
each of these well-meaning but ill-thought-out reforms is helping to
play havoc with the temper and the common life of the country.

Half the Population on Means Tests

Indeed it is now possible to marshal fully the arguments against a
welfare state which subjects so many members to the Poor Law tradition of subsistence on a means test alone. Figures so far presented give
information on the individual claimants to means-tested benefit. And
individuals may be entitled to claim income support and housing benefit as well as council tax rebate, or family credit and housing benefit
as well as council tax rebate. Adding together the claims for each
benefit tells us only about the numbers of such payments. It does not
tell us about the number of individuals and families on means test, for
families can legally be entitled to a number of means-tested benefits.
Table 5.5 plots the information for the numbers of people drawing a
major means-tested benefit and accounts for any double counting. It
shows that while there are very nearly 16 million individual claims for

TABLE 5.5
Number of Claimants on Means Tested Assistance Spring 1993:
Great Britain

		(000s)
Income support (May)		5,643
Family credit (April)		487
Housing benefit (May):	*receiving income support*	2,852
	receiving family credit	115
	other	1,562
Council tax benefit (May):	*receiving income support*	3,020
	receiving family credit	129
	other	2,104
Gross total		15,912
Net total		9,796

Source: Social Security Statistics 1993

means-tested assistance, the number of heads of households whose income from welfare is at least in part dependent upon a major means-tested form of support is a little under 9.8 million. This amounts to just under one in two of all households in the country.

There are no detailed breakdowns of the figures showing the pattern of increase since 1979, as detailed figures are not available on a consistent basis over this period. But it would seem likely that the number of households claiming at least one of the major means-tested benefits in 1978–9 was in the range of four and a half to five million. Thus the number has roughly doubled during the following decade. An alternative source of information is the DSS analysis of Households Below Average Income. This shows that there were an estimated 13.8 million recipients of means-tested benefits in 1991–2. This includes partners and dependants and compares unfavourably with an estimate of 9.3 million for 1979. There are a number of differences between the HBAI estimate and the administrative count. It is clear however that there has been an increase in the number of means-tested recipients, who represented an estimated 17 per cent of individual households in 1979 compared with 24 per cent in 1991–2 (House of Commons Library Note 28 December 1994).

The growing dominance of means tests under the Tories can be seen from the information and the amount spent on each of the major groups of benefits: contributory or national insurance, non-contribu-

TABLE 5.6
Social Security Expenditure on Each of the Main Categories of Benefit,
1978–9 and 1993–4 (in 1993–4 prices)£bn

	1978–9	1993–4
NI	30.705	39.451
Non-contributory	1.920	6.694
means tested	12.869	34.797

Source: DSS

tory and non-means-tested, and finally means-tested benefits. This information is presented in table 5.6.

By far and away the greatest growth in expenditure is in means-tested support—up from £12.9bn in 1978–9 to £34.8bn by 1993–4. The role of means testing in our social security system would be even more visible if the Government produced a breakdown of benefit expenditure for non-pensioner claimants. This they do not do. But the information on the growth in the numbers on income support, for example, shows that overwhelmingly this has been concentrated amongst primarily single parent-families and, to a lesser extent, the unemployed.

Who could be against any of those advocating means tests as a way of targeting help on the poorest if the judgement is limited only to the present? It is only when a longer-term time span is adopted that the full horror of post-war welfare can be seen. Means tests have spread their tentacles across society to a growing extent in the post-war world. Within the lifespan of the present Government the number of households trapped on means-tested benefit has probably doubled. If we estimate the number of dependants in the 9.8 million households claiming a major means-tested benefit (assuming a ratio of 1.5 dependants per claimant) we find that something in the order of half of the entire country is now ensnared in means-tested welfare dependency. A welfare system increasingly shaped to concentrate help on the poor has turned out to have a monstrous effect on human motivation and honesty—the fundamental forces which determine the very nature of society.

It is in this sense that means tests are a poverty trap from which it is almost impossible to be sprung but from which one would wish to be sprung. The reason is that these men and women, like most others, wish to maximise their income. The eligibility rules ensure that most effort by economic men and women will be channelled into working the system, i.e., of maximising help from welfare rather than striving for independence from it.

Let us consider the example of a divorced woman with no children. Any number of other examples could be cited. The position in which this 50–year-old woman finds herself was written about recently by Bishop Montefiore. Her husband had disappeared and, as there were no children, the Child Support Agency was uninterested in her welfare. She claimed income support and housing benefit and thereby qualified for nil council tax contributions. She qualified in addition for free medicines. She cannot afford a holiday, hardly gives herself any treats and frequents 'nearly new' shops for clothes.

Part-time work is open to her. It is unlikely that she will gain a full-time job in present circumstances. She can work for up to 30 hours but she can keep only £5 of her earnings. So even if she were lucky enough to earn £100 a week she would only be about £10 a week better off once she had paid her increase in rent and picked up her council tax bill and met the charge from the Inland Revenue. In these circumstances what should she do?

An increasing number of people in this position either opt to do nothing—welfare dependency par excellence—or commit fraud. As Hugh Montefiore concludes: 'quite widespread fraud hardly induces public sympathy. [Yet] no one in their senses wants to produce a nanny state which creates increasing dependency'. ('Pushed into dishonesty', *Church Times*, 23 December 1994).

It is here that we are brought face to face with the reality of how human nature operates. Politicians, above all people, are not in the business of being able to change the deepest of human motivations. What politicians should be concerned about is creating a framework of rules which strikes most people as fair and reasonable and which at the same time attempts to harness self-interest and self-improvement in a manner which is conducive to the public good.

Cheating the Taxpayer

Cheating the welfare, as it is called, is now a major business. Taxpayers' money comes under attack from organised gangs. Two activities are particularly lucrative. Order books are stolen in bulk. The most public side of this trade is the usually bleak announcement of a postal train robbery. Sacks of order books are what the gangs are usually after. Understandably the Government discloses very little information about the range of organised warfare against the DSS. We do not know, for example, whether criminal groups have been able to take one step back from stealing order books and begun to print fraudulently their own supply. Given the value of such a regular supply it would be very surprising if a number of such operations were not being carried out in different parts of the country at any time.

The other known major organised criminal warfare action against the DSS is the buying of order books from claimants. In most poorer areas certain pubs will be known as points where the trade takes place. Order books can be worth well over £2,000 each. Claimants sell them for a knockdown rate. These books then re-enter circulation under new covers and are cashed by part of a very wide gang network at post offices in other parts of the country. The claimant who sold his or her order book then reports its 'loss' to the DSS. A new one is issued shortly afterwards. For obvious reasons there is no known value put on the size of this trade.

Much greater concerted action should be taken against gang-based fraud. This should be a priority and it is an issue separate from the concern of this book, which is, fundamentally, about the principles on which welfare should be reconstructed. The main concern here must necessarily be how the motivation and actions of individual claimants are affected by the operation of today's welfare state. The typography of fraud encompasses the following activities.

Many claimants drift, or find themselves slowly being pulled into, fraud. The way the labour market works, and the DSS's inability to respond quickly and effectively, acts as an effective recruiting sergeant to the ranks of the fraudulent. Consider the position of a young mother on benefit working part time in a local pub. She declares her earnings to the DSS. One week one of the other part-time workers is ill. The employer asks her to work more time. What should she do? To refuse may result in the loss of her job. To report the extra earnings will invariably result in her benefit being recalculated with the chance of payments not being made to her on time, and probably not for some weeks. Even if she does tell the DSS staff she may be told by one of the officers to forget it and just pocket the extra money. But once her employer knows she will work more hours the chances are that she will be asked to become more 'flexible' in her working week. What started out as an act of goodwill to her employer, and her own self-interest to keep the job, can very quickly degenerate into the beginnings of regular fraudulent claims of income support.

There has been, understandably, great disappointment with the effectiveness so far of the Child Support Agency (CSA) operations. Given its apparent inability to function with even a modest degree of success in establishing regular payments by non-custodial parents, it is not without irony that its one clear success has been in an area where no claim was ever made for the Agency. By accident it has turned into being an effective agent against fraud.

In the first year of operation mothers who were drawing benefit as single parents returned order books to the value of £1170m. In most incidences the supposed absent parent had never left the family home and these families returning the order books did not have the wit to lie and think up another address. This gigantic total, however, is only the tip of the iceberg of fraud in this area. Families invent fictitious desertions and back them up with another address for the supposed absent parent. Others do not even bother to do this. With the cessation of routine home visiting by the DSS, neighbours have little idea of who is on benefit and who is not. If couples live together but claim as independent households from different addresses, no one will know, least of all the poor old DSS who, shorn of home visitors by the Tories, have not the faintest idea of what is really going on. Nor will they get tip-offs from neighbours who in the past would have seen DSS officers visiting in their area families who are known to be at work. Claimants can also work on the side and again be in little danger of ever being found out. Their greatest chance of being rumbled by the authorities is when their employer wishes to get rid of them with the minimum amount of fuss. A call to the DSS, followed by charges, does just that. Thus the morality of the state is further undermined. The employee abuses the system. The employer manipulates the employee.

The Government claims it is making major headway against these kinds of claimant abuse. But its own figures are bogus. When a single mother is found to be living with a boyfriend who works, her order book is taken away. The value of the weekly benefit is multiplied by 32 weeks—an arbitrary figure guessed at by the Department for the average number of weeks a fraudulent claimant will be off the books. Within a couple of days of course the mother will have no money, the children will be hungry and the family, quite rightly, will be back on benefit.

Fraud officers, set meaningless targets by the Secretary of State, meet these objectives by picking on single mothers. The benefit 'savings' are achieved and duly published. But if most families have made a new claim within days there cannot be in reality a 32–week benefit saving. For that is how the figures are presented.

This fraud on the part of the Government about its anti-fraud success rate leaves untouched the much more sinister and costly individual claimant fraud. Large numbers of claimants draw benefit and work full time. Fraud officers find it massively difficult to track down these claimants. The claimants are usually adept at giving the fraud officer the slip. How best to tackle effectively the fraud of single mothers living with boyfriends or working part time will be considered in the final chapter as it has to be a major consideration when reconstructing welfare rules. (At that point non-claimant fraud is also considered.) But fraud by claimants working full time can be dealt with easily and effectively by any government that wishes to act. Claimants so suspected should be required to register three or four times a day. At each registration claimants would be told the time of their next appointment. Identification cards would be a necessary accompaniment of this reform. Without such a change claimants working full time would begin employing other claimants to pose in their place at the registrations. In return such claimants would demand a stake in the fraudulent benefit claim.

Policy Conclusions

Welfare dependency has grown like Topsy during the post-war years. Ten million householders draw at least one of the major means-tested benefits. Once dependants are included, half of the population now has their standard of living determined to some extent by means-tested welfare provision. While means-tested dependency dominates Britain's welfare provision it offers millions of people the stark choice of cheating or inaction.

This horrendous scenario was never envisaged by war-time reformers. It has occurred from a combination of politicians going for the short-term cheap option of means testing and then paying no attention to the direction in which they have set the welfare agenda.

Welfare's whole *raison d'etre* has to be radically overhauled and redirected so that it can offer opportunities for self-improvement and self-advancement while allowing a vast body of citizens to keep within the law.

Agreement is crucial on three inter-related responses. First, there is the urgent need to recognise just how fundamental is the challenge welfare now poses to a free, honest and open society. Second, to accept that there is no short-term cut to reform. A twenty-year programme is needed which is spelt out and against which every action and welfare reform can be judged. That programme must be based on a clear objective of the role of welfare in a free society and, at the same time, to take full account of human nature. Third, and simultaneously, it is crucial not only to make effective the whole series of anti-fraud measures but also to construct pathways back to legitimacy for those who are currently defrauding the welfare state.

6

The Disintegrating
Socio-Economic Landscape

Today's Uncertain World

The world for which Beveridge devised his welfare state has, largely, passed away. While millions had waited patiently for work during much of the 1920s and 1930s, Beveridge's scheme assumed there would be full employment. Indeed, he stressed that his proposals were based on this assumption. So fundamental was full employment to Beveridge's scheme that he moved quickly from publishing *Social Insurance and Allied Services* to commence a freelance enquiry on this very topic.

The Coalition Government, rattled by Beveridge's activities, rushed through the publication of its own White Paper *Employment Policy*, in June 1944 (Cmd 6527, HMSO) so as to head off the impact of Beveridge's labours. Beveridge's efforts appeared five months later under the title *Full Employment in a Free Society* (Allen & Unwin, 1944).

The post-war welfare state was designed for a world where a fully employed male labour force brought home reasonable wage packets, where women often worked in the home, where the overwhelming proportion of young people moved straight from school into work, and where once a satisfactory job had been found (there is evidence that young people initially swapped jobs quite frequently) it would last until retirement forty-five or more years later.

The world has changed in a number of fundamental ways since these early post-war years.

- Employment prospects for most people have been transformed. The phrase 'a flexible labour market' would have been unintelligible to Beveridge.
- The numbers working part-time have transformed the labour market, both because such a pattern of work was largely unknown to Beveridge, and also because it has heralded the growing importance of women workers.
- In the 1940s the number of single mothers on benefit was insignificant: even then most of these parents were widows. Now the largest group of claimants with children on welfare are mothers who have never married.
- Beveridge was no innocent when it came to human frailty. He assumed that some claimants would cheat. But he would be staggered by the extent of welfare fraud today. He attached the main responsibility for abuse of the system to politicians who placed temptation in the way of claimants.
- He would no doubt be pleasantly surprised by the extent to which life expectancy has increased—he wrote his famous report at an age when most people would now have retired—but even he would have been taken aback by the number of people who now live for more years in retirement than they spend in work.

Each of the ways in which British society has been transformed over the past 40 years throws up a serious challenge to what is required of a welfare state and how it can operate. Indeed these challenges, once knitted together, have thrown our welfare system into deep trouble. We need to consider each of these major changes in turn as they will set the framework within which new policies have to be developed.

Revolution in the Job Market

There have been two near revolutionary changes in the composition of those in employment: the number of women working and the growth of part-time work.

Every woman turning up to work in 1948 was accompanied by two male colleagues. Less than fifty years later there are already more women than men working in some industries. Shortly there will be more women overall in employment than men. This significant change in the employment stakes occurred in the 1980s. Although this trend was clearly visible in the previous decade, the position when Mrs Thatcher was first elected was not that dramatically different from 1971 (the first date for which we have reliable data on full- and part-time employment). In 1978 9.4 million women were in employment as opposed to 13.4 million men. In 1993 the 10.8 million total of male workers had only just managed to keep its nose ahead of the 10.48 million women workers.

The second near revolutionary employment change has been in the number of hours worked, and again a significant change occurred during the 1980s. Almost nothing is known about why people work the number of hours they do. Presumption must therefore take the place of hard data. Women fit in major household responsibilities with working and it is presumed that the hours worked reflect this. But the hours worked by both women and men are also presumably affected both by domestic budgetary pressures as well as by expectations about improving living standards. It is the rise in the real value of wages and salaries which has allowed the dramatic reduction in hours worked and thereby in what is thought of as full-time work. A workman a hundred years ago would think of what today constitutes full-time work as being clearly part time. In 1861 fitters and turners in London, to take one example, worked an average of 58.5 hours a week. By the 1920s this total had fallen to 47 hours, falling again to 42 hours in the 1960s and to 39 hours in 1980. And there the total number of hours worked has remained constant as it has across most industrial sectors. If the same pace of this long-term reduction in the number of hours worked had continued through the 1980s, Paul Gregg estimates that a million jobs could have been created ('Share and share alike', *New Economy*, IPPR, Spring 1994). Why, when living standards rose at an average rate of a third over the decade, the number of hours worked did not continue to decline is a mystery awaiting explanation.

The changing composition of the labour force, and the mix between full-time and part-time, have thrown up major challenges for the social security system and must be a pivotal consideration in any reconstruction of welfare. This challenge is not limited to ensuring that part-time workers are adequately covered by the social security system. For what role do we assign to the large group of unskilled males for whom there is currently no prospect of work?

The Rise and Rise of Part-Time Work

It is important to discuss both these trends in more detail. It is true that large numbers of females work part-time. The DE estimates that 6.5 million out of a total workforce of 24.6 million are part-time workers. This total of part-time workers is composed of 5.2 million women workers as opposed to only 1.4 million male workers. Yet part-time jobs are making up a greater proportion of all jobs. Since 1978 the number of full-time posts in the economy has dropped by almost 3 million, whereas the number of part-time jobs has risen by just under 2 million. (Frank Field and Paul Gregg, *Who Gets What, How, and for How Long?*, Mimeograph, 1994). One-third of all part-time working in the EU now takes place in the United Kingdom.

Part-time working is defined as employment offering not more than 30 hours a week. In the 12 months to the end of 1993 the number of part-timers working up to 7 hours a week rose by 150,000, an increase of twice the rate of those gaining jobs of between 16 and 30 hours a week, and three times the rate of those working between 8 and 15 hours a week. Workers putting in up to only 7 hours a week now account for over one-third of all the hours worked by part-timers. During the same period the numbers working 31 hours a week or more fell by 316,000 (Philip Bassett, 'Part-time solutions that mask full-time problems', *The Times*, 18 April 1994). *The changing nature of the number of hours worked is a factor which needs to be taken into account when refashioning welfare. Benefit rights must adapt to the changes in the numbers of hours worked, particularly the growth in the number of part-time workers.*

This growth in part-time earnings is already having an important impact on the social security budget and the welfare state's coverage. This is particularly so for a social security system based on insurance rights. As we have seen, the fastest growing group of part-time workers are those working under 7 hours a week. The vast majority of this group, and of other part-time workers, do not earn enough to participate in the national insurance scheme. We have consequently seen, for the first time since 1945, a very substantial and growing army, composed almost totally of women, who will not qualify for any national insurance cover—unemployment or sick pay, and most important of all, a national insurance pension in their own right.

The Government attaches so little importance to this scenario that no official figures are collected on the size of this group of disenfranchised workers. The only data available relate to the number of workers who fail to make a single national insurance contribution during a given year. The figures are staggering. Over 1.5 million workers at the end of 1992 failed to earn in any of the preceding 52 weeks a sum above the national insurance threshold (*Hansard*, 9 May 1994, cols. 36–8w). This snapshot figure is, however, an underestimate of the number of workers disenfranchised from eligibility for the main non-means tested benefits.

There are 5.4 million people in paid employment who are excluded from the New Earnings Survey largely on the grounds that their income is below the PAYE tax threshold, itself usually only a little above the national insurance threshold. In addition, there will be large numbers of workers who pay contributions in some weeks, but not on a systematic basis, who gain no national insurance cover. It is crucial in planning a restructuring of welfare that detailed information is gathered on this large and growing body of disenfranchised workers (for the case for Employment Audits see Frank Field, 'Employment Audits' in *The Full Employment Seminar*, The Prudential, 1995, and Frank Field and Paul Gregg, 1994). In the absence of such information it is important to build into the assumption underpinning the reform that there is a large group of workers who pay over the year varying amounts of national insurance contribution and who gain no national insurance benefit rights. How these contributions can be converted into benefit rights is considered in the policy chapter at the end of the volume.

We also need to consider the impact not just of part-time working, but of the growth of contract working and of self-employment, as each of these trends must be allowed to help determine the kind of insurance-based welfare which is being proposed here. The latest information on these two trends shows each becoming a more important source of employment.

The Disinherited Male

It is also claimed that the labour market in Britain is fast moving into a clear division between two-wage households on the one hand and no-wage households on the other. That is the conclusion to which, for example, Paul Gregg has come. An analysis of trends over a thirty-

TABLE 6.1
Population by Economic Status of Family

	1961		1991	
	Share of total	Share of 'in work'	Share of total	Share of 'in work'
Self-employed	7.4%	13.2%	9.9%	18.7%
All full-time	23.5%	42.1%	23.5%	44.3%
Full-time/Part-time	13.4%	24.1%	13.8%	26.0%
Full-time/not working	36.3%	65.1%	14.6%	27.6%
All part-time	2.6%	4.6%	6.2%	11.7%
Over 60	11.6%	n.app.	17.6%	n.app.
Unemployed	0.7%	n.app.	6.0%	n.app.
Other	4.6%	n.app.	8.5%	n.app.
Total	100.0%	n.app.	100.0%	n.app.

Source: IFS *For Richer, For Poorer*, table 3.2

year period by the Institute of Fiscal Studies refines the Gregg position (Alissa Goodman and Steve Webb, *For Richer For Poorer*, IFS, 1994). It is not so much that the two-wage households are composed of a full-time, probably male, earner together with a part-time, probably female earner. The most significant growth has been in households with an absence of full-time workers, but an increase in the number of members working part-time.

What is also clear is that a large group of males who were previously in work are no longer and that the unemployment figures underestimate the size of this group. Alongside the trend in long-term unemployment we need to consider what is called the inactivity rates, i.e., the ratio of people of working age who are not in work but who do not appear amongst the unemployment figures.

What has happened to this group, and particularly the unskilled male who is least advantageously placed as far as employment opportunities are concerned? The unemployment rate for this group of males rose by 8 percentage points between 1977 and 1991 and the inactivity rates by a further 16 percentage points. By 1991 1 in 5 of all males, and 1 in 3 of unskilled male workers, had no job (Edward Balls, *Work and Welfare: Tackling the Jobs Deficit*, IPPR, 1993).

That is a dramatic change from the employment position in the late 1970s. At around that time approximately one million men of working age were inactive. By 1992 this total had more than doubled. So what does this group do? Here again is another question on which the official data maintain a resolute silence.

This trend of rising inactivity amongst male workers is not confined to the United Kingdom. A summary of the inactivity and non-employment data shows:

- Non-employment rates rose during the 1980s in almost all OECD countries.
- In continental Europe this rise was largely reflected in the unemployment statistics.
- In the UK, Sweden, Canada and Austria the rise in inactivity was as important as was the rise in unemployment.
- The big exception to all these trends is the US. Here non-employment rates fell only very slightly in the 1980s after rising during the 1970s.

Now let us consider what is happening behind these trends and specifically for the prospects of men aged between 25 and 55 during this period. Non-employment rates for this group of males have doubled in the US since 1970, despite that country producing by far and away the best record on job creation. The same rates have tripled in the UK, France and Germany.

Despite all the encouraging noises about job creation in different countries across the Western world, one fact stands out in stark relief. The numbers of what are called prime-aged male workers who are non-employed have risen significantly not only in France, Germany and the UK, but also in the United States, which has the best employment creation record of any western country (Balls, 1993).

Here the argument leads us to another clear choice. The limitations of an insurance-based social security system have to be faced. The Poor Law tradition in England has resulted in a widely held belief that, in the absence of work, the unemployed have an indefinite right to maintenance by the state. The workhouse poor originally gained help after entering the workhouse. This policy was then adapted by the offer of outdoor relief, first through the Poor Law, and then through public assistance provision. After 1948 this income of last resort was organised through the National Assistance Board, which was succeeded in 1966 by the Supplementary Benefits Commission and is now organised through the current income support system which commenced operation in 1988.

The case for building up a public works programme was first proposed in the late 1880s as an alternative to the Poor Law. Its success over the following two decades has never been properly appreciated (Frank Field and Matthew Owen, *Beyond Punishment: Hard Choices on the Road to Full Employability*, ICS, 1994). Given the plight in which the disinherited unskilled male worker now finds himself, a renewal of this approach assumes a new urgency.

In contrast to the position of some men, the position of women generally is improving. Women now account for an increasing proportion of the declining numbers in full-time jobs. Moreover, while the numbers of full-time workers earning low pay have increased since 1979, the number and proportion of women working full-time but earning low wages actually fell. And, as we have already seen, an increasing number and proportion of full-time workers are women. It is not therefore possible to argue that they have gained these jobs by undercutting men. A different position however emerges when we consider a similar analysis of what has been happening to part-time workers' pay. By far and away the biggest increase in the numbers of part-time workers earning low pay is accounted for by women workers. (The likelihood here though is not that women have undercut male workers, but that male workers refuse to consider most of the new jobs which they regard as 'women's work'.)

So, three trends have been at work in the role of women workers in the labour market.

- They have been winning a growing share of full-time jobs.
- Similarly, more of those full-time jobs are paying good wages and salaries.
- However, the biggest increase in employment over the recent past has been amongst part-time workers. Those jobs are generally poorly paid, and have gone overwhelmingly, although not exclusively, to women.

The Pay Revolution

I want to discuss a phenomenon which is of enormous importance—probably the single most significant social change affecting the UK and most other Western countries. That phenomenon is not the ageing of the population. Nor the breakdown of the family. Nor the increasing proportion of women at work. Rather, it is a phenomenon which is strangely largely unrecognised—the growing dispersion of earnings power.

TABLE 6.2
Number of Individuals in Households with Net Equivalised
Incomes Below 50 Per Cent of Average Where at Least One Person
in the Family Is in Employment

Period	Before housing costs (*millions*)	After housing costs (*millions*)
1979	1.5	1.7
1987	2.9	3.5
1990 & 1991	3.5	4.5
1991 & 1992	3.5	4.6

Source: *Households Below Average Income, 1979–1990/91*, HMSO, 1993 and *1979–1991/92*, HMSO, 1994.

So spake the Social Services Secretary towards the end of 1994 (Peter Lilley, speech to the Northern Ireland CPC, 18 November 1994). I for once could not accuse him of underestimating the trend to which he had drawn attention.

The European norm is to consider those earning below two-thirds average earnings as being low paid: 4.6 million full-time workers in the UK in 1979 earned below this threshold. By 1992 this total had risen to 5.8 million full-time workers. In respect of part-time workers the crude figures are 7.8 million in 1979 and 10.3 million in 1992.

So one trend is clear and widely understood. Over the Thatcher years inequality in earnings became very much more marked. Indeed the gap between the poorest 10 per cent of male workers compared to the average male wage packet is wider now than at any time since 1886 when the data were first collated.

The numbers of very low paid show up clearly in the Households Below Average Earnings series (HBAE). Table 6.2 sets out the position in 1979 and 1992—the latest year for which data is available.

The growing number of low-paid workers impacts in a number of different ways on the social security budget. There is the question of pension entitlement, to which we shall return later. Low pay also impacts through the eligibility it gives to means-tested wage supplements. The first in modern times was introduced in 1971 under the family income supplement scheme. In the last year of the scheme's operation, 1988, 84,000 FIS awards were in operation, covering 320,000 people. In that year FIS was superseded by the family credit scheme.

The latest family credit figures show 570,000 claims in payment, covering a little over 2 million people.

Inequality in Incomes

The Government's analysis of households below average incomes broadens out the analysis from the narrow confines of earnings to the broader measurement of incomes. Mrs Thatcher promised greater inequality on this score and much greater inequality was delivered during her stewardship. The IFS, in *For Richer For Poorer* (Goodman and Webb, 1994) has analysed the distribution of income over the 1961–91 period. Four findings are of key importance. During these three decades:

- The increase in inequality during the 1980s dwarfed all previous fluctuations over the previous two decades.
- Real incomes on average before housing costs grew by 84 per cent. The poorest 10 per cent experienced only a 57 per cent increase, while the richest notched up gains of twice this rate.
- After housing costs the real income of the poorest 10 per cent fell in real terms and the living standards of this group in 1991 had been pushed back to the level at which they were in real terms 25 years previously.
- Mass unemployment has changed the composition of the poor. The eightfold increase in unemployment between the early 1960s and the mid 1980s has resulted in families with children making up half of the poorest decile. As a consequence, pensioners—many of whom are now beneficiaries of the State Earnings Related Pension Scheme (SERPS) or occupational pensions—form less than one quarter of the poorest decile, compared to almost a half in 1961.

This drop in the proportion of poor pensioners occurred at a time when the number and proportion of pensioners in the population grew— from 13.4 per cent in 1961 to 16.9 per cent three decades later.

Other important trends emerged from the IFS 30–years-span analysis. The proportion of the population living in families with a full-time worker fell from 80.6 per cent in 1961 to 61.7 per cent 30 years later. Not surprisingly therefore the contribution of net earnings to total income also fell, from 76.8 per cent to 61.4 per cent over the same period. The gap from this falling share of earned income was filled from three sources. The contribution of social security benefits to total income rose from 8.9 per cent to 16.2 per cent over the last two decades. Investment income over the same period rose from 3.2 per cent to 6.8 per cent and the contribution of non-state pensions—also investment income—rose from 2.2 per cent to 4.7 per cent over the 1961–1991 period. This investment income at that date therefore made up 11.5 per cent of all personal income.

The Impact of Tax Changes

How important were the Thatcher tax cuts and benefit changes, the rise in unemployment and changes in earnings in bringing about the record growth in inequality during the 1980s? Looking at these three factors in isolation, the most important was the government-directed tax and benefit changes. It was principally the tax rather than the benefit changes which accounted for around half of the increase in income inequality. Changes in the pattern of economic activity accounted for around a third of the record increase in inequality, while the differential earnings growth explained around one-sixth of that inequality increase.

There are two important lessons to be learned here. The tranches of tax increases announced by Norman Lamont and Kenneth Clarke will have made some impact on the pattern of inequality described in the IFS study. But these findings throw up a direct challenge to the Labour Party and its debate on tax and welfare changes. If half of the recorded inequality of the 1980s has been brought about by tax and benefit changes then a Party serious about reversing this trend will need to focus an important part of its manifesto on countering these very tax and benefit changes.

The other lesson stems from the proportion of pensioners who are poor. This has been brought about by both negative and positive forces. Many pensioners have been shoe-horned out from the bottom of the income pile as unemployed workers and their families have been thrust on to even lower incomes. But other pensioners have seen their incomes rise due to a significant number being recipients of occupational pensions. This again is an important finding which will impact on the policy recommendations.

The Rise and Rise of Single Parents

A favourite trick of governments not wishing to act on urgent issues is to set up a committee of inquiry. All questions pertaining to the issue are then easily deflected. Ministers are waiting with bated breath for the committee's report. Action will then follow—or so the story goes.

Harold Wilson was a past master of this approach. The Child Poverty Action Group (CPAG) was formed in the spring of 1965. It believed that it was only necessary to tell the Government what was wrong and action would follow, in the same inexorable fashion that night follows day. So confident was CPAG about the ease with which reform would be won that it saw no need to open a bank account, let alone a membership list, so quickly would the campaign against poverty be successfully completed. Thirty years later, CPAG is not only still very much around, but has been transformed from a body of voluntary enthusiasts into a very effective and large professional lobbying organisation.

While the Wilson Government expressed genuine concern about the issues CPAG raised, there was no member of the Government with the political clout and the intellectual ability to steer the issue towards the top of the political agenda and keep it there. The Government's response instead was to establish official committees of inquiry. To the reformers this appeared to be a time-wasting device. To ministers it meant that difficult issues were kicked into the long grass and stayed there until after the election.

One such committee of inquiry was the Finer Committee on One Parent Families (*Report of the Commission on One Parent Families*, Cmnd 5629, HMSO, 1974). The committee defined single-parent families as 'a mother or father living without a spouse (and not cohabiting) with his or her never-married dependent child or children aged either under 18 or from 16–19 and undertaking full time education'.

It has been this definition which has been used when estimating the number of such families. No one source is used and the 'best estimate' comes from a range of data (John Hasky, 'Estimated numbers of one-parent families and their prevalence in Great Britain in 1991', *Population Trends*, 78, 1994). These estimates tell an amazing story. In 1971—when the series began—there were 570,000 single parents responsible for a million children. The 1992 provision estimates the totals having

DIAGRAM 6.1
**Proportions of Lone Mothers with Dependent Children in
Each Age Group by Marital Status: 1986–92: Great Britain**

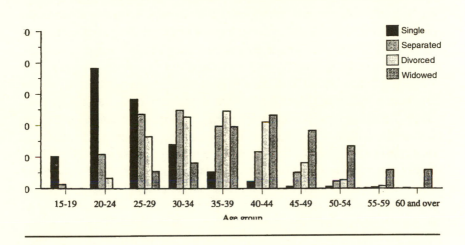

soared to 1.4 million single parents—a near trebling in the space of a little over 20 years. The number of children rose to 2.3 million, a somewhat smaller growth than the rate of increase in single-parent families themselves. However, the trend of single-parent families with few children may be at an end. Between 1990 and 1992 the number of children in single-parent families rose by 300,000.

The reason for this recent growth in the number of children in one-parent families is due largely to the very significant increase in the number of never-married mothers. This is now the fastest growing group of one-parent families—increasing from 90,000 in 1971 to 490,000 in 1992, and at a rate of 13 per cent a year. As diagram 6.1 shows, these mothers are overwhelmingly young and are therefore likely to become part of a growing group of single parents who have a series of children by different partners.

What the social and psychological impact is on children spending their leisure hours watching television with a whole sequence of male partners sitting behind them is impossible to judge at this stage. The old adage that children should be seen but not heard is certainly still true in respect of the children of single parents.

The growth of single-parent families should concern us for four major reasons. The first is that we do not know what the long-term effects will be for the 2.3 million children currently living without two parents. Over the life of a child, for example, it is calculated already that a third of children experience being in a single-parent family for part of their childhood. This phenomenon may be unimportant. No one, however, can make such a statement with any degree of certainty.

Second, children of single parents are much more likely to be condemned to poverty. Not all are. But eight out of ten are and this is a very significant proportion. So it is no use anyone arguing that it does not matter whether the children live with both their parents or not. Setting aside the social and psychological impact, it matters simply on economic grounds. Let me put these figures another way. While as many as one in four of all children live in families with incomes at or below the income support rates, that proportion rises to nearly three out of four where these children are in single parent households. Children growing up in the care of only one parent amount to less than one in five of all children. But these children account for 1.8 million of the 3 million—or very nearly 2 out of 3—children living on income support.

Third, more and more single parents are having to resort to means-tested income support. In 1971 43 per cent of single parents drew supplementary benefit, as income support was then called. Today that proportion has risen to over three-quarters.

Fourth, single parenthood is the major cause of family poverty. The widely held view that the major cause of poverty amongst families in our country is unemployment is wrong. There can be no question about the evil of unemployment. But if we look at the income support data and consider only families with children the picture is transformed. By far and away the largest family group on benefit is single parents—with 983,000 recipients. The next most important reason for families being on benefit is unemployment. The number of families claiming income support where the breadwinner is unemployed is 386,000—a mere 30 per cent of the numbers of single parent families on benefit.

Should the fastest-growing group depend upon means tests to be brought within a new national insurance scheme? There is no question that such provision could be made. It would not be a move which would command much political support, however. The objections Beveridge felt and which the Attlee Government articulated are as valid today as they were 50 years ago. Insurance benefit should not be offered where choice may lead to eligibility. Moreover, the vast majority of voters believe that, wherever possible, children should be nurtured in two-parent families (and that includes parents who are cohabiting or are remarried) than in single-parent families. Voters are also wise enough to know it would be as wrong to deduce from their preference that mothers should be pressurised into unsatisfactory relationships merely to provide a father figure for their children, as it is to propagate policies which favour single-parent households as opposed to two-parent establishments. Likewise voters are aware of the heroic endeavours of most single parents to bring up their children to the very best of their abilities, compensating as far as possible for the lack of two parents.

Fraud

One of the advantages of friendly society welfare to Beveridge was its self-policing nature. Recipients, he thought, would be less likely to defraud colleagues they knew. And if they did, those colleagues would take quick and effective action. Beveridge was under no illusion about human nature and particularly its darker side. But he would have been surprised by the extent today of social security fraud, and the reflection this is of an endemic collapse of honesty, stretching from boardrooms to benefit office.

It is important not to get social security fraud out of context. It needs to be seen as part of a marked increase in dishonesty which is apparent in most areas of life. A single company, KMPG, Peat Marwick's Fraud Investigation Unit, identified 27 significant cases involving the attempted theft of £254m in the first six months of 1994 alone. The Metropolitan Police Company Fraud Office claims to have prevented international and national fraud worth £66m in 1993–4 and additionally prevented the loss of standby letters of credit worth £6.7 bn. The Association of British Insurers estimates that fraudulent claims now run at £400m a year. The Audit Commission estimates that, between 1990 and 1993, there was an increase in the proportion of all organisations suffering incidents of computer fraud and abuse, from 12 to 36 per cent, with a 38 per cent increase in the number of reported frauds and an almost eightfold increase in the use of illicit software. In terms of the total value of reported incidents, there was a 183 per cent increase, with an average of £28,170 per incident. The British

Retail Consortium puts shop thefts at 1.5bn a year. Even solicitors are not exempt, with 100 firms currently being investigated for defrauding the legal aid scheme alone.

It is against this background that it becomes clear that DSS fraud is not the only or indeed the most important of fraudulent activities. It is, however, the one with which we are concerned here. Social security fraud ranges from single individual acts to big-time gang operations. Fraud against the DSS encompasses the following activities, with:

- claimants working part-time and failing to declare their earnings;
- claimants working full-time and drawing benefit as though they are unemployed;
- claimants selling their order books which are then recycled by gangs with a network operating throughout the country;
- gangs stealing shipments of order books;
- individuals and gangs possibly operating within the Department itself.

The recent government announcement on the introduction of Benefit Payment cards belatedly begins a counterattack. But while social security fraud is given too low a priority, fraud against housing benefit has an even lower priority. Here fraud is committed not only by claimants drawing benefits for any number of fictitious addresses, but also by landlords who make extensive claims for non-existent tenants.

Being concerned about fraud, and taking adequate steps to prevent it, should not be thought of as an exclusively right-wing concern. It is only recently that the Left has allowed this perception to take root. Trade unions and friendly societies were only too well aware of the extent of the problem. Josie Harris describes the measures trade unions took to protect their funds.

> All leading trade union members were disqualified from sick pay if their illness was brought on by drink, physical violence, or sexual misconduct. Recipients of sick pay were subject to compulsory medical inspections and were regularly visited by brother members, who checked that they were genuinely ill, that they were not secretly employed in work and that they were not engaged in practices harmful to their recovery.

She describes how curfews were imposed on those who were ill, how unemployed members lost benefit if they had been sacked for poor workmanship or if they had given up their job and only offered a trivial excuse. Unemployed members were required to follow up rumours of vacancies and accept reasonable offers of work offered at the standard rate. Those breaking these rules were fined and then disqualified from benefit. Fellow members were expected to report abuse and were fined if they failed to do so.

Josie Harris cites how the Amalgamated Society of Engineers responded in 1910 to a member prosecuted for altering a benefit cheque for 5 shillings. The Union

> felt that this was a matter that should be brought forward as a warning and deterrent against the committal of similar offences. When this particular offender was sentenced to five months' imprisonment with hard labour he was expelled from the Society: 'we are well rid of such characters' was the comment in the Union's monthly report. (Josie Harris, 'Victorian values', *Proceedings of the British Academy*, 78, 1992, 175 and 176)

That large-scale fraud is committed and is likely to increase is one of the facts of welfare life which reformers ignore at their peril. The two important lessons to draw from this change in moral values are, first, that it is necessary to devise welfare systems which not only make it harder to commit fraud but, even more important, make it easier for claimants to remain honest. Second, given the numbers of claimants committing fraud it is important not only to increase welfare policing, but also to construct pathways back to legitimacy so that, hopefully, increasing numbers of claimants opt for the straight and narrow.

The Very Elderly

Beveridge completed his report during his 63rd year. The contributory pension introduced in 1925 provided for flat-rate payments for all pensioners over the age of 65. It was only in 1940 that the women's pension age was lowered to 60. While some people lived to a good age—Beveridge himself lasted until he was 84—most men in particular did not live long after retirement. Ill-health, poor housing conditions, and tough working conditions left many middle-aged people 50 years ago looking, by today's standards, well past their allotted three score years and ten. The 1980s saw a change in retirement practices. For many males the chance to retire at 60, or at 55, or even earlier, offers major opportunities for leisure, part-time work, and what, not so long ago, would have been labelled as self-improvement. The same trend affects women workers, but not to the same extent. But for some—possibly a great number—ceasing to work has a totally different connotation. For this group it is not a voluntary decision. It is rather like being handed down a death sentence. For such workers, who are euphemistically termed 'prematurely retired', a whole way of life is ripped apart, comradeship destroyed, and far from entering a period of gentle leisure, this phase marks the beginning of a life of hardship.

In addition to retiring earlier, people are also living longer. The number of years worked has decreased, and the number of years when people are outside the labour market (while at school, or while retired) has grown. Yet this trend of a much shorter working life occurred at the same time as life expectancy increased significantly.

At the turn of the century life expectancy for men and women was respectively 45 and 49 years. By the end of this century it will be 73 and 79 years respectively for men and women. In addition, Adam Smith's Hidden Hand also appears to be working, protecting those who are able to survive to a great age. A woman, for example, if she reaches 70, can expect to live to 84. However, life expectancy figures have all the advantages and disadvantages of averages. They tell us very little about the tail-end of the distribution. And, as far as elderly people are concerned, that tail is now pretty substantial. In 1961 a little over one million people reached the age of 80. Now well over 2 million have already crossed that threshold. Indeed over a quarter of a million individuals have burst through a 90th-birthday tape.

Most people will not only reach retirement, but will also enjoy a long retirement. This was not the assumption when pensions were first introduced. The first old age pensions were paid in 1909 and were targeted at the very poorest pensioners aged over 70. Only a minority survived to draw a state pension, and the drawing of these pensions was for a very limited period. Indeed, at the time old age pensions were being introduced for people over 70, life expectancy for males was, as we have already noted, a mere 45 years. It was quite understandable that retiring was an eventuality to insure against.

Now the position is quite different. The standard retirement pension is paid at 65 and 60 respectively for men and women, and, on average, is drawn for 14 and 22 years respectively. The Government intends to equalise pension ages at 65 from the decade beginning 2010.

All of us are dependent when we are very young. For a growing group dependency again occurs when we become very elderly, and often become consequently very frail. This dependency shows up in public costs in a number of ways. In the early 1950s, for example, the over-65s commanded 20 per cent of NHS expenditure. This proportion had risen to a fraction over 50 per cent 35 years later. In addition, a growing part of government expenditure is directed to the community care budget.

How our income can match the growing cost of care is one of the major considerations of the following chapter.

Policy Conclusions

Successful reformers need to read aright the political culture in which reforms are being suggested. The shape of the welfare reconstruction proposed in this volume has been directed to this end. The option for an insurance-based system is one which both fits the hour and the British character. How such a scheme is made universal is discussed in the next chapter. Here the argument has been deployed that the shape of reform has to be very much determined by what is happening in society. In particular seven key trends need to be reflected in welfare policy.

Two trends illustrate that an insurance-based welfare has limits no matter how intelligently and sensitively it is crafted. One overall aim must be to achieve full employability. The apparently natural movement to share work which has occurred this century, and which is illustrated in the shrinkage of the length of the normal working week, came to an abrupt halt in the 1980s. A full employability strategy is needed to break this particular log jam.

Similarly it is vain to suppose that a successful economy will produce jobs at a sufficient spread and range to lift free from idleness the large and growing army of unskilled disinherited males. Action here is crucial for two reasons. The first, and most important, is that unless a totally new approach is taken to the unskilled male worker left like a beached whale by the quickly receding tide of unskilled jobs, a growing army of the least advantaged citizens will be kept in enforced idleness from now until they retire. Secondly, if Britain's Poor Law tradition is finally to be laid to rest we need to move from the passive handing out of maintenance to offering work opportunities.

The relative importance of tax changes, as opposed to benefit changes, in accounting for the growth in income inequality calls for a radical response from Labour. As half of the observable increase in inequality in the 1980s was due to the Thatcher Government's tax changes, Labour's fair tax strategy has to take this point as its starting block.

Recent earnings changes impact on the welfare debate in two distinct ways. First they draw attention to the need to rethink the role and importance of national minimum standards in public life. Later Victorians and Edwardians saw the need to establish such standards as part of a strategy on national efficiency. The case for a similar approach which takes into account the profound changes over this century is proposed in the next chapter, as Britain again approaches a new century, indeed a new millennium.

The second impact stems from the newly emerged pattern of earnings, and particularly the rise of low part-time earnings. While establishing national minimum standards will encompass wage levels, welfare has its part to play in reflecting a world of growing labour market flexibility and uncertainty. Any redistribution through a new national insurance scheme must be open, above board and, in particular, matched by specific grants from the general body of taxpayers. It is also necessary to prevent millions of workers falling outside the national insurance scheme because of their low or fluctuating earnings. Eligibility for insurance must begin with a yearly-hours-of-work count. Eligibility for part-time workers should be cumulative over the year and all contributions must be banked towards specific benefits. This contrasts with the current practice of many part-time workers paying national insurance contributions.

The four final trends discussed in this chapter impact differently on welfare's reconstruction programme. A general decline in honesty is reflected in the extent of social security fraud. Three reforms are urgent. Welfare rules must be reformed so that it is easier for the poor to remain honest. Instead of berating dishonesty, politicians would be better employed devising initiatives which build pathways back to honesty for those currently defrauding the system. In addition the Government should become serious about tackling fraud. At the moment only the rhetoric meets the challenge.

Earnings are a falling total of all income and this gap has been filled largely by a doubling in 30 years of social security payments as a proportion of total income—up from 8.9 per cent to 16.2 per cent. There is clearly a limit, in the short term at least, to the extent that taxpayers will be willing to fund an even greater proportion of personal incomes in this way. It is therefore crucial to consider mutually beneficial partnerships with the private sector. The most outstanding success on this front concerns pensions.

The growth in the number of very elderly people suggests how the national insurance scheme should develop to meet new needs. The cost of care at the end of life can present families and taxpayers with crippling bills. A new national insurance scheme should cover nursing care costs for those for whom it is medically determined to be necessary.

The escalating growth in the number of single parents, the doubling of the proportion of benefit and the growing dominance of never-married mothers within this group, underline both the limits of a national insurance scheme and the need for proactive action. The age-old arguments on the moral hazards against extending national insurance coverage to single parents endure. But if the Poor Law tradition is to be finally dispensed with it is necessary radically to change the terms of operation of the income support scheme. It must move from being an agency passively paying out benefits to one which, while fulfilling this role, also becomes proactive, seeking out the best ways of building exits from welfare dependency.

7

A Stakeholder's Welfare

Two Destructive Forces

The two trends which run through the previous chapters are increasingly pivotal to the welfare debate as Britain approaches the millennium. *The first trend has been the recent violent polarisation of British society and the concentration of its poorest into ghetto areas.* Without decisive action this growing polarisation will threaten the stable way Britain has lived and governed itself in modern times.

A distinctive feature of British political culture has been the manner with which those rising in the social and economic hierarchy have been incorporated into the governing classes. Of similar importance has been the more recent trend of the past three hundred years or so whereby an ever-growing proportion of the population has been incorporated into the wider body politic.

The eighteenth century was characterised by the struggle to establish the rule of law and equality before the courts. The politics of the nineteenth century were dominated by the extension of the franchise, and agitation on this front spilled over into this century. By the mid-twentieth century it was believed that economic and social rights enshrined in full employment and the abolition of Want, to use Beveridge's phrase for the last time, were both universalised and enshrined in Britain's unwritten constitution (T H Marshall, *Citizenship and Social Class*, Pluto Press, 1992).

From the mid 1960s it was clear that this belief represented a far too optimistic view of human progress. More recently, changes brought about by the Thatcher Governments have not only weakened social solidarity, but have also actually expelled members from the body politic. Britain, as it approaches the millennium, is a very different country to what might have been envisaged even two decades ago.

Welfare reconstruction is therefore important on most political grounds. It is also crucial in a necessary counter-offensive against this socially dangerous polarisation. There is a clear need for a programme of reconstruction which appeals to the majority of voters, and part (but only part) of this appeal is the role which welfare should play in knitting the ghetto areas back into the mainstream of society. This joint endeavour is best achieved through mobilising self-interest in a way which also promotes the common welfare. Such a strategy would also lay the basis for countering the second destructive force at work in British society.

The balance of welfare has been shifted from an insurance to a means-tested base. The impact of this change has been so profound that it is difficult to over estimate its importance. It has moreover occurred at a time when a commitment to honesty has undergone a fundamental change. If it were possible to measure the degree of honesty in the country, then such an index operating in Britain would regrettably show a marked decline over the past 40 years, with an accelerating collapse in the index during the 1980s, as individuals and families responded to the 'get rich quick' atmosphere of those heady times. It is against this background that the ever-growing dominance of means testing has to be viewed.

Today almost half the population live in households dependent upon one of the major means-tested benefits. Means tests penalise all those human attributes—such as hard work, work being adequately rewarded, savings, and honesty—which underpin a free, let alone a civilised, society. The present welfare system, therefore, reinforces this shift in morality, further eroding the fundamental law-abiding principles and wealth of the country. Lying, cheating and deceit are all rewarded handsomely by a welfare system which costs on average £15 a day in taxation from every working individual. Again it is difficult to overestimate the destructive consequences welfare now has for our society.

Advent of a Social Philosophy

A major reconstruction is long overdue and the arguments in the previous six chapters are designed to support these two main conclusions. The task now is to map out an alternative welfare state. Previous efforts have failed to be clear about the objectives which a reconstruction of welfare should pursue. Peter Lilley is a notable exception here, although, as I have already made clear, his vision is not one which I endorse. Proposals for reconstruction have simultaneously failed to take into account the most basic ingredient of political activity, namely the forces which drive human beings.

Why is the human character so fundamental to these discussions? An answer has been given implicitly in the previous chapters. Now it is time to be explicit. The politics of welfare used to be seen as part of a vigorous social philosophy debate. It was within this theatre that reformers spelt out how they saw human beings operating, their motives and aspirations. The goal was the promotion of the good life and welfare was viewed as one channel directed to that end. This was the way the British welfare debate ignited again during the last years of the nineteenth century.

Many people contributed to this debate, but two groups stand out, and their contribution helps focus our debate. One such group was the Charity Organisation Society (COS), which coalesced around the Bosanquets, Helen and Bernard, together with Charles Loch. The other alliance centred around the Fabians, where the Webbs played a dominant role. Membership of the two groups was not fixed and there was some movement from the COS to the Webbs' camp. The climax of this debate was reached during, and in the aftermath of, the report of the 1905–9 Royal Commission on the Poor Laws, and this clash of philosophies is captured in A M McBriar's *An Edwardian Mixed Doubles* (Oxford, 1987).

Beatrice Webb was a member of the 1905 Royal Commission on the Poor Laws. So too were Helen Bosanquet and Charles Loch. Beatrice viewed the Royal Commission as yet another platform for promoting her views, and decided early that a minority report would be the best way of achieving this objective. A minority report was duly produced and a national campaign initiated with the object of securing the implementation of its recommendations. Part of that debate was an attack on the majority report, large parts of which had been drafted by Helen Bosanquet (McBriar, 1987, 282–5). The Webbs skilfully marshalled their forces by inflaming all the hatred that rightly existed against the old Poor Law. In the rough and tumble of that debate the similarities between both majority and minority reports were deliberately obfuscated by Beatrice and her team of campaigners (J H Muirhead, *By What Authority?*, P S King & Son, 1909). But in pulling the debate their way the Webbs had a much more profound impact on this country's wider debate on welfare.

It was Sidney, Beatrice's husband, who not only coined the phrase a national minimum, but who also brilliantly linked it to the political issue of the hour—the urge for national regeneration which swept the country in the wake of the Boer War (Sidney Webb, 'Lord Rosebery's escape from Houndsditch', *The Nineteenth Century*, September, 1901). Their studies had taught the Webbs how the skilled trade unions had begun to transform the living standards of their members. How could these advantages be spread to all groups, particularly the semi—and unskilled? The Webbs' answer was to use the law to universalise the progress made by the skilled trade unions.

The Pivotal Role of Human Character

The leaders of the COS had the same objective, but their means of achieving this outcome were very different. Both groups had fallen upon what they saw as the organisational form which could promote the good life by improving character and the values associated with it. (See Stephan Collini, 'The idea of "character" in Victorian thought' *Transactions of the Royal Historical Society*, 35, 1985, for the role character played in the philosophy of Victorian reformers.) The skilled working class of the late Victorian and early Edwardian times had given birth to a multitude of voluntary organisations concerned with securing improvements in living standards. These trade union and friendly societies were highly disciplined, highly successful self-gov-erning organisations. As a means of spreading the best practice of these self-governing voluntary organisations, the Bosanquets coined the phrase social, or popular, collectivism, as opposed to state collec-tivism. It was crucial that collective action should be organised on a voluntary basis. The COS feared that the Webbs' statist approach would cut through the sinews motivating the action of these voluntary bodies.

Unfortunately the weight of the campaign against the COS was such that the two most valuable aspects of this group's views were trodden underfoot in the rush to achieve reform. The value attached to the role of human character and motivation was downgraded, even though their opponents were agreed upon its importance. Yet the campaign against the COS marked the high-water mark for the social philosophy movement. From now on the role that individual character ought to play in securing social advance ebbed away from the centre of the political debate. A growing emphasis was to be placed upon the role of institutional change, devoid of its impact upon human motivation.

The campaign's success against the COS was relatively easy to achieve. So much of this Society's activity was a casework approach to the poor, where charitable effort was centred on those characters who could and would benefit by charitable help. Benefit was defined in terms of an individual's chance of progressing towards self-suffi-ciency. It was very easy for the politicians to slip into attacks on the spurious distinction between deserving and undeserving. No doubt many of the COS caseworkers were harsh in their judgement of, and insensitive in dealing with, poor families. The COS was in any case an easy target. Voters generally do not approve of people who refuse them help. So the COS was from the outset designed to flourish with-out mass support, and it was never popular amongst working-class and trade union groups. Yet the central importance the COS attached to the development of an individual's character, and how we are moti-vated, is a subject which is as important to the general political debate as it is to the debate specifically concerned with the reconstruction of welfare.

The second of the COS beliefs is much more difficult to reinvent in today's changed world. Welfare was then provided through voluntary groups, and in the rush to universalise such bodies were painted as reactionary forces. Not until recently has the Left begun to take an interest in this approach (Frank Field, 'Moore gives the trade unions a chance to steal the ball', *Sunday Times*, 16 October 1988; Mai Wann, *Building Society Capital*, IPPR, 1995. For a right-wing view see David G Green *Reinventing Civil Society*, IEA, 1993). The designers of the 1911 National Insurance Act were anxious to put the friendly societies in the pivotal position of delivering the new state benefits (William J Braithwaite, *Lloyd George's Ambulance Wagon*, Methuen, 1957). How-ever, under political pressure, Lloyd George awarded a similar status to the industrial and collecting societies, as they were known.

Companies such as the Prudential proved too attractive an alterna-tive for an ever-growing body of working-class adherents, when mem-bership of a friendly society demanded not only regular savings but also commitment to, and participation in the life of, that society. The call at the door from the 'man from the Pru' was too convenient an option for most people to resist. The 1911 Act, far from heralding a new advance for friendly societies, marked the start of their decline as the great purveyors of welfare. And, despite Beveridge's wish to see their role enhanced, they were relegated to promoting a range of topping-up benefits in the new state universal scheme he outlined in *Social Insurance and Allied Services* (Cmd 6404, HMSO, 1942). We will return to what can be learned and salvaged from this debacle later.

This story of the down-grading of the importance which should be attached to human character is, like so many, not without its ironies. The Webbs, and particularly Beatrice, had very firm views about human nature and how it needed a rigorous disciplinary framework if it was to operate satisfactorily. Both the Bosanquets and the Webbs realised the importance of training armies of foot soldiers to carry their respective ideologies into battle.

The COS established the School of Sociology where teaching was clearly within the social philosophy framework. Significantly the School's not too distant precursor was entitled the Ethical Society (see John Henry Muirhead, *Reflections by a Journeyman in Philosophy*, Allen & Unwin, 1942, chapter 6). The Webbs were instrumental in founding the LSE. Unable to gain university recognition without an adequate endowment, which the relative deprivation of the COS prohibited, the School of Sociology merged with the LSE. Apart from strengthening the latter, the Webbs saw this development as crucial to satisfying the demand for staffing the new bureaucratic organisations they were successfully establishing and through which the national minimum of welfare standards would be enforced.

Yet, as Josie Harris recalls, the character of the social teaching at LSE changed (Josie Harris, 'The Webbs, the COS and the Ratan Tata Foundation', in *The Goals of Social Policy*, ed. Martin Bulmer, Jane Lewes and David Piachaud, Unwin Hyman, 1989). From a clear-cut stance of being part of the social philosophy tradition, and adding to it, LSE's cast of eye narrowed to a concern about social policy, and then adopted an even more limited gaze focusing on social administration. From a vision about the good life, and the part which collective or social action, together with individual character, played in nurturing it, the subject deteriorated into a compilation of rules, statutes, entitlements, and statutory instruments as its staple diet.

When lifted up again as a subject with vision it was R M Titmuss's approach which prevailed. His view was that welfare should be given as of right and free of any restrictions or stigma. The delivery of benefit should not therefore suggest that individuals were responsible for their circumstances. 'Taken to the extreme, this seemed to push Titmuss into a position of almost total determinism and a rejection of personal responsibility in almost any circumstances' (Alan Deacon, *Rereading Titmuss: Moralism, Work and Welfare*, University of Leeds Review, vol. 36, 1993–4, 91). The Webbs, in contrast, held strong views about people's characters and motivations which would sometimes appear extreme, even to middle class audiences. To talk of 'social drainage', as Beatrice was fond of doing, tells practically all there is to be said. The residuum, which played such a dominating role in Victorian and Edwardian concern about the condition of the people, was to be siphoned off, according to the Webbs, either to labour colonies at home or to the colonies proper abroad. With Beatrice's emphasis on punishing the malingerers it should come as no surprise that Charles Masterman, the Treasury minister responsible for the day-to-day handling of the 1911 National Insurance Act, uttered the plea that should he ever become unemployed, he hoped to be spared falling into the hands of Mrs Webb. So, although the first results of this mixed doubles appeared to be a victory for the Webbs, the longer-term impact was not even a draw. Both parties lost as the social philosophy approach of both couples fell first into contempt, and then disappeared completely from the political agenda. (Readers wishing to pick up on this debate should begin with Andrew Wright and Raymond Plant, *Philosophy, Politics and Citizenship*, Basil Blackwell, 1984.)

The initial marginalisation and subsequent ignoring of a social framework for any discussion of welfare helps to explain the lack of any clear long-term welfare thinking by the Left. The social philosophy approach needs to be re-established as the framework for welfare debate. Within this approach the aims and objects of welfare need to be spelt out. This approach is necessary not only in order to advance clear thinking and thereby increase the chance of policies fulfilling their objectives: such an exercise would also mobilise support amongst the electorate.

Reasserting a Public Ideology

All societies have public ideologies which lay down the moral framework within which their members operate. Usually these ideologies come from, or are supported by, religious beliefs. Edmund Leach, an agnostic anthropologist, observed: 'The most important thing about religion is that it provides the believer with an ideology—a world view about how I am related to the world around me and how parts of the world are related to one another' (cited in Peter Pilkington 'Morality in a society without an agreed system of values', *Seek Ye First the Gospel*, St Mary's Bourne Street, 1992, 98). Religious ideologies present a system of rules for human behaviour within a wider framework of order which justifies the demands being placed on individual actions. Such an ordered framework is not only necessary for mankind's collective endeavours, which seek to control the external environment, but is also similarly important for bringing order and sense to an individual's personal life.

If this sense of structure breaks down, the whole society becomes uncertain of its purpose. We see such uncertainty vividly illustrated today. The behaviour of the younger members of the Royal Family is unlikely to be due to any wilful desire to shock, let alone to bring disdain upon themselves. Rather, it occurs because the members feel that the framework within which they are required to work is becoming, or has already become, irrelevant. They no longer instinctively comprehend the function and duties of a ruling family.

Uncertainty about how to behave now characterises an increasing proportion of the community. This is a general phenomenon sweeping across Western Europe. 'It is possible that we are the first society in history to experience this phenomenon—Our generation does not have an agreed system of values and insecurity and uncertainty results from this development' (Pilkington, 1992, 98). Into the vacuum created by a collapsing public morality stepped Mrs Thatcher. It is little wonder that her privatised approach, emphasising with great force the place of private or personal morality, which was the only one on offer, met with such a positive response.

Here then is both a challenge as well as an opportunity for welfare's reconstruction. Which of the verities can be reaffirmed in constructing a framework for welfare reform? And what part can this exercise play in the wider objective of providing beliefs and hopes which, by being affirmed on the welfare front, will spill over into the wider political arena and so affect public conduct?

How then do we view ourselves and, within this view of mankind, what are the chief mechanisms for bringing about successful social change?

One characteristic which separates men and women from the rest of creation is our ability to make moral judgements. Indeed, the making and upholding of such judgements is, as we have commented, crucial to our sense of security and well-being. The ability to act as moral agents is central to our understanding of human behaviour and development. An attribute of a good society is the nurturing and enhancement of our moral awareness. Indeed any social change which is not based on this objective inevitably adds to social instability.

The Centrality of Self-Interest

Our moral decision-making does not operate in a human vacuum. A fundamentally important part of human nature is the promotion of self-interest. Indeed it is because this is the most immediate and powerful of our urges that codes detailing what is right and wrong become doubly important. *Part of the necessary moral order is not about decrying or thwarting our self-interest, but of attempting to satisfy it in a way which is consistent with the public good. The most deadly charge which can be made against Britain's welfare state is that it increasingly ignores this cardinal principle. Welfare is pitted against self-interest in a way in which the public good can only be the loser. Hard work is penalised by the loss of entitlement. Incentives reinforce welfare dependence. Honesty is punished by a loss of income. It is in this sense that welfare is the enemy within. Its rules actively undermine the moral fabric of our characters. In so doing it eats into the public domain and so helps erode the wider moral order of society.*

Dominant as self-interest is, it is not the only force shaping our characters and actions. Other attributes lie deeply embedded within us. A wish for self-improvement is one such force. Altruism is another. Welfare's reconstruction needs to be shaped to take account of these varying human attributes which themselves need to be weighed carefully.

Self-interest is clearly the dominant force. Self-improvement is also important, even if it has to be given less weight. Yet much of the aggressive force of self-interest is channelled into self-improvement. In contrast, altruistic feelings vary according to the object of the altruism. It is usually expressed most strongly in the family, and indeed here it can even be a more powerful influence than self-interest. But the further we move away from the family—to more abstract concepts such as our neighbourhood, our town, our country—the weaker usually are such altruistic feelings. Yet these weaker motivational forces are not only important parts of our true characters, needing to be reflected in the world we make around us; they are also those which, though less characteristic of individual human beings, are nevertheless more important when it comes to measuring how civilised the society is in which we live. To take an extreme example, the most plutocratic capitalist knows the value of a freely given blood bank (R M Titmuss, *The Gift Relationship*, Allen & Unwin, 1970).

Welfare reconstruction needs to reflect this wider canvas of human motivation. To stress disproportionately one aspect will set welfare operating in varying degrees against rather than with the grain of human nature.

Some on the Left may view this approach as being at worst an immoral and at best an amoral stance. Such accusations spring from a most perverse understanding of moral behaviour. Such critics appear to argue from the basis that Christ's Second Commandment instructs us to love our neighbour *more* than ourselves, rather than *as* ourselves. The proposed framework is not a plan to sell out on the moral force which welfare can and should play in our society. It is rather to build its moral worth on secure foundations including a proper acceptance of what motivates us. Only then can self-improvement and altruism play their true part in human affairs.

The Pace of Change

The next question we need to ask is how best can welfare advance self-interest, self-improvement and altruism, and do so in the world we have been describing in the previous chapters? And can the reconstruction of welfare be achieved in a way which remains true to these objectives when there are now masses of our fellow citizens with a vested interest in the continuation of means-tested welfare?

Timing is of crucial importance. General budgetary restraints alone make it a near impossibility to move other than at a modest pace, although this pace of change will in part depend on how quickly the electorate wishes to proceed. The Chancellor announces his financial proposals for the coming year in the November Budget. Expenditure plans are approved and taxes levied to pay for these programmes. Government expenditure currently totals £290bn. But when the Chancellor of the Exchequer of the next Government stands up to deliver the first budget he or she will find, as does the current Chancellor, that five-sixths of the spending programme will in fact have been committed by governments led long ago by Clement Attlee and Neville Chamberlain, or even by Prime Ministers before them (Richard Rose and Phillip L Davies, *Inheritance in Public Policy*, Yale University Press, 1994). There can therefore be no instant result, no immediate solution.

While welfare reconstruction is one of the most pressing of political objectives, its transformation cannot be achieved overnight. As *Making Welfare Work* has argued, the size of the task is enormous. But this is not a reason for despair. It is rather the basis for laying out clearly the objectives of reform and a programme of action which allows these goals to be achieved over a more realistic 20–year time span.

The 20–year duration needs explanation. It signifies the magnitude of the changes which must be made. Hope will be engendered by facing the size of the task realistically, by setting clear objectives of what and how welfare should be reconstructed and why, and by the laying out of a detailed programme of how such a goal can and will be realised. Each welfare reform can then be judged in terms of whether or not it moves Britain towards this objective.

What are the other lessons from the previous six chapters which now need to be brought together in order to begin a discussion on the political framework for welfare's reconstruction?

The Strategy of the Reform Programme

Severe budgetary restraints will leave Chancellors with little room for manoeuvre. The only options open are to cancel programmes—an improbable move given the inevitable backlash from irate voters who will be worse off as a result, or to increase taxes—which politicians have convinced themselves amounts to near political suicide. Another alternative is to gain additional revenue from the proceeds of economic growth—which will only increase the Chancellor's revenue if its product is distributed in forms of income or dividends (and therefore liable to personal taxation) or subjected to corporation tax. Yet consumer-led booms in this country have proved short-lived and are therefore a very unstable basis on which to plan long-term revenue gains.

But, it may be asked, if Beveridge's plans could be implemented at a time when national income was a little over a third of the size it is today, why isn't a 'big bang' approach to welfare reconstruction being seriously considered? There are four important reasons why it would be mistaken to argue by comparison with war-time conditions and circumstances.

First, the war engendered a strong feeling of a shared purpose. The ever-present common enemy gave rise to a sense of social cohesion, commitment and fellowship, which were particular to that time and its events. It was these values which Beveridge believed should underpin his proposed welfare state and to which he appealed. Beveridge's report received a rapturous reception because it reflected the feelings and aspirations of the time. Today's circumstances are totally different. There is no strong feeling of a common purpose 'out there'. *The aim of any welfare report now is not to assume that it will catch a radical tide waiting to be directed. Rather the task is to help raise hopes and aspirations that reform is still possible and so help create the demand for a radical government.*

Second, there are the budgetary restraints which have just been touched upon. To argue that national income is two and three-quarters greater than it was when Beveridge published his proposals is only partly relevant. Clearly a small tax increase raises that much more money on an economic base which is approximately three times the size of the economic base over 50 years ago. But the revenue from such a small taxation increase achieves less now as expectations of what is adequate (and therefore the impact it has on cost) are now so much higher. More important is the state of the budget when the Government introduced the Beveridge Report. Taxation was at a record high level at the end of the war. The cessation of hostilities was accompanied by a rundown of defence commitments, at least until the outbreak of the Korean War. The massive cuts in the defence budget consequently allowed new programmes to be financed without having to raise new taxation. That option is not open on the same scale today.

Third, voters are sceptical of politicians claiming to have the skills to introduce successful monumental institutional change. The Child

Support Agency is a very pertinent example here of what can all too easily happen. The DSS's Liable Relative Unit was charged with collecting maintenance payments from the fathers of children in one-parent families dependent upon benefit. As part of the introduction of the CSA the activities of this Unit were discontinued. Immediately the CSA was given the task of arranging maintenance settlements for an additional two million broken families. In its last year of operation, with a renewed interest from the Government in securing maintenance payments for single parents drawing income support, the Liable Relative Unit raised £231m. One year later, and after an expenditure of £113m to finance the introduction of the CSA, only £15m of additional maintenance was being paid. Two years later, and with the cost of running the Agency soaring towards the £185m mark, the Government cannot quantify how much additional new maintenance on top of the £15m is being paid and collected. The political lesson from this ongoing CSA saga is surely to implement major welfare changes by building, step by step, on the existing working framework. That was, moreover, Beveridge's approach, although the electorate was then willing to support a major increase in welfare expenditure to facilitate the implementation of the total Beveridge package.

Fourth, there is a vested interest against reform: the existing means-tested system has whole armies of supporters. For the genuine poor it provides a bulwark against destitution. Life would be really impossible without such help. However, those cheating or legitimately working the system have turned means tests into a de facto citizens' income. Benefits are seen as an income floor on which earnings from work are added to meet the claimant's income target. Both groups, the first from fear of the consequences, the second from knowing the impact which the phasing out of means tests would have on their standard of living, may be opposed to reform. The pace of change, guaranteeing that no one will be made worse off by any changes, should assuage the fears of the first group. A much more determined anti-abuse strategy will convince the second group that their time is up anyway (see the section below: *A pro-active Benefits Agency*).

The Key Political Commitments

The first crucial political commitment for a party poised to become a radical reforming government must be to phase out means-tested assistance over what will, in all probability, amount to a 20–year period. The proposal in *Making Welfare Work* is to achieve this end by phasing in a stakeholder's national welfare state. Once these two commitments are given, each and every move of a government's economic and welfare programme can be judged by whether they are being implemented. Both programmes, the phasing out of means-tested benefits and their replacement by a stakeholder's insurance scheme, need to be spelt out carefully and are detailed below.

This re-establishment of insurance-based welfare is not the traditional Left programme. In the past the emphasis of Centre Left radicals has been on raising the relative value of insurance benefits so as to float claimants off means-tested support. Such an approach would be prohibitively expensive. It also ignores the role human nature should play as an engine force within the welfare state. An alternative strategy for freeing individuals from means-tested dependency is advanced here. What is missing from the debate is the very simple fact that insurance cover is fast collapsing. The emphasis of *Making Welfare Work* is on establishing a near universal insurance coverage and then harnessing self-interest to add to this insurance-based income. In this approach self-interest can work within the law as other family members are free to work without fear of financial penalties being applied to the claimant's benefit. In addition, it is proposed that the housing benefit scheme's escalating number of claimants and costs will be countered by tackling the massive fraud currently organised by landlords and then cash-limiting all new claims to benefit to a rent officer's assessment of a fair rent.

Two other commitments are also required. Large numbers of people will continue to rely on means tests until the stakeholder's welfare state is brought to fruition. Indeed, for reasons explained later, single mothers will still draw income support after the reform is complete. It is crucial therefore to transform the income support machinery from a passive into an active body. From an agency which merely pays out benefit, and occasionally checks on fraud, income support needs to become an agency primarily concerned with tailoring exits from welfare for those able and anxious to move back into the labour market (see below: *A proactive Benefits Agency*).

The final commitment concerns striking a genuine partnership with the private sector. The section below entitled "Universalising private provision" will argue for a radical extension of the Left's concept of universal coverage. Traditionally, the Left has seen this commitment as being secured within a state-delivered welfare system. The Left has to decide what is sacred about this approach. Is it the state-delivery element, or is it the guarantee of a universal coverage? The proposal in *Making Welfare Work* is for the universalist approach to be applied to the private sector in respect of pensions. The aim will be for everybody to gain a dual universal coverage of both private and public pension provision.

The Politics of Reform

So much then for the strategy. What of the politics of welfare reform? Specifically, where are the pressure points in our political system and how best can maximum pressure be applied to these strategic targets? Fundamentally, how can the self-interest of the middle classes be mobilised in a way which allows the development of a welfare state which simultaneously promotes the interests of the poor?

The proposal for building a stakeholder's insurance scheme rests on the assumption that the political climate is one where individuals require:

- that the uncertainty created by a flexible labour market is matched by a welfare flexibility offering security;
- that the best way of achieving this objective is a stakeholder's welfare scheme where contributions and benefits are both linked and carefully spelt out;
- that while this reform has to be paid for, it is a crucial part of the philosophy that the stakeholder should have a decisive say in the question of its finances;
- that stakeholders will want to have a maximum say in how they spread their earnings from their working life over the rapidly expanding periods of non work;
- that stakeholders will want a mix of funded and unfunded schemes, and public and private schemes, in order to maximise security and minimise risks.

Making Welfare Work rests on the assumption that the electorate feels a growing sense of insecurity which is not registered in public debate and hardly addressed by politicians. In one sense this is another success for Mrs Thatcher. The big issues no longer surface in the same way. The political agenda, both because of the impact of her governments, and their impact coinciding with global economic changes, has become privatised. *The rewards for the political party which can voice*

*and address these private fears and aspirations could be very consid-
erable indeed.*

The political ability of Sidney Webb was shown in his identification of a topic which became the focal point of radical politics—
establishing a national minimum—and linking it with the issue of the
hour—the physical standards required for an effective functioning of a
great imperial power recently humiliated at the hands of the Boers.
Through such connections the idea of establishing national minimum
standards, underpinning the life and well-being of the entire population, became a subject of mass concern.

Radical reformers today need to link their proposals for welfare
reconstruction to an issue which similarly commands broad support. A
hundred years ago the chanting of jingoistic crowds guided politicians
towards the issue of the moment. Today, where protest has been largely
privatised, opinion polls are a means of gauging the importance the
electorate attaches to their varying concerns.

The polls show that the climate of opinion has changed dramatically over the past few years. From the high confidence of the Thatcher
years, increasing numbers of voters now express deep concern about
the future. Central to this concern is a growing sense of insecurity.
While uncertainty about the future of house prices clearly registers
amongst voters, the primary concern is about their future employment
prospects. With 54 per cent of the working population experiencing
job changes during the previous three years, this finding should come
as no surprise. Within the space of a generation, the jobs-for-life era
associated with the full employment of the early post-war years has
unravelled as the uncertainties and practices associated with the flexible labour market have gained an increasing ascendancy. No matter
how clever the euphemism used to disguise what is happening,
'downsizing' is much in vogue at the moment: the reality of redundancy and long-term unemployment are an ever-registering threat with
voters. While some may thrive on uncertainty, most people crave a
known framework within which they can order their lives.

The dark shadow of uncertainty is cast beyond the individual right
through to the extended family. How are children going to fare when
they leave school or university? The story of a grandson who laughs at
having the worst degree of all the porters at Harvey Nichols (one of
London's premier stores) highlights the scramble for jobs amongst
young people. And if graduates are taking the portering jobs, what are

the prospects of lesser-qualified individuals? And then there is the confusion of grandparents who, if they are lucky enough still to be in work, find themselves continuing to support financially and in kind their unemployed married children and their families.

There is a sense of hopelessness and resignation abroad. Work plays such a key role in defining our worth that people are usually only too pleased to accept part-time or contract work, even if they would prefer alternative offers. It is not only professional people who question how it will be possible to conform to the cry from politicians for more stable families when their only chances of work are short-term fixed contracts and of being moved around the globe, never mind around this country, as one contract gives way to another. If both partners work and are subjected to these demands, how can a stable environment be created for the raising and nurturing of children?

No welfare reconstruction can put the clock back and offer a tempo of life which individuals and families experienced during the 1940s and 1950s and this is not what I propose. What welfare reconstruction can and should do is to offer as much certainty in respect of income as is consistent with the country's overall economic wealth, together with a realistic view of the need to maintain work incentives.

Few reforms come without a price tag, least of all a reconstruction of welfare. *The centre of the reform is to offer people the opportunity of spreading their income from work more equitably over the totality of their lives. But few voters are going to subscribe to this approach if they think the scheme is actually aimed at redistributing their income to other people. A clear distinction has to be made between savings and redistributory taxation.* (See *Averting the Old Age Crisis,* World Bank, 1994, for a clear distinction here.) *A commitment must therefore be given, as part of a stakeholder's welfare, that any redistribution will be clear and above board. It should come from general taxation and not by sleight of hand on the part of fund administrators. Here welfare's altruistic role comes to the fore.*

How can this guarantee of the security of funds be offered and consolidated? The stakeholder's welfare will be a genuine partnership between public and private provision. And both kinds of provision need to be organised and guarded by their own corporations. The two new corporations, one governing the public provision of insured welfare and a separate corporation governing the private provision of welfare, would be established and would be given a legal identity distinct from that of the Government. Their legal standing would be similar to that granted to the great merchant venturer companies who were delegated many of the tasks of government, although only for their operational activities outside this country.

Stakeholder's Insurance Scheme Framework

The public welfare provision would be administered by a newly constituted stakeholder's insurance corporation. This must be clearly independent of government. Its constitution must lay down a new structure of contributions, with its board reflecting the weight of the contributions of the different parties—employers, employees and the Government. If such a corporation were currently operating, and reflecting accurately the different 'pay-masters', then the employers' representatives would have 49 per cent of the seats, employee representatives 31 per cent, the self-employed 3 per cent and the Government the remaining 17 per cent of the corporation's seats.

The proposals detailed later for higher stakeholder insurance contributions will inevitably change the composition of the board. If employees agree to contribute a greater share of their income in contributions, so would their representation on the stakeholder board grow at the expense of other representatives.

The new stakeholder board, the governing body of the corporation, would be a proactive body charged with the following responsibilities:

- It would have a duty to comment on economic and social trends and how these might affect the funding of the stakeholder's insurance scheme.
- It would be charged with linking clearly the level of contributions to the level of benefits paid.
- While the Government would initially retain the say in determining the rates of contributions, the new stakeholder insurance constitution would lay down that, once the scheme is fully operative, this power of the Exchequer would be reconsidered. Ultimately the Exchequer's power would be limited to a veto. Up until now questions of devolution have been thought through merely in geographical terms. Other forms of devolution—such as direct say over the level of insurance contributions—might be thought of by the voters as of greater importance. The corporation would collect and publish the views of stakeholders on changes to the scheme and the impact these changes would have on contributions and benefits.
- The scheme's comprehensiveness would be maintained by the Exchequer paying in contributions for the lowest-paid workers, for whom part

of the reward of work would be a partial stakeholder contribution, as well as for those individuals outside the labour market who are accorded stakeholder status. This group would include the long-term sick, unemployed and carers.

Building Up a New System

Setting the welfare reconstruction exercise within its proper perspective—how best to guarantee an adequate income flow over each individual's lifetime—establishes the parameters of welfare's role. Welfare has a role to play in its own right as well as acting as the handmaiden of the labour market for the employee. This joint endeavour with the labour market has to be accomplished in a way which offers security to the individual while not undermining the best operation of the labour market itself. How that can be achieved can only be considered in a practical manner by bringing back into discussion the earlier material on the changing nature of Britain's labour market. The overall aim is to detail the part a stakeholder insurance-based welfare system can play in offering an adequate income flow to individuals in a manner which strengthens rather than undermines national prosperity.

At the present time the 24.7 million of Great Britain's working population is not a homogeneous group. It breaks down into male and female workers with differing family and other responsibilities: those who work for an employer and those who work for themselves, those working full time and those working part time, those workers who have only one job and those workers with more than one job, as well as workers who are established and those who work on a contract basis.

Yet even these categories fail to catch the full variety in the labour market—those who are self-employed, work part-time, and in addition work also for an employer. Nor do these categories give any sense of the dynamics of the labour market: of those moving from part-time to full-time work and those who are making the opposite journey; the movement from employee to self-employed status, and those who are journeying in the opposite direction; of employee status and temporary work status, and the movement between these two groups as well as the combination of full-time and part-time work for each of these categories. In addition, the movement from any one of these positions to unemployment or inactivity needs to be considered, as does the journey from inactivity or unemployment into one of the categories so described. In addition there are at any one time employees moving between employers without there necessarily being any periods of unemployment. Movement between jobs is considerable. The Labour Force Survey of June–August 1993 shows that only 46 per cent of employees had been in continuous employment with the same employer for three years or more.

It is therefore apparent that the insurance framework must be both appropriately complex and flexible if it is effectively to shadow the dynamics of the labour market. Yet a major goal of the reconstruction must be to devise an inclusive insurance base into which people can fit irrespective of the variety of their pattern of work.

Here the first stage of the new enterprise is embarked upon. The description of an inclusive framework is outlined. The second stage will be to seek funds from a Foundation, and to commission the Government Actuary to carry out a study. This would test the growing comprehensiveness of the reform programme, the costing of a staged reform programme and its impact on contributions over the 20–year period suggested for restructuring welfare.

A Policy of Inclusion

Full-Time Employees

The easiest group to which one must extend insurance cover are those in regular employment although, as with each group we consider, it is important to emphasise once again that the figures we use (as in table 7.1), as in practically all labour market data, are snapshots. They tell us much about the labour market frozen at the point when the data were collected, but nothing about the constancy or otherwise of the picture so painted. Again it is appropriate to stress the need for employment and social security audits—giving a moving picture of the labour market and its interaction with the social security system— if a more rational discussion is to take place. Such audits are of particular importance at a time of rapid flux in the labour market.

The figures in the table suggest a large measure of order and stability in the labour market, with 16 million out of a total of 24.7 million employees in full-time employment (10.3 million men and 5.6 million women). At this point the limitations of the snapshot approach to

TABLE 7.1
Labour Market Characteristics
Great Britain *(000s, seasonally adjusted)*

| | Males | | | | | | Females | | | | | |
| | Employees | | Self employed | | Second job (a) | | Employees | | Self employed | | Second job (a) | |
Spring	Full time	Part time (b)	Full time	Part time (b)	Employ-ees	Self Employed	Full time	Part time (b)	Full time	Part time (b)	Employ-ees	Self Employed
1984	11,189	418	1,849	137	211	161	5,033	3,973	308	314	234	85
1985	11,206	428	1,901	135	233	164	5,081	4,057	336	332	285	96
1986	11,104	442	1,929	124	229	178	5,134	4,156	344	318	298	108
1987	10,965	486	2,084	157	220	170	5,203	4,225	382	362	345	99
1988	11,211	560	2,214	149	262	189	5,436	4,322	399	367	393	116
1989	11,370	538	2,433	181	266	206	5,795	4,454	433	368	442	140
1990	11,401	586	2,448	186	287	220	5,905	4,462	455	372	436	129
1991	11,074	620	2,355	164	291	209	5,791	4,488	435	352	445	127
1992	10,649	648	2,181	179	249	189	5,689	4,499	398	362	424	100
1993	10,415	667	2,109	199	258	204	5,632	4,559	400	381	434	131
1994	10,379	726	2,179	211	295	202	5,565	4,658	407	395	494	142

Notes: (a) not seasonally adjusted
(b) where part time employment is main job

Source: Labor Force Survey

employment data become very obvious. We in fact know next to nothing about the work careers of this group of people. For how long has each person been in full-time employment? How many have moved recently from part-time employment into full-time employment, especially from jobs paying below the national insurance contribution threshold? And how many of this total are among the 54 per cent of workers who have changed their jobs in the last three years? Moreover, of that 54 per cent, how many workers have periods of unemployment between jobs, even though they are now back in full-time employment? All these discontinuities could affect a worker's contribution record and thereby eligibility for national insurance benefits. We will consider in a moment the changing pattern of insurance cover.

Part-Time Employees

Once we move beyond those employed in full-time work—a group which makes up around three-fifths of the labour force—we move into even more uncertain territory. The number of males primarily working part-time has grown from 418,000 in 1984 to 726,000 in 1994. These totals, although important, are dwarfed by the number of women part-time workers. Here we see a total of 3.9 million rising to 4.7 million over the same time span.

But once again the snapshot figures produced by the Government tell us nothing about the careers of these workers. Given their numbers it is reasonable to assume that the majority of part-time workers have had, or wish to have, long-term careers on this basis. Part-time working is defined as working for 30 hours or less a week. The snapshot total tells us nothing about the number of hours worked over time by each part-time worker, and particularly the numbers who choose or who are pushed into jobs paying wages below the national insurance threshold (£59 per week from April 1995). What is known is that in the 12 months up to the end of 1993 the fastest-growing group of part-timers were those working for up to seven hours a week.

We do not know how many of this group of part-time workers had two or more such part-time jobs, although we now have a little information on the total numbers of workers with more than one job. Again there are many more women than men with second jobs: 494,000 women in 1994 compared with 295,000 men had a second job working as an employee. For self-employed second-job workers the figures are smaller in total and show a slight majority of male workers: 202,000 compared to 142,000. We do not have any data on the number of workers in this category who do not declare their earnings. The Government has only just started to collect further data on very low-paid wage earners and it has yet to be used in an insurance context. During 1992 1.5 million workers failed to earn in any of the preceding 52 weeks a sum equal to the lower earnings level. This tells us nothing however about the number of workers who, because of low, fluctuating earnings, are unable to make a complete record. The LEL is usually around the tax threshold. Current figures estimate that 3.5 million workers are below this income point and practically all will be unable to make full national insurance contributions.

Self-Employed and Contract Workers

Despite the Government's efforts to persuade unemployed people to consider becoming self-employed, the numbers of self-employed have not risen greatly since 1984 when the Annual Labour Force Survey was introduced or, it would appear, from the war years when Beveridge calculated the size of this group. The number of men whose main occupation was self-employment rose from 1.8 million in that year to 2.2 million by 1994. The number of part-time self-employed men rose, as we can see from the table above, from a total of 133,000 to 211,000. Combining these data gives a total of nearly 2.5 million male self-employed workers. The number of full-time self-employed women workers has increased over the same period, from 328,000 in 1984 to 407,000 in 1994. The number of part-time self-employed women has also increased from 318,000 to 395,000, giving in 1994 a total just in excess of 800,000 self-employed women workers. While almost 3.5 million people are registered as self-employed, this is only a million more than was estimated by the Government Actuary in calculations he undertook in 1942 for the Beveridge Committee (Joan Brown, *A Policy Vacuum*, Joseph Rowntree Foundation, 1992, 5).

To these totals we need to add contract and temporary workers. The numbers of fixed contract workers have changed most over the period since figures were collected in the mid-eighties. A total of 428,000 contract workers in 1985 rose to a peak of 495,000 in 1987 and fell thereafter. The numbers began rising again in 1992 and totalled almost three-quarters of a million by 1994. The number of temporary workers rose from a fraction over 1.1 million in 1988 to almost 1.4 million in 1994.

Reduced Insurance Cover for Married Women

Beveridge accorded married women a special status in his thinking. Using the 1931 Census (the latest available to him) he deduced that over 80 per cent of married women of working age regarded marriage as their sole occupation. Even if a wife worked, Beveridge argued she was in a different position to a single working woman. The married woman would have time out of the labour market while she nurtured her children and her earnings were 'a means, not of subsistence but of a standard of living above subsistence' (para 108). Such beliefs led Beveridge to conclude that married women did not therefore require the same insurance cover for sickness and unemployment as other women who were breadwinners. Married women who were earning were therefore given in Beveridge's scheme the possibility of opting out of insurance cover and, depending on their husband's insurance record, of gaining thereby retirement pension and maternity grants. Alternatively they could opt for full insurance cover. From 1946 until 1975 this was largely the position.

By the 1970s over 60 per cent of married women of working age were in the labour market. This married women's option, as it was known, was then abolished. But those married women or widows who had opted out were allowed to choose between a full or a reduced contribution. The numbers paying the reduced contribution for re-duced benefits show that this gap in the national insurance scheme is righting itself. There are no reliable figures prior to 1978. Since then the number of women who continue to exercise the right to pay re-duced-rate contributions has fallen continuously, from 1.9 million in 1978–9 to an estimated 763,000 in 1993–4 (*Hansard*, 14 February 1995, cols. 603–4w)

Insurance Cover Since 1948

We now need to consider how well the national insurance scheme has worked in the post-war world. In particular we need to judge how well the 1948 scheme has performed in extending cover to both full—and part-time workers as well as to self-employed and contract workers. The concern here, however, is not the usual one of the extent to which national insurance cover has prevented people from drawing means-tested assistance in addition to their insurance entitlement (i.e., the debate about the adequacy of benefit levels). The primary aim of *Making Welfare Work* is to gain comprehensive coverage for a new stakeholder's scheme. The reason for this switch in objective will be explained shortly. The question here is the extent to which people gain insurance cover when they are unable to work or when they have retired. Our primary concern is how this pattern of entitlement may have changed over the post-war period. We will then be in a position to attempt an analysis of the extent to which millions of individuals now working within a flexible labour market are constrained by an inflexible welfare state just at a time when they need help in underpinning their living standards. Indeed we shall be examining whether during this period of growing labour market flexibility the welfare state has moved in the opposite direction, becoming less rather than more flexible in the way it meets needs.

Table 5.1 depicts the main groups dependent upon means-tested income support: pensioners, the unemployed, the long-term sick and disabled and single mothers. Here we consider the first three groups. The unemployed are clearly the group most affected by changes in the labour market and, as the stakeholder's insurance scheme has a primary aim of bringing welfare out from the ghetto and into the mainstream of labour market and economic policy debate, it is here we begin our discussion.

Table 7.2 details the emergence of a broken-backed unemployment insurance scheme. The years of peak unemployment are those to which particular attention should be given. By 1958 a clear trend had been established: the growing ineffectiveness of insurance cover for workers losing their jobs. Picking up the story in 1972, when unemployment peaked at 873,000 claimants, only 39 per cent drew unemployment benefit and a further 13 per cent claimed the latter as well as what is now called income support. Thirty per cent of the unemployed drew means-tested income support alone, while a little over 18 per cent claimed no benefit whatsoever at the time of the count.

Six years later, with the unemployment count peaking at 1.28 million, only 32 per cent of this total were entitled to unemployment insurance benefit. A further fall was recorded in the numbers and proportion drawing both unemployment and supplementary benefit—

TABLE 7.2
Number and Percentage of Claimants by Benefit Entitlement(f) *(000s)*

Year	Total unemployment count (a)	Unemployment benefit only (b)		Unemployment benefit and IS/SB/NA (c)		IS/SB/NA only (d)		No benefit (e)	
1951	303	202	*67%*	33	*11%*	32	*11%*	36	*12%*
1952	400	269	*67%*	59	*15%*	41	*10%*	31	*8%*
1953	322	167	*52%*	48	*15%*	<u>45</u>	*14%*	62	*19%*
1954	256	118	*46%*	30	*12%*	50	*20%*	58	*23%*
1955	216	101	*47%*	20	*9%*	40	*19%*	55	*25%*
1956	297	138	*46%*	30	*10%*	42	*14%*	87	*29%*
1957	335	<u>161</u>	*<u>48%</u>*	41	*12%*	55	*16%*	79	*23%*
1958	532	268	*50%*	66	*12%*	85	*16%*	113	*21%*
1959	421	199	*47%*	42	*10%*	113	*27%*	67	*16%*
1960	365	146	*40%*	31	*8%*	97	*27%*	91	*25%*
1961	389	174	*45%*	29	*7%*	102	*26%*	85	*22%*
1962	566	258	*46%*	55	*10%*	147	*26%*	106	*19%*
1963	460	208	*45%*	46	*10%*	139	*30%*	67	*15%*
1964	349	146	*42%*	26	*7%*	105	*30%*	72	*21%*
1965	319	139	*44%*	24	*8%*	75	*24%*	81	*25%*
1966	295	128	*43%*	25	*8%*	65	*22%*	78	*26%*
1967	543	260	*48%*	76	*14%*	94	*17%*	114	*21%*
1968	559	236	*42%*	70	*13%*	135	*24%*	119	*21%*
1969	532	218	*41%*	63	*12%*	129	*24%*	122	*23%*
1970	576	237	*41%*	65	*11%*	140	*24%*	134	*23%*
1971	736	302	*41%*	94	*13%*	177	*24%*	163	*22%*
1972	873	343	*39%*	114	*13%*	255	*29%*	161	*18%*
1973	621	196	*32%*	58	*9%*	234	*38%*	133	*21%*
1974	546	176	*32%*	59	*11%*	190	*35%*	121	*22%*
1975	808	301	*37%*	95	*12%*	251	*31%*	161	*20%*
1976	1,200	446	*37%*	141	*12%*	413	*34%*	200	*17%*
1977	1,229	408	*33%*	130	*11%*	489	*40%*	202	*16%*
1978	1,283	413	*32%*	113	*9%*	511	*40%*	246	*19%*
1979	1,106	366	*33%*	85	*8%*	466	*42%*	188	*17%*
1980	1,304	489	*38%*	105	*8%*	486	*37%*	225	*17%*
1981	2,195	940	*43%*	225	*10%*	735	*33%*	294	*13%*
1982	2,573	731	*28%*	251	*10%*	1,202	*47%*	390	*15%*
1983	2,864	713	*25%*	253	*9%*	1,539	*54%*	359	*13%*
1984	2,999	750	*25%*	223	*7%*	1,661	*55%*	364	*12%*
1985	..	..	..	..	..	..	..	..	..
1986	3,079	732	*24%*	194	*6%*	1,684	*55%*	469	*15%*
1987	2,752	645	*23%*	152	*6%*	1,514	*55%*	442	*16%*
1988	2,264	504	*22%*	132	*6%*	1,254	*55%*	374	*17%*
1989	1,649	278	*17%*	100	*6%*	997	*60%*	274	*17%*
1990	1,432	251	*18%*	48	*3%*	914	*64%*	220	*15%*
1991	2,048	453	*22%*	102	*5%*	1,212	*59%*	280	*14%*
1992	2,546	545	*21%*	124	*5%*	1,564	*61%*	313	*12%*
1993	2,759	543	*20%*	116	*4%*	1,765	*64%*	335	*12%*
1994	2,551	428	*17%*	113	*4%*	1,729	*68%*	281	*11%*

from 13 per cent to 9 per cent. The proportion claiming supplementary benefit only rose to almost 40 per cent. The numbers of unemployed gaining no benefit at all rose to 9 per cent.

Eight years later, in 1986, the unemployment count peaked at a little over 3 million. The proportion gaining insurance cover fell once again, to 24 per cent of the total. Similarly the proportion of unemployed drawing unemployment benefit and income support, as supplementary benefit was renamed in 1986, fell to 6 per cent. The proportion totally dependent upon means-tested income support grew by nearly 15 percentage points—up to 55 per cent. The proportion gaining no benefit fell four percentage points to 15 per cent.

The unemployment count peaked again seven years later, in 1993, when 2.76 million claimants were registered as unemployed. But less than 20 per cent were eligible for unemployment benefit and a mere 4 per cent for unemployment benefit and income support. However, the numbers and proportion of unemployed claimants gaining only income support rose 9 percentage points to 64 per cent. The latest data in the table show that the trends of falling national insurance cover and rising means-tested benefit support continues, even after the unemployment count begins to fall.

The national insurance scheme could not give complete coverage even in the early post-war years. Yet the transformation has been dramatic: 87 per cent of the unemployed in 1951 gained the insurance benefit, together with a further 11 per cent who supplemented their benefit with means-tested support. Only 11 per cent of the unemployed were totally dependent upon a means-tested income. Even so, one lesson is very clear: as unemployment has become an ever more serious problem in the later post-war years, employment benefit schemes

Notes to Table 7.2
Notes: (a) Until 1964 average of December registrants, from 1964 at second Thursday in May.
      (b) Until 1957, December figures, from 1957 to 1964 November and from 1965 at second Thursday in May.
      (c) December figures until 1964. second Thursday in May from 1965.
      (d) November figures until 1953, then December until 1964 and second Thursday in May from 1965.
      (e) Calculated as a residual until 1964.
      (f) 1951 to 1964 not strictly comparable with later years, in particular the split between National Assistance claimants and unemployed receiving no benefits.
Sources: Annual Abstract of Statistics, various editions; Social Security Statistics 1972; Ministry of Pensions and National Insurance Annual Reports; National Assistance Board Annual Reports

TABLE 7.3
Recipients of Invalidity Benefit and Sickness Benefit(a) *(000s)*

	Invalidity benefit recipients				Sickness benefit recipients			
Year	All	With IS/SB only(b)	With IS/SB and HB	With HB only	All	With IS/SB only(b)	With IS/SB and HB	With HB only
1948	..	..	..	..	..	..	..	..
1949	..	..	..	..	..	..	..	..
1950	..	..	..	..	884	..	..	..
1951	..	..	..	..	791	..	..	..
1952	..	..	..	..	811	..	..	..
1953	..	..	..	..	882	..	..	..
1954	..	..	..	..	904	..	..	..
1955	..	..	..	..	877	..	..	..
1956	..	..	..	..	881	..	..	..
1957	..	..	..	..	859	..	..	..
1958	..	..	..	..	851	..	..	..
1959	..	..	..	..	857	..	..	..
1960	..	..	..	..	894	..	..	..
1961	..	..	..	..	878	..	..	..
1962	..	..	..	..	889	..	..	..
1963	..	..	..	..	921	..	..	..
1964	..	..	..	..	876	..	..	..
1965	..	..	..	..	923	..	..	..
1966	..	..	..	..	900	..	..	..
1967	..	..	..	..	903	..	..	..
1968	..	..	..	..	934	..	..	..
1969	..	..	..	..	923	16	..	..
1970	..	..	..	..	932	16	..	..
1971	..	..	..	..	857	21	..	..

have become progressively less effective in offering insurance cover. By 1994 only 21 per cent of the unemployed gained national insurance cover, of which 4 per cent were also drawing income support. The reverse trend is apparent on the means-tested benefit front, up from the 1951 position, when 11 per cent of the unemployed were totally dependent upon means tests, to 68 per cent in 1994.

The inadequacy of benefit rates is the usual criticism made of the insurance scheme. This does not appear to be borne out by the figures. There would have been only a marginal improvement to this trend if unemployment benefit had been paid at the higher level. Only 11 per cent of claimants supplemented their insurance cover in 1965. The proportion in 1994 had fallen to 4 per cent, although two qualifications should be added. While the percentage of claimants had fallen,

TABLE 7.3 (*Continued*)
Recipients of Invalidity Benefit and Sickness Benefit(a) *(000s)*

	Invalidity benefit recipients				Sickness benefit recipients			
Year	All	With IS/SB only(b)	With IS/SB and HB	With HB only	All	With IS/SB only(b)	With IS/SB and HB	With HB only
1972	414	110	..	..	455	20	..	..
1973	435	..	..	..	449	..	..	..
1974	442	72	..	..	455	18	..	..
1975	450	54	..	..	403	15	..	..
1976	..	48	..	..	..	17	..	..
1977	505	45	..	..	452	17	..	..
1978	557	42	..	..	472	16	..	..
1979	610	33	..	..	430	11	..	..
1980	615	34	..	..	384	13	..	..
1981	633	43	..	..	353	19	..	..
1982	683	55	..	..	393	24	..	..
1983	737	63	..	..	338	21	..	..
1984	797	83	..	..	190	24	..	..
1985	849	..	..	..	180	..	..	..
1986	899	92	..	..	179	25	..	..
1987	968	112	..	..	110	20	..	..
1988	1047	97	..	..	117	23	..	..
1989	1126	102	..	189	109	27	..	9
1990	1209	110	4	205	103	12	11	9
1991	1306	51	53	237	110	13	17	13
1992	1439	65	65	260	138	16	16	11
1993	1580	80	77	267	147	16	17	11
1994	..	..	..	..	..	..	..	..

Notes: (a) May figures until 1964, May/June from 1964 to 1982 and March/April thereafter. Prior to 1966 may include a number of cases where benefit was not in payment.

(b) All supplementary benefit/income support claimants prior to 1990.

Sources: HC Deb 7 February 1995 c201–4w

Ministry Pensions and National Insurance Annual Reports

the actual numbers of this group record a substantial rise—from 33,000 in 1951 to 113,000 in 1994. In addition, the Government is unable to say how many unemployed claimants are drawing means-tested housing benefit in place of income support. Yet the figures do seem to suggest that, if a claimant is able to claim national insurance benefit, the likelihood is that his or her partner continues to work and therefore raises the household income above income support levels.

So a fundamental conclusion which will shape the recommenda-

tions of **Making Welfare Work** *is already clear. It is not the inadequacy of the unemployment benefit which can explain the rise of seven out of ten unemployed claimants being totally dependent upon means-tested income support. It is, rather, the failure of claimants to qualify or requalify for the insurance benefit.*

We now need to examine the trends that emerge from data on sickness and invalidity benefit as well as the pattern of support given to the national insurance retirement pension. The data on sickness and validity benefit for which the Government was able to collect information are presented in table 7.3.

The routes by which claimants qualify for these two benefits are very different. National insurance sickness benefit has been largely replaced since 1985 by statutory sick pay (SSP), run by employers. Employers were initially compensated for the payments they made under this scheme. In future most of them will not be compensated. Currently a little over 5 million individuals make an annual claim for benefit (*Hansard*, 7 February 1995, col. 204w).

Those who do not have a job, but become sick, or whose sick pay is not payable by their employers, may qualify for the national insurance sickness benefit which has been largely replaced by SSP. The contributory rules are explained later. Entrance to invalidity benefit is by way of the qualifications for sickness benefit. The vast majority of workers who are ill for any length of time draw SSP. Yet, at the end of six months, the claimant may qualify for invalidity benefit only if he or she would have qualified for the national insurance sickness benefit.

The data in table 7.3 confirm the trend apparent in the previous table on unemployment benefit claims. And this trend is crucial to the main argument of *Making Welfare Work*. While national insurance unemployment benefit and sick pay is paid at a low level, and the value of these benefits is below the income support level plus rent, the vast majority of claimants do not claim additional means-tested support. The reason for this, I contend, is that other members of the family do work, because they do not suffer the penalty of seeing practically the whole of their earnings deducted, pound for pound, from their partner's benefit. In other words insurance benefits, unlike means-tested help, act as an income floor allowing other members of the household to increase the household income, sometimes substantially. The result is not only the freedom of action by those individuals, improving their own lot by honest effort and actions, but the public good is also promoted with fewer individuals and families dependent upon means tests, and fewer still having to resort to deceit to improve their income.

Rather different but important conclusions emerge from the data on claimants for retirement pension which are presented in table 7.4.

Here the surprise is that almost one in ten individuals over retirement age failed to qualify for the state retirement pension. Yet this finding should not be overplayed. A significant number of this group will continue to draw invalidity benefit rather than a taxed retirement benefit, which they are entitled to do for five years once they have reached the retirement age. This 'loophole' for pensioners previously claiming invalidity benefit will be closed from April 1995. Nor should the trend over time be ignored; there has been a dramatic fall, from 42 per cent in 1950 to 9 per cent in 1993, in the total who gained no retirement pension.

Much more important is a converse trend from those apparent in table 7.3. The retirement pension is paid at a level below the income support and rent levels, and large numbers of pensioners claim income support and/or housing benefit: in all 22 per cent. The reason for this outcome is obvious. The possibility of large numbers of pensioners being able to work is slight, particularly in today's labour market. In fact only 630,000 people in the UK receiving the state retirement pension also have an income from earnings (*Hansard*, 13 February 1995, col. 537w). Moreover, most of the very poorest pensioners supplementing their retirement pension are the very oldest: 62,000 aged between 60 and 64 draw income support with their pension compared with 671,000 over-80–year-olds (*Hansard*, 13 February 1995, col. 541w). Age and increasing sickness, together with growing frailty, prevent this group from being able to supplement their insurance benefits by working. Of even more significance is the fact that these figures ignore the number of claimants with reduced pensions. The numbers of people in this position are given in table 7.5. Here two trends need to be highlighted. The first concerns the rising number and proportion of male pensioners who gain a reduced pension. The second trend concerns the growing number and proportion of women gaining a reduced pension on their own earnings record.

The proportion of men gaining only a reduced pension has risen from 3.1 per cent to 5.2 per cent over the past 30 years—from 2 million to 3.3 million individuals. This rise, and particularly the rise of

TABLE 7.4
Claimants Over State Retirement Age With and Without
Retirement Pension(a) *(000s)*

Year	All (b)	With IS/SB only (c)	With IS/SB and HB	With HB only (d)	All (b)	With IS/SB only (c)	With IS/SB and HB	With HB only (d)
		People with retirement pension				People without retirement pension		
1948	..	..	..	..	..	..	..	..
1949	3,690	..	..	..	..	..	..	..
1950	3,858	..	..	..	2,766	..	..	..
1951	4,146	..	..	..	..	..	..	..
1952	4,184	..	..	..	2,599	..	..	..
1953	4,309	..	..	..	2,548	..	..	..
1954	4,435	..	..	..	2,516	..	..	..
1955	4,548	..	..	..	2,469	..	..	..
1956	4,644	..	..	..	2,457	..	..	..
1957	4,755	..	..	..	2,329	..	..	..
1958	5,320	..	..	..	..	..	..	..
1959	5,447	..	..	..	..	..	..	..
1960	5,563	..	..	..	1,928	..	..	..
1961	5,676	..	..	..	1,901	..	..	..
1962	5,814	..	..	..	1,869	..	..	..
1963	5,981	..	..	..	1,772	..	..	..
1964	6,158	..	..	..	1,747	..	..	..
1965	6,357	..	..	..	1,710	..	..	..
1966	6,540	..	..	..	1,622	..	..	..
1967	6,769	..	..	..	1,560	..	..	..
1968	6,973	..	..	..	1,497	..	..	..
1969 (e)	7,170	1,662	..	..	1,457	208	..	..
1970 (e)	7,363	1,700	..	..	1,396	200	..	..
1971	7,515	1,735	..	..	1,404	185	..	..

over a percentage point during the last five years, is not without significance. A male pensioner retiring today has a contribution period spanning perhaps the previous 50 years. The contribution rules lay down, roughly speaking, that a pensioner should have worked for 90 per cent of their potential working life, and paid contributions above the lower earnings level, or gained credits for periods where no contributions were made. The rise by 1.3 million in the numbers of men gaining only a reduced pension indicates how the flexible labour market is detrimentally affecting insurance rights, even during a period when there seems to be little public appreciation of changes beginning to work their way through a more settled employment pattern.

TABLE 7.4 (*Continued*)
**Claimants Over State Retirement Age With and Without
Retirement Pension(a) (*000s*)**

Year	All (b)	People with retirement pension			All (b)	People without retirement pension		
		With IS/SB only (c)	With IS/SB and HB	With HB only (d)		With IS/SB only (c)	With IS/SB and HB	With HB only (d)
1972	7,668	1,733	..	..	1,367	177	..	..
1973	7,688	..	..	..	1,467	..	..	..
1974	7,822	1,654	..	..	1,454	156	..	..
1975	7,985	1,538	..	..	1,399	142	..	..
1976	8,155	1,547	..	..	1,295	143	..	..
1977	8,266	1,590	..	..	1,242	150	..	..
1978	8,397	1,593	..	..	1,138	147	..	..
1979	8,528	1,599	..	..	1,032	121	..	..
1980	8,681	1,576	..	..	1,032	114	..	..
1981	8,780	1,624	..	..	1,030	116	..	..
1982	8,877	1,683	..	..	990	97	..	..
1983	8,936	1,549	..	..	946	101	..	..
1984	9,003	1,565	..	..	907	115	..	..
1985	9,085	..	..	..	936	..	..	..
1986	9,210	1,592	..	..	892	128	..	..
1987	9,310	1,613	..	..	863	117	..	..
1988	9,298	1,431	..	..	923	109	..	..
1989	9,305	1,314	..	1,057	974	116	..	108
1990	9,391	595	789	1,033	919	59	60	109
1991	9,380	595	677	1,026	976	68	65	124
1992	9,425	692	626	1,031	955	76	64	123
1993	9,448	674	712	952	943	80	75	120
1994	9,442	..	..	..	..	..	..	..

Notes: (a)   Until 1972, pensions include a small number of pensions paid to persons overseas.
(b)   Including AP only from 1979.
(c)   All SBAS claimants prior to 1990.
(d)   All claimants 60 or over.

Sources: HC Deb 7 February 1995 c201–4w Ministry of Pensions and National Insurance Annual Reports

Even greater surprises are revealed in the information on women's pension rights. The pension rules operate so that a woman's pension is based either on her husband's contribution record or her own, depending upon which alternative is more advantageous to the woman. The number of women being awarded a reduced pension has risen by 50 per cent over the past 30 years, and the proportion of women finding

TABLE 7.5
Number of Claimants Receiving Less than 100 Per Cent of Standard Rate Contributory Retirement Pension in Great Britain in the Last 30 Years

	Men			Women				
	All Men	Reduced Rate	Per cent	All women	All reduced rate women	Per cent	All women on their own insurance	Reduced rate women on their own insurance
31.12.64(d)	2,048,160	63,420	3.10	4,110,160	263,040	6.40	1,654,040	175,140
31.12.65(d)	2,120,780	68,120	3.21	4,236,340	275,380	6.50	1,723,720	183,840
31.12.66(d)	2,191,560	71,900	3.28	4,348,420	286,280	6.58	1,788,160	194,960
31.12.67(d)	2,291,460	79,780	3.48	4,477,720	301,420	6.73	1,857,780	209,200
31.12.68(d)	2,373,320	84,780	3.57	4,600,120	313,220	6.81	1,917,040	219,720
31.12.69(e)	—	—	—	—	—	—	—	—
31.12.70(e)	—	—	—	—	—	—	—	—
31.12.71(d)	2,591,360	121,620	4.69	4,907,490	373,480	7.61	2,020,980	264,210
30.11.72(d)	2,653,509	126,277	4.76	4,999,553	384,259	7.69	2,024,053	266,685
30.11.73	2,719,684	136,217	5.01	5,092,180	391,267	7.68	2,023,678	269,826
29.11.74	2,784,488	147,528	5.30	5,177,185	404,000	7.80	2,021,174	277,079
28.11.75	2,796,047	98,129	3.51	5,181,664	323,249	6.24	1,958,555	239,580
26.11.76	2,883,681	102,198	3.54	5,263,672	328,126	6.23	1,929,910	245,333
25.11.77	2,932,847	103,394	3.53	5,327,166	323,574	6.07	1,878,553	243,265
30.11.78	2,993,060	103,660	3.46	5,399,160	330,020	6.11	1,577,030	214,050
30.11.79	3,049,140	105,850	3.47	5,474,400	355,130	6.49	1,596,680	238,490
28.11.80	3,084,590	105,800	3.43	5,590,800	407,370	7.29	1,676,190	295,810
30.06.81	3,099,920	105,530	3.40	5,674,060	438,810	7.73	1,729,530	329,010
30.05.82	3,107,940	103,650	3.34	5,761,550	490,690	8.52	1,805,320	385,480
31.03.33	3,096,620	107,670	3.48	5,830,760	547,530	9.39	1,883,400	443,400
31.03.84	3,078,490	107,480	3.49	5,913,380	626,280	10.59	1,987,760	526,590
31.03.85	3,107,140	118,520	3.81	5,966,010	659,080	11.05	2,034,650	547,980
31.03.96	3,160,600	122,310	3.87	6,036,480	687,300	11.39	2,098,850	583,640
30.09.87	3,219,820	123,300	3.83	6,074,680	680,850	11.21	2,142,850	589,230
31.03.88	3,215,530	124,590	3.87	6,066,410	682,570	11.25	2,152,390	591,120
31.03.89	3,224,120	128,450	3.98	6,062,620	681,660	11.24	2,173,730	591,780
30.09.90	3,263,520	136,220	4.17	6,107,570	709,320	11.61	2,241,070	620,100
31.03.91	3,260,930	139,080	4.27	6,096,910	716,090	11.75	2,252,250	627,420
31.03.92	3,280,200	148,730	4.53	6,122,330	740,270	12.09	2,295,740	646,780
31.03.93	3,293,560	161,030	4.89	6,130,820	764,210	12.47	2,336,620	666,780
31.03.94	3,302,300	172,310	5.22	6,114,590	782,760	12.80	2,370,040	682,870

Notes: (a)   Paid to widows on the basis of the late husbands' contributions—excludes pensions paid at a reduced rate on the basis of age at widowhood.

(b)   Full-rate Category B(L) and A/B(L) paid to married women is equal to approximately 60 per cent of the full Category B pension.

(c)   Category A/B(L) is based on a combination of the woman's own contribu-

TABLE 7.5 (*Continued*)
Number of Claimants Receiving Less than 100 Per Cent of Standard Rate Contributory Retirement Pension in Great Britain in the Last 30 Years

Women (continued)

Per cent	All women partly on their husband's insurance (b)(c)	Reduced rate women partly on their husband's insurance	Per cent	All widows on their husband's insurance (a)	Reduced rate widows on their insurance	Per cent	All women completely on their husband's insurance (b)	Reduced rate women completely on their husband's insurance	Per cent
10.59	—	—	—	1,332,320	62,420	4.69	1,123,800	25,480	2.27
10.67	—	—	—	1,345,460	64,180	4.77	1,167,160	27,360	2.34
10.90	—	—	—	1,351,640	62,820	4.65	1,208,620	28,500	2.36
11.26	—	—	—	1,361,660	60,560	4.45	1,258,280	31,660	2.52
11.46	—	—	—	1,376,640	59,840	4.35	1,306,440	33,660	2.58
—	—	—	—	—	—	—	—	—	—
—	—	—	—	—	—	—	—	—	—
13.07	—	—	—	1,433,720	55,370	3.86	1,452,790	53,900	3.71
13.18	—	—	—	1,481,547	58,402	3.94	1,493,953	59,172	3.96
13.33	—	—	—	1,535,426	60,138	3.92	1,533,076	61,303	4.00
13.71	—	—	—	1,573,907	62,962	4.00	1,582,104	63,959	4.04
12.23	—	—	—	1,626,723	44,250	2.72	1,596,386	39,419	2.47
12.71	—	—	—	1,682,695	42,820	2.54	1,651,067	39,913	2.42
12.95	—	—	—	1,755,972	39,873	2.27	1,692,641	40,436	2.39
13.57	—	—	—	2,097,080	76,140	3.63	1,725,050	39,830	2.31
14.94	7,990	70	0.88	2,121,380	75,730	3.57	1,748,350	40,910	2.34
17.65	30,270	230	0.76	2,127,270	71,290	3.35	1,757,070	40,270	2.29
19.02	45,260	180	0.40	2,143,730	69,780	3.26	1,755,540	40,020	2.28
21.35	73,310	330	0.45	2,140,400	66,660	3.11	1,742,520	38,550	2.21
23.54	103,520	960	0.93	2,133,060	64,370	3.02	1,710,780	39,760	2.32
26.49	140,430	820	0.58	2,121,170	59,330	2.80	1,664,020	40,360	2.43
26.93	183,700	1,010	0.55	2,104,820	70,970	3.37	1,642,840	40,130	2.44
27.81	265,870	1,510	0.57	2,079,320	65,910	3.17	1,592,440	37,750	2.37
27.50	368,160	1,910	0.52	2,035,060	53,830	2.65	1,528,410	37,790	2.47
27.46	396,060	1,950	0.49	2,015,980	53,100	2.63	1,501,980	38,350	2.55
27.22	447,250	2,210	0.49	1,985,330	51,420	2.59	1,456,310	38,460	2.64
27.67	525,320	2,790	0.53	1,926,850	50,040	2.60	1,414,330	39,180	2.77
27.86	546,330	2,800	0.51	1,908,660	48,990	2.57	1,389,670	19,680	2.86
28.17	589,040	2,770	0.47	1,873,880	50,810	2.71	1,363,070	42,680	3.13
28.54	628,490	2,930	0.47	1,834,970	51,640	2.81	1,330,740	45,790	3.44
28.81	664,110	2,910	0.44	1,788,700	52,090	2.91	1,291,740	47,800	3.70

tions and those of her husband and was introduced with effect from 6 April 1979.

(d)   Figures include a small number of pensions paid to persons overseas.

(e)   Figures not available.

Source: HC Deb 13 February 1995 c537–40w

themselves so treated has doubled. By far and away the most important reason for this is the rise in the number of women gaining a reduced pension on their own insurance record. The Government does not collect figures on the number of women who are long-standing cohabitees who would have gained a larger pension on the basis of their partner's earnings record. Only a husband's contributions can be called into account. The figures therefore mean that despite the very significant increase in the number of women working over the past 30 years, and the earnings threshold for national insurance contributions being set at a fairly modest level (£59 a week from April 1995), a growing proportion of women have found themselves recipients of a reduced pension. The total number of women involved is also important. Half a million more women now gain a full pension in their own right. But so too do a further half a million women who gain only a reduced pension on their own contribution record. The number with only a reduced pension has more than doubled during the 1980s when the contribution record will have been built up over the previous 40 years. So, again long before flexible labour markets had become the buzz phrase, employment opportunities for women were polarising between those getting a secure place at work and those whose much more precarious footing was leading to only partial insurance coverage.

A Broken-Backed Insurance Scheme

We need now to consider the causes of the broken-backed welfare system. Is the cause due to the entrance requirements—i.e., the contribution conditions—being set at too high a level in the first place, or has the height been increased since? Or has what is called the system of credits for non-workers changed, disenfranchising people from cover? Alternatively, have working conditions so changed that an increasing number of individuals cannot gain entrance to the insurance scheme? Or does a mixture of both reasons explain the deepening failure of the national insurance system to fulfil its primary objective?

First, have the contribution conditions been made more onerous? The current conditions for the major benefits we have considered can be summarised as follows.

For *unemployment and sickness benefit* there are two conditions which have to be met. The first is that the claimant must have paid in the contribution year the appropriate class of contributions, producing what is called an earnings factor of at least 25 times that year's lower earnings level (i.e., in 1995–6 25 times £59, or in total £1475). For sickness benefit these contributions may have been paid in any tax year, but for unemployment benefit the claimant's contribution must have been paid in one of the last two complete tax years before what is called the relevant benefit year, i.e., the year beginning with the first Sunday in January during which the period of interruption of employment claim is made.

Claimants, in order to fulfil the second condition, must have paid or been credited with contributions producing an earnings factor equal to 50 times the lower earnings limit in each of the last two complete contribution years ending before the relevant benefit year.

For the payment of a *retirement pension* two conditions also have to be fulfilled. In any tax year before pensionable age, contributions the same as those for unemployment and sick benefits but at 52 times the lower earnings level. In addition, a claimant must have paid or been credited with contributions with an earnings factor of at least 52 times that year's lower earnings level for the requisite number of years. These years are determined by the length of a claimant's working life, and this calculation is based on the years between 16 and until the year in which the claimant retires. From this total is subtracted a set number of years, of between one and five, varying directly according to the actual length of the claimant's working life (i.e., the longer the person is in the labour market the larger will be the reduction of years when the contribution conditions do not have to be fulfilled). How have these conditions for each of these benefits changed since 1948?

For all of these benefits there are really only two main changes, those in 1975 and those in 1988. The 1975 changes were largely concerned with the changeover from flat-rate to earnings-related contributions. In broad terms they did not change the actual entitlement to contributory benefits, but provided a basis for calculating contributions in relation to the lower earnings limit.

The 1988 changes were more significant in terms of unemployment and sickness benefit. They made contribution conditions considerably more onerous for these benefits. Effectively they doubled the number of necessary weeks' contribution from one to two years (or the equivalent in terms of multiples of the lower earnings limit).

For retirement pensions the 1988 changes affected the standard pension, although there were significant changes (making it less generous) to contributions counting towards the SERPS element. The requirement for a full standard pension is that the contribution record must show contributions above the lower earnings limit for around 90 per cent of the contributor's working life. Working life is currently 49 years for a man and 44 years for a woman.

Claimants may qualify for any one of nine credits which count towards their entitlement to benefit, although it is important to note that credits by themselves do not qualify claimants for unemployment and sickness benefit. The combination of the two conditions detailed above ensures that a claimant must have worked and paid minimum contributions, i.e., paid in the appropriate contribution year a sum through the appropriate class of contribution equal to 25 times the lower earnings level, i.e., in 1994–5 contributions valued at a minimum of £59 per week.

The Government has undertaken no studies of the extent to which the contribution rule changes have disenfranchised individuals from national insurance cover. The picture is rather different when we turn to consider the question of how the system of credits has changed over the post-war period. Here the Government has produced a detailed account of the changes in the system of accreditation since the conception of the national insurance scheme and the impact these changes have had in the level of insurance cover (*Hansard*, 3 March 1995, cols. 761–4w). There have in fact been a number of changes to the rules governing insurance credits, the bare outlines of which cover three columns of *Hansard*. The Government concludes, 'It is not possible to estimate the impact of these changes on the number who have lost national insurance cover' but adds, 'Since the majority of changes have been favourable there have been more gainers than losers in benefit terms.' In coming to this conclusion what the Government does not do, however, is distinguish the impact of these changes on the rights to retirement pension, and the rights to what are called short-term national insurance benefits such as unemployment and sickness benefit.

Three factors need to be taken into account when discussing the transition to the stakeholder's scheme: countering the greater restriction on entry into the scheme, making the system of creditation effective and, above all, ensuring that the contributory system matches the changing nature of the labour market.

Transition to a Stakeholder's Scheme

We are now in a position to begin describing the process of transition and the outline of a new stakeholder's insurance scheme which will over time replace the current national insurance scheme. It is possible only to give an outline of the reform. Funds will be sought to commission the Government Actuary to calculate the full impact of *Making Welfare Work*'s proposed changes on the key issue of the new scheme's comprehensiveness. Only the Government Actuary has the information or, as is more likely, if the data are lacking, is in a position to begin collecting it, and to undertake the necessary range of calculations about how the steps to reform will be matched by increasing insurance cover. Will the proposed reforms bring into insurance cover practically all those now in work but presently excluded? The Government Actuary will moreover be asked not only to calculate the cost of the changes proposed in *Making Welfare Work* but also what the distributional impact might be on the three parties to the scheme: the employers, employees, and taxpayers.

There is also the need to encourage the Government, the academic community, or a joint effort by both, to begin compiling an employment and social security audit. At present, practically all the Government's data in this area are of a snapshot variety. Employment and social security audits will track the same individuals over time. The audit will position voters and politicians to judge the pace of change in the flexible labour market and how best to compensate for these changes by adapting the entry requirements into the stakeholder insurance scheme. The audit will also alert voters and politicians to the need constantly to review the adequacy of the insurance base as the labour market continues to evolve new working practices.

What will the new scheme look like? In respect of entry into the scheme three reforms are urgently required on the basis of the evidence already presented in *Making Welfare Work*.

- The first reform centres on the need to reconsider the relevance of the earnings threshold.
- The second reform looks at the contributory year requirements for benefit eligibility.
- The third reform concerns judging the comprehensiveness of the credits offered to those unable to earn a contribution record.

In addition it is also necessary to

- consider the introduction of graduated benefits;
- reform more generally the financial base of the system.

Earnings Conditions

All examples in *Making Welfare Work* assume that the lower earnings level is the appropriate point for contributions to gain full insurance cover. Given the very significant changes in the distribution of earnings, one question which the Government Actuary will be asked to consider is the relevance of this level, set as a proportion of average earnings back in 1975, and the distributional impact of changing the level on the costs of the new scheme and the rights to benefit. But taking the current LEL for illustrative purposes, *Making Welfare Work* proposes:

- All earnings would count towards the contribution conditions of the scheme.
- Workers below the current lower earnings level would pay contribution as would their employers, and gain percentage credits towards all stakeholder insurance benefits.

So if a person paid half of what is currently the lower earnings level they would gain half the relevant benefit, providing the time contributions were met, or they had gained a credit qualification.

Those earning above the lower earnings level for some but not all weeks of a contributory year would have the entitlement to benefit calculated accordingly. So claimants with half of the 50 contributions at the full rate, and half of the contributions at only 50 per cent of the full rate, would have contributions entitling them to three-quarters of the standard rate of benefit.

Again the precise details of the reform will have to await both the report of the Government Actuary working in association with the pilot studies of the employment and social security audits already called for in this report. On this aspect of the reform we need to know the career paths of part-time workers. How temporary or long-term are these posts, what proportion lead to unemployment and how important are family responsibilities to the choice of part-time work? Are part-time posts stepping stones to full-time jobs, and what proportion of part-time jobs are held by workers coming to the end of their careers who do not wish to work full-time?

There are, of course, a number of other possible career paths for this group. This kind of information on what is actually happening in the labour market is crucial in planning the details of the reform. One assumption on which the reform is currently built is that the great majority of part-time workers choose jobs which allow these work duties to be combined with household responsibilities. If this is so, then the model here of thinking about a lifetime's earnings, and similarly a life time's national insurance contributions, can give an adequate insurance coverage. But if a more typical part-timer's career is one where time at work is regularly interspersed with periods of unemployment, so that some of these spells are prolonged, and there is almost no chance of expanding this time at work, then the insurance coverage advocated here is going to need to be built on different assumptions.

Qualifying Time

- The qualifying time for all the short-term benefits should be simplified to 50 paid contributions within the relevant year. It is worth recalling that in the 1911 Insurance Act, relating to unemployment entitlement, benefit was payable not only on today's basis of two very strict conditions, one of which stretches over a two-year period, but also on condition that the claimant had been employed as a workman in an insured trade in each of not less than 26 separate calendar weeks in the preceding five years (Section 86, 1911 National Insurance Act).

Two new controls would operate to ensure that the right to unemployment benefit, or the qualification for national insurance sickness benefit passport to invalidity benefit, was not abused. The 'actively seeking work' rules would continue to operate for the unemployed, with an additional and crucial safeguard. Employers would have a duty to report to the public employment service all vacancies for jobs expected to last for more than 10 days. Currently, only 30 per cent of vacancies are reported to Jobcentres. (For further details see "A proactive Benefits Agency" below). A doubling or more of this rate of notified vacancies would allow the Department to offer actual jobs as a test of actively seeking work. (For details see Frank Field and Matthew Owen, *Beyond Punishment: Hard Choices on the Road to Full*

Employability, ICS, 1994.) A severe tightening up of the rules against abuse will therefore protect the fund while ensuring that a much more flexible welfare system is built to deflect the disadvantages of a flexible labour market. Members, once they are in full control of their own organisation, will take an active interest in its anti-fraud strategy.

The argument against the self-employed being full members of an insurance scheme has largely rested on the concern about benefit abuse. How can unemployment insurance cover, for example, be offered when there would be little or nothing to stop some self-employed claiming to be unemployed, drawing benefit while continuing to work in their own trade or profession?

The simple truth is that under current checks against abuse one has to agree with the argument against extending coverage to the self-employed. But if an effective battery of controls was in place—i.e., either reporting regularly a number of times each day to a Jobcentre or, more effectively still, agreeing to become full-time members of a Job Club searching for work—then the case against unemployment insurance cover for the self-employed falls. Again the Government Actuary will need to advise on the contribution rates necessary for both sickness and unemployment cover.

Invalidity benefit would, as now, be conditional upon fulfilling the contribution conditions for sickness benefit as well as the separate medical criteria. This latter criterion would be kept regularly under review. In the past many claimants were put on invalidity benefit as part of an unspoken agreement when massive redundancy took place in manufacturing industry, affecting as it did a preponderance of older male semi-skilled and unskilled workers. (Many of these workers do not possess the skills necessary for the new IT jobs.) As well as specifically targeting training courses to this group the creation of community-based jobs is an essential part of building up a comprehensive reform package. (For the range of these jobs see Frank Field, Liam Halligan, and Matthew Owen, *Europe* Isn't *Working*, ICS, 1994). Many of the men (78 per cent of invalidity benefit claimants are men) currently on invalidity benefit might well look differently at their disabilities if other suitable work was available. Similarly the availability of such work will probably slow down registration for invalidity benefit.

The qualifying time for retirement pension also needs to be reconsidered. The growing number of pensioners failing to gain a full entitlement is testimony both to the changing labour market and to the failure of the system whereby individuals do not gain credits when they are unable to work.

Contributory Year

Next, the contributory year basis for calculating entitlements similarly needs to be revised. Calculating on a 50–week year contribution record was an acceptable basis when the vast majority of workers were employed every week of every year from joining a firm until retirement. The increasingly flexible labour market challenges the appropriateness of this model for insurance cover. Contributions should in future be based on the fulfilment of a required number of weekly contributions only.

System of Credits

The last aspect of the current rules needing reform concerns the offering of credits to those unable to work. Is this coverage adequate, or are the inadequacies a source of disenfranchisement from insurance cover particularly for unemployment and sickness benefit (the latter being important as it acts as a gatekeeper to invalidity benefit)? Moreover, in a stakeholder's scheme, should the basis of credit be replaced by actual contributions? Again, perhaps quite unsurprisingly, the Government has no information whatsoever on the extent to which the current system of insurance credits is in itself an important cause of the lack of insurance cover. What is clear however is that the current system of credits, where the Exchequer makes a bookkeeping adjustment in people's insurance records but makes no actual contribution into the fund, has to cease. The effect of such a system is to place the cost of the credits on the employer and employee contributions. As has been argued at length earlier, *Making Welfare Work* insists that any redistribution to the lower paid, or to those outside the labour market, must be done openly, be above board, and be agreed by the voters themselves. The quid pro quo of this approach is that Exchequer credits need to be converted into Exchequer contributions into the fund.

It is here that the altruistic side of the new welfare will become operative, and which politicians will have a responsibility to sell to the electorate. On the current system of credits, payments to the fund would have been in the region of £7.7bn in 1992–3 if those for whom contributions were being paid, had been earning two-thirds of average earnings (House of Commons Library Note, March 1995).

Graduated Benefits

The next major reform concerns the type and range of benefit. The original Beveridge scheme has moved from a flat-rate contributory system (albeit with a generous Treasury supplement as we shall shortly see) and flat-rate benefits, to a proportional tax base over a set income range with graduated benefits, and back to a flat-rate benefit system but with graduated contributions over income between the lower and higher earnings level.

The argument for moving back to a graduated system of benefits appears overwhelming. Together with ensuring a fully comprehensive insurance cover, graduating benefits to contributions will be one of the major selling points for the reform. Whereas a state-run insurance scheme does not vary the contribution levels as does a private scheme, according to the risks attached to the member, graduated contributions for flat-rate benefits strike at what is perceived to be the strength of a national scheme i.e., benefits related to contributions. The abolition of the lower earnings limit on employees (the upper earnings limit on employer contributions was abolished in 1985) makes inevitable the reintroduction of graduated benefits for those below the current LEL.

Whether the LEL is a proper and fair cut-off point for a new range of reduced benefits should be considered in the light of the report from the Government Actuary. There are, however, two main reasons why there should be this range of graduated benefits for those making the smallest contributions. The first relates to the replacement ratio of benefits to earnings. To pay too high a level of benefits to part-time workers will create a disincentive problem. Moreover, such payments might well undermine the appeal to fairness which the scheme must seek to engender. The second reason is that what is being proposed is an insurance system and there must be some link between payment of contribution and benefits. But the logic of this position should not be sidestepped. A task of the new stakeholder's insurance corporation will be to consider whether all benefit should be earnings related. Part of this decision would naturally cover the question of the upper earnings level for employee contributions. What would be the contributors' views if the abolition of the upper earnings level were linked with the introduction of fully integrated benefits over the whole of income contributions? Indeed, would the question of the upper earnings limit be viewed differently by contributors if this were one of the alternatives proposed for them to consider?

The Scheme's Finances

Writing in *Social Insurance and Allied Services* Beveridge made a clear distinction between taxation and insurance contributions: 'taxation is or should be related to assumed capacity to pay rather than the value of what the payer may expect to receive, for insurance contributions are or should be related to the value of the benefit and not the capacity to pay.' (para 272). Beveridge then crucially qualified this contributory aspect of the scheme's financing which must be re-established in the new insurance scheme: 'whatever monies are obtained—from insured persons as contributions and from their employers as employers, it is certain that the Exchequer, that is to say the citizen as taxpayer, must continue to meet a substantial part of the total expenditure' of the scheme (para 273).

Here again is a sign of Beveridge's intuitive skill as a reformer. The above quotation leaves the reader in little doubt about the importance of the insurance principle of relating payments to benefits. Because he was opting for a flat-rate range of benefits, contributions had to be fashioned as a poll tax—or so Beveridge thought. There would be, in addition, a progressive element in the scheme's financial structure.

Contrary to various statements which have been made, the Beveridge Report did contain details of the size of this progressive element for both 1945 and 1965: a 36.5 per cent contribution from the Exchequer in 1945 was expected to rise to a 50.7 per cent contribution of the total cost of the fund 20 years later. More detailed estimates of the Exchequer's role were given in the White Paper *Social Insurance*, published in 1944 (HMSO, Cmd 6550). Here is detailed an Exchequer contribution rising from 54.1 per cent in 1945 to 59.6 per cent 10 years later, rising further to 63.6 per cent in 1965, and reaching 67 per cent in 1975.

The Exchequer contribution is in no immediate danger of reaching these proportions. In 1955 it stood at a fraction over 13 per cent of the Insurance Fund, rising to 15.5 per cent in 1965 and falling back to 15

TABLE 7.6
The 1945 White Paper Projections—Percentage Shares

	1945	1955	1965	1975
Employer/employees	43.5	38.3	34.5	31.2
Interest	2.3	2.5	1.9	1.8
Exchequer	4.1	59.6	63.6	67.2

Source: Social Insurance and Allied Services, Table XIII, 112

per cent in 1975. It stood at 16 per cent when Labour lost office at the 1979 General Election.

The phasing out of the progressive element in the financing of insurance entitlement became part of the Thatcher Government's hidden welfare agenda—hidden only because few politicians (excluding this author) appreciated the importance of what was afoot. From contributing 16 per cent of national insurance funding in 1979 (itself a proportion of only about a quarter of what was envisaged by the wartime Coalition Government) the taxpayers' element was abolished entirely in 1989–90. It has only since been reinstated to finance the payment of the subsidies to persuade individuals to leave the SERPS scheme and take out a private pension. The size of this subsidy—or bribe—is significant. From 1993–4 the subsidy will amount.3bn in 1994–5. Thereafter the grant will be limited to a maximum of £4bn a year (*Hansard*, 13 March 1995, col.457w).

Apart from any Exchequer contributions, the scheme was dependent upon monies paid in by employers and employees. From 1948 employers and employees paid a flat-rate contribution, or stamp as it was commonly called. In 1961 employees then began paying in addition an earnings-related contribution of between £9 and £15 a week.

From 1961 to 1966 there was one rate of graduated contributions between the lower and upper earnings limit. Graduated contributions were payable only on earnings in excess of the lower limit. From 1966 until 1975 there were two rates of graduated contribution. The lower rate applied to earnings between the lower and what was called the intermediate earnings limit, and a second rate from this point up to the upper earnings limit.

The measure which came into force in 1975 abolished the national insurance stamp and these earnings-related contributions and substituted in effect a social security tax of 5.5 per cent on earnings. The ceiling was maintained in the new scheme and the social security levy was applied on earnings between £11 and £69 per week. A further development occurred in 1978–9 when those employees who did not come into the State Earnings Related Pension Scheme (SERPS), or who were later opted out from the Scheme, were allowed what was called a contracted-out rate on payments between the lower and upper earnings limit for both employee and employer.

Gradually the 5.5 per cent rate for employees was raised to 9 per cent by 1983–4. Employers' contributions, which began at 8.5 per cent in 1975–6, had risen to 10.45 per cent by 1984–5. From October 1985 contribution rates were broken into different income bands of both employers and employees. A further change was made to the rules of contribution from October 1989. The first band of income attracted a 2 per cent tax, whereas other incomes up to the upper earnings level attracted a 9 per cent contribution. Employers' contributions continued over a five-band range of income although, as we have noted earlier, the ceiling on employer contributions at the upper earnings level was abolished in 1985.

The contribution base for the current national insurance scheme has therefore been something of a movable feast. Benefits too have changed, from universal flat-rate benefits to flat-rate plus earnings-related schemes and back again to flat-rate benefits only.

The lessons are clear. The rates levied and the contribution base have been largely settled by the Government of the day's wish either to phase out the Exchequer contribution, or its realisation that the cost of the national insurance contribution was becoming so great that the original flat-rate stamp contribution had to be reformed, even if only step by step, or lastly to begin paying bonuses to individuals transferring out of SERPS into a private pension scheme.

There is also a lesson here for the reconstructed scheme. There will be a need for a significant Exchequer contribution, in particular to pay for the credits earned by designated groups of the population. As we have seen, had the current system of credits led to Exchequer contributions into the fund sums in the region of £7.7bn would have been paid over in 1992–3. The fund is self-financing and needs only to balance its accounts on an annual basis. So the increase in cost to the Exchequer for its contribution would have been offset in contributions paid by employers and employees. The distributional impact of such changes would depend on how the revenue is raised for the Exchequer contribution and how the reduction in the national insurance contributions was spread between employers and employees.

The commission to the Government Actuary would request the costing and measurement of the comprehensiveness of the major alterations to the national insurance scheme which are being proposed here and this will hopefully herald a clear debate on the future of insurance-based welfare for the first time since 1942.

One of the duties of the new stakeholder's insurance corporation would be to report on emerging needs which are likely to put major strains on the welfare system. As well as developing responses to greater flexibility in the labour market, an effective stakeholder insurance scheme must also respond to new demands which have little or nothing to do with changes in the functioning of the economy. The most important of these new issues centres on the simple fact that Britain's population is rapidly ageing. We now turn to look a how a new stakeholder insurance corporation might respond to this new need.

Care Pensions

It is true that, in contrast to many of our partners in Europe, the impact of this severe greying process on the population's profile is already well advanced. It is nevertheless expected to continue apace in the coming decades. While ageing is not the only factor influencing the demand for nursing and residential care (fast becoming one of the most costly items in the welfare budget), it is by far the most important. It has already led the Government to make what is likely to be the most significant alteration to the NHS since its inception in 1948. An assumption on which the Service is founded is that most of the care being offered would be short-term. It inherited the geriatric beds when the NHS was formed in 1948. But for decades this hospital population was fairly static. As the number of geriatric patients rose, the Government deflected the pressure on NHS budgets by allowing poor pensioners to be awarded additional supplementary benefit payments to cover the cost of residential care. As that bill exploded the Government, in true fashion, panicked, transferring the task of deciding who would qualify for assistance to local authorities. It cash-limited the budget after generously increasing it. Now the Government has issued guidelines laying down that the charges should be met where possible from beneficiaries. A free service has been transformed, almost without debate, into a means-tested one.

Calculating the level of care needed in 10, let alone 50 years' time, is fraught with difficulties. It is impossible to estimate what the impact of scientific advance might be in slowing down the ageing process, and then whether any such breakthroughs will further impact on human longevity.

It is, however, irrefutable that the likelihood of requiring nursing care increases with age. One way therefore of constructing a crude index of need is to take a cut-off point of 85 plus years, i.e., the onset of extreme old age. This will give us some idea of the size of the growth in that part of the population which will put most demands on nursing and residential care. Obviously younger groups of the population will similarly make such demands, but not in anything like the numbers that will come from the oldest group. For it is amongst this latter group that the numbers are projected to grow very rapidly. In 1991, for example, 881,000 pensioners were aged 85 or more. By the year 2021 it is estimated this total will have almost doubled to over 1.5 million and will double again to over 3 million thirty years later.

Over the immediate future in Britain the pattern of long-term care will change as a result of the Government's community care policy. There will be a contraction of private sector institutions, although this is likely to be far less than the reduction in what is called local authority Part III Accommodation. Here I would expect to see the 100,000 or so beds be rapidly reduced as local authorities assume the role of purchasing agents, rather than direct providers of services. It is, after all, another aim of the Government's community care strategy. This reduction will be matched by an increase in the amount of care given to a person while still at home. But there will still be a need for long-term residential care for very frail elderly people. What might the size of this need be?

The current community care legislation will reduce significantly the numbers in residential care. For the sake of trying to cost this sector in the future, let us assume that the numbers in residential care will fall to half the current level. This sector will then resume growing from this reduced level along with the rise in the numbers of the very elderly. As access to nursing home care for those on income support is judged on medical needs alone I have assumed that there will be no reduction in the numbers in this sector, and that the size of the market will grow in step with the increase in the over-85s. On this basis a bill of £2.4bn for 1991 will have risen (in 1991 prices) to £4.4bn by 2020 and will increase further to 8.3bn by 2051.

How might the cost of nursing home fees be met by individuals? We could assume that the new system now in operation will expand and local authority social services departments will be given the cash by taxpayers to meet the bill. That is not, I must add, a very likely scenario. An alternative and more realistic approach, given the record of this Government, is to consider ways of ensuring that all those in need of nursing home care have the money to meet the fees. How might these sums be met?

There are a number of alternatives which ought to be considered.

- Is the need for long-term care a risk which should be covered through the new stakeholder's insurance scheme?
- Should this risk be met by universal, targeted or means-tested benefit?
- What part might private insurance play in covering this risk?
- Should we be thinking of adapting private and company pension provision so that weighted payments are given to the oldest pensioners?
- What are the best ways of enabling pensioners to realise the capital to meet the costs of long-term care?

So far the private sector has made little headway in providing cover for people who may need to purchase long-term care. Very few pension schemes currently weight payments towards the very oldest members. Modest moves to allow greater choice in the holding of pensions capital and buying into annuities are contained in the Pensions Bill going through Parliament. On this basis, effort should be made to allow pension-fund owners to weight the payments of their pensions towards the end of their lives. Similarly, little headway has been made in unlocking housing capital as a means of meeting long-term care bills.

Action on each of these fronts is important. None of them should be dismissed from playing a part in building up a comprehensive coverage of need in this area. But if policy is limited to these areas alone the ability of people to gain the long-term care they require will, at best, be patchy.

Part of the immediate debate must therefore centre on wider provision. The key elements here are contained within the first two questions: should the risk of long-term care be met from the new stakeholder's insurance scheme or should it be targeted and means-tested?

As stated above, the number of very elderly pensioners aged 85 or more will rise over the next 50 years, from the current total of 881,000 plus to the three million mark. Most of the increase will occur after the Government begins implementing the decision to equalise age eligibility for the retirement pension at 65 for both men and women. This policy is to be phased in over the decade beginning in 2010. Savings will be in the order of £400m at first and rising to give a total saving on the annual pensions bill of £4bn by 2025. This total falls to £3bn a decade later. These data are in 1993–4 prices.

Here is a political opportunity for reform. The Right will argue that the savings should be used to provide tax cuts. The Centre Left in Britain have a chance again to make the case for universal benefit. Such use of savings from the social security budget is totally different from proposing tax increases. An increasingly ageing electorate will appreciate the need to channel such savings into universal long-term care provision.

There are two reasons why new care pensions should be universal rather than means tested. As a general principle I believe it is in society's interest that capital is saved and passed on within the family. An aim of government policy should be to increase, not to reduce, the number of families in the position to transfer capital. To link the care pension to income would require many old people to sell their homes rather than pass these assets on to their family, or to lie about their capital. There are already too many existing rules penalising thrift— or, as we have seen, encouraging dishonesty—to add yet another penalty. Moreover, central to *Making Welfare Work* is the contention that set, clearly defined increases in insurance contributions are a price that should be paid by a country that believes in seeing the family as the basis on which society is built. (The decision to fund a care pension will of course be made by the new National Insurance Corporation which will have to approve the expenditure and the contributions to pay for the reform.)

These arguments point conclusively to the introduction of a new insurance benefit—a care pension. A very large part of the cost could be financed from the savings generated by equalising the pension ages. The pension would be payable to people in need of residential or long-term nursing care. It should not be linked to age, but instead targeted to need. Payments should be triggered on the basis of a GP's recommendation, if confirmed by a DSS doctor.

Two other initiatives need to be linked to this new stakeholder insurance care pension. The first is to build on the invalidity care allowance so that it becomes a much more adequate income for carers. Despite the Government's trumpeting about initiating a community care policy, care has predominantly been carried out in the community and been provided by families. This major source of informal care should be strengthened and rewarded. Linked to this is a third initiative which is to continue to build towards a comprehensive system of respite care for the millions of people who bear the burden of full-time caring. New national initiatives here must learn the lessons of the pilot schemes which are already in operation and being backed by companies such as the Prudential.

How do the costs look for these proposals? The savings to public expenditure occurring during the first decade after 2021 from the equalisation of pension ages could more than pay for the additional cost of nursing home care, the cost of doubling in real terms the ICA and increasing significantly the available respite care. But these savings can in no way pay for the reforms before 2021, even though the demand for nursing home care will increase substantially over the next 25 years. And, more importantly, very significant growth in the very elderly in Britain after 2021 puts even greater pressure on the health and welfare budgets in the following decade.

Additional funds will be required both in the period leading up to the equalisation of pension ages and to add to the size of the budget after 2020. How might these funds be raised?

The national insurance system in Britain owes a great deal (although not everything) to the original development of the idea in Germany (E P Hennock, *British Social Reform and German Precedents*, Oxford, 1987). Again, it would be useful to look East for ideas. Despite the major economic problems associated with reunification, the German Parliament introduced, at the start of this year, new long-term care insurance. From January 1995, employers and employees pay an additional one per cent social security contribution, rising to 1.7 per cent in 1996, towards the cost of long-term care needs. The package of reform provides for:

- DM2010 per month (about £910, depending on the exchange rate) for those requiring hospital care and lower amounts for those requiring full-time or part-time home care.

- A substitute carer is provided for a four-week period while the carer has an annual break.

The new stakeholder insurance corporation would be charged with drawing up and costing a similar package of reform to that now in operation in Germany, together with changes proposed in the ICA and the provision of respite care. Attention would be paid to the ways in which any carer's holiday entitlement would affect the extent of need for respite care. Maximum flexibility should be built into the scheme with cash payments or packages of care being on offer. The corporation would be charged with reporting on the costs over time of such a scheme, the views of carer organisations and other interested bodies, and how different aspects of the reform might be phased in and funded.

Care pensions are certain to be an issue which grows in importance. Retirement pensions are already very much one of the big issues of welfare reform today. How can private pension provision best be universalised so that each of us draws a pension from at least two sources—from the stakeholder insurance fund as well as from a private source? Our discussion now turns to lifting the Left's key concept of universality, which has up until now been applied only to the provision of public services, and planting it firmly in the private sector.

The Stakeholder Corporation

Already some of the functions of the corporation have been touched upon. But how is this body to gain a legitimacy beyond being established by an Act of Parliament? Above all the corporation must be a truly independent body with a life and an agenda of its own. The Government will play a part in this, but only to the extent that contributions from taxpayers to the fund warrant this. The Government will, of course, retain the power of veto (but not initiation) on benefit and contribution rates. That statement sounds tougher than it probably will be in practice. The private negotiations and public discussions attached to the making of these decisions will usually pull parties together.

But how will the corporation be elected with a representation reflecting the contribution value of the constituent parts: employees, employers, self-employed and the Government? One way would be by indirect election. An alternative would be a much more direct form of representation. Indirect election will be the easiest to arrange and this could be the form at the establishment of the corporation. It will facilitate a quick advance in the scheme's working. Employer and small business organisations would be allotted the appropriate number of seats with trade union and staff organisations being similarly treated. The government would then fill its places with ministers and MPs.

Direct elections to the corporation could then be planned as a second stage. The three interests would seek to gain support from their various constituencies. But the form of the election would be different from a parliamentary or trade union election. The House of Commons would vote on the Government delegation to the corporation. All employers paying contributions, and not just those who are members of an employers' organisation, would need to be involved in choosing that group's delegation. The contributory record would become in effect the electoral register. There would similarly be a need to involve employee representation from beyond the trade unions and staff associations, and also for the election of a delegation from the self-employed. The contributory record would again act as the list of those eligible to vote. It is a fact, though, that the long-established organised groups in each of these three areas are going to be in very strong positions when it comes to seeking election. But as a subsidiary aim of the reform is to strengthen the role of non-governmental organisations in our democratic process there is a clear advantage in this happening.

It will be from the corporation's wider membership that the executive will be drawn to act as the governing body at its general meetings. This body would have a similar role to that given later to the Private Pensions Corporation's executive.

Private Pension Stakeholding

Even if Mrs Thatcher had not decoupled increases in the state retirement pension from either earnings or prices, taking whichever formula was the more favourable to pensioners, the status quo could not have held. Eight forces are placing increasing pressure on existing state pension provision. These are:

- The growing inadequacy of the basic state pension.
- The converging size of the economically active and inactive groups in society.
- The casualisation of working practices.
- The growth of numbers experiencing long-term unemployment.

- The rise in the number of full-time carers.
- The increase in the proportion of marriages breaking up.
- The reduction in the number of employees in each firm.
- The security of existing pension arrangements, given that employers no longer need to offer generous pension schemes in order to attract and retain employees.

Alternative Reforms

There are three major alternatives as far as reforming pensions is concerned. Two are not serious runners. The first needs only to be mentioned for it to be dismissed. It is to rebuild the State Earnings Related Pension Scheme. This approach has such major disadvantages attached to it that it is hardly worth considering. The impact on national insurance contributions would be substantial. Yet the increased contributions would not necessarily guarantee future benefits. SERPS is a pay-as-you-go scheme, with today's contributions paying for today's benefits. Moreover, the scheme has received such a political mauling since 1979 that it would be difficult to convince taxpayers—even if some politicians convinced themselves—that their benefit rights were secure. In addition, many taxpayers are likely to prefer to have pension guarantees spread over a pay-as-you-go scheme, as is the national insurance retirement pension funding, and a funded scheme which is completely independent of politicians' sticky fingers, as are the vast majority of occupational and private schemes.

What then are the other two alternatives? Again the first of these is hardly a serious option. The growing inequality in the income of pensioners stems from the partial provision of company and private pensions. The poorest pensioners are those dependent upon the national insurance pension and any supplementary income support. One way of preventing this inequality from spreading would be to make the provision of private pensions unlawful. Merely to state this alternative highlights its fundamental absurdity, quite apart from the undoubted impact which such a proposal would have on the Labour vote at the next election, should the Party ever be so foolish as to advocate such a scheme. Implicit in this approach, however, would be an attempt to persuade taxpayers either to agree to vote major tax increases to pay for increased national insurance benefits, or voluntarily to embrace such a policy.

There is a further objection to this approach. To rely solely on the state retirement pension or increasing tax rates to pay for higher pensions is out of step with the tempo of the time. This is no new phenomenon. Liberal ministers in the 1906 Government believed they faced such pressure from the electorate in respect of income tax rises, although at the time no working people paid income tax. Hence the attractiveness to the Cabinet of building up a national insurance fund (McBriar, 1987, 331).

Taxpayers are increasingly demanding a greater say in, and control over, the funds which they vote in taxation. Hence the attraction of the last alternative as far as major pension reform goes. This is to rely on private pension provision and to integrate this second tier of pensions into the stakeholder welfare concept. The only question left to consider is whether the securing of a second pension should be left to voluntary efforts of employers and employees, or whether compulsion should be used to ensure that everybody is in the scheme, and that both employers and employees make contributions.

The only way to guarantee universal coverage is to make the scheme compulsory and that is the approach advocated here. (For full details see Frank Field and Matthew Owen, *National Pensions Savings Plan*, Fabian Society, 1994.) The proposal is to compel, by law, every employee and self-employed person to become members of a private pension scheme. Already employees are covered either through a company or a private pension scheme. To say that this approach of universalisation of private pension provision is one which seeks to build on an existing success story underestimates how effective this non-state pension provision of welfare has been. *Private pension contributions already amount to a larger sum than that paid to cover the cost of the national insurance retirement pension, as can be seen in chart 7.1.*

Stakeholder's Private Pension Corporation

How could the universalisation of private pension provision come about? The first move would be to establish a legal framework which would ensure, over a set timescale, that every employee, employer and self-employed person would begin to make contributions towards adequate private pension cover. In other words, membership of a second scheme—running parallel to membership of the state pension scheme—would become compulsory. The task of implementing such a

DIAGRAM 7.1
Pension Contributions (Gross) (a)
Occupational, Personal & National Insurance
1992

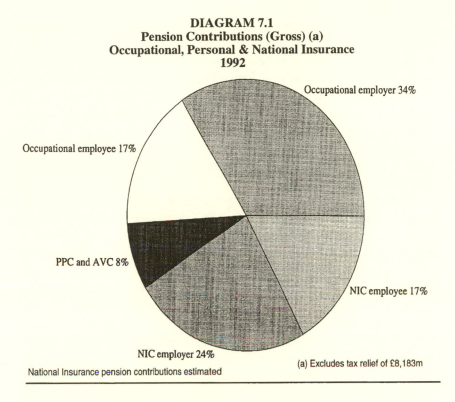

Occupational employer 34%

Occupational employee 17%

PPC and AVC 8%

NIC employee 17%

NIC employer 24%

National Insurance pension contributions estimated

(a) Excludes tax relief of £8,183m

programme would be allocated to a stakeholder's pension corporation which would operate alongside the corporation established to run the stakeholder's national insurance scheme.

The board's task would be fourfold. First, it would set the rate of contributions for employee and employer as the scheme envisages compulsory participation by both parties. Initially the contributions would be modest, but they would be progressively raised. Contribution rates during the build-up of the scheme would of course have to vary according to the age of the employee.

Second, the corporation would be given the task of ensuring that the current patch work of provision—covering company as well as personal pension schemes—is woven into a greater fabric of universal coverage. The aim is therefore not to destroy any of the existing provisions, but to integrate them into a broader provision. It is likely, however, that few if any new company pension schemes will be initiated in the present climate. Part of the pension debate must therefore be over what is best: a defined benefit scheme or more personal pension provision.

Third, the office of the new pensions regulator, to be established under the Pensions Bill slowly winding its way through Parliament, would be transferred to the corporation. The office would be transformed from the largely passive role envisaged in the Bill into a proactive agency determined to root out fraud and malpractice. The corporation would have a duty to report annually to Parliament on the adequacy of private pension provision as well as on the question of security of funds.

Fourth, the corporation would be charged with establishing a National Pensions Saving Scheme (for full details see Field and Owen, 1994). This proposal stems from one put forward by Joel Joffe. Responding to the original proposal for universalising private pension provision (Frank Field and Matthew Owen, *Private Pensions for All*, Fabian Society, 1993) Joel Joffe argued that the best way forward was to market through the National Savings Network a National Savings Personal Pension Plan (NSPPP) which would be sold on a money purchase basis and invested in gilt linked investment. The main advantages of such a scheme were as follows:

- The NSPPP could be linked to one or more index tracking funds (or specially created funds where no suitable index was available). Funds would cover the main range of sound investments including equities, and corporate bonds.
- In accordance with current government policy, administration and possibly the marketing of the NSPPP would be subcontracted on tender to the financial sector.
- When pensions became payable an open market option would be made available to enable pensioners to purchase annuities from the most competitive life companies. A minimum standard could be assured to a National Savings annuity.
- The basic NSPPP would be kept as simple as possible to meet the needs of the most unsophisticated investors, leaving it to the financial services companies to compete by offering more elaborate products including life assurance and other protection.

If contributors are asked about the kind of pension scheme in which they are investing considerable sums of money, the reply is usually that their pension scheme is a kind of savings scheme for their retirement provision. That belief should be capitalised upon and the saving mechanism should reflect what most people believe the scheme is about. Hence the name of the National Pension Savings Scheme. The National Pension Savings Scheme differs from Joel Joffe's proposal in that the scheme is compulsory if workers are not members of an alternative adequate private pension scheme. Adequacy would be defined initially in terms of minimum standards of disclosure, relative fund performance, client service and security and then, once the scheme is operative, in terms also of contribution levels.

There is, however, nothing particularly novel in this approach. The Commissioners on Friendly and Building Societies (1875) considered an idea that annuities should be sold through local post offices (William Beveridge, *Voluntary Action*, Allen & Unwin, 1948, 66–9). The collecting companies saw this as such a threat that they mobilised swiftly to kill the idea. They were only too successful.

By imposing universality the new scheme will assume some of the important characteristics and advantages of SERPS. The main difference from SERPS will be that the new scheme will be funded and that it will be independent of the state. This last aspect is vital. Huge sums will accrue into the national scheme. Decisions about investment will need to be independent of day-to-day political interference. Presumably, trustees will take into account the long-term needs of the British and European economies and in this sense will clearly act both economically and politically. In addition to these advantages the National Pension Savings Scheme has one further attraction for the Left. It is the only offer currently being discussed where new forms of collective provision, independent of the state, are being advocated.

This reform offers the Left a way out of the present cul-de-sac in which it finds itself. The National Pension Savings Scheme should be viewed as the first, hopefully, of a number of schemes where social and individual efforts are collectivised in a manner acceptable to voters. In this sense the National Pension Savings Scheme rejoins the debate which occurred earlier this century between the state collectivists, with the Webbs as the main protagonists, and the social collectivists, represented by the Bosanquets and Charles Loch. The state collectivists won that argument. The new front being opened up for the new millennium is designing forms of social or popular collectivism which are acceptable to the growing individualism of our times.

How will this new stakeholder corporation be elected and controlled? There will be two bodies in fact. The first will be the governing body of the NPSS. The second will be concerned with governing the Private Pensions Corporation. Just as the detailed calculations on the formula required to make the stakeholding insurance scheme comprehensive will have to await the Government Actuary's report, the proposals on the institutional arrangements of these new bodies—as with the Stakeholder National Insurance Corporation—are given here to initiate rather than preclude discussion.

The governing court of the NPSS's scheme could be elected from a constituency of all savers. The ballot could be distributed with the annual presentation of accounts and the details on the value of each saver's own deposit. From this general council an executive would be chosen to manage the NPSS business between annual meetings. The annual meeting could be given, in addition to the crucial powers of any annual meeting:

- responsibility to debate the long-term plans prepared on the NPSS's investment strategy and progress reports on the universalisation strategy of private pension provision.
- duty to draw attention to the emergence of trends which could affect the long-term stability of the scheme.

The executive would have the responsibility analogous to a board of directors of a public company.

The role the NPSS would play in the Private Pensions Corporation would depend on the success of the savings scheme in capturing a large part of the new savings resulting from this reform. The legal framework of the corporation will guarantee it independence from government interference (over and above the regulating role the government plays in setting the legal framework for any constituent body of the state). The corporation membership should reflect both the current institutional pension providers as well as the NPSS.

So the commission membership will be composed of representatives from company pension schemes and from those holding personal pensions as well as a delegation from the National Pensions Savings Scheme. In the first instance the National Association of Pension Funds would have the task of electing the delegation covering company pension schemes. The annual statement from the sellers of personal pensions would contain details of candidates standing for election from this constituency. Indeed the industry would have the responsibility of informing members each year how individuals can seek election. The corporation of the National Pension Savings Scheme, which itself will be elected from its membership, will elect its delegation to the Private Pensions Corporation.

There remain two issues which need to become part of the reform agenda. The first concerns that old chestnut, rent, which so effectively undermined Beveridge's original proposals. The second is the need to transform income support into a proactive form of welfare.

Rent Payments

Beveridge's aim was to ensure that everyone gained an income above what he defined as the poverty line. Chapter 3 set out why he failed to achieve this objective and *Making Welfare Work* argues that whatever the merits of this approach at that time, it is wrong for Britain as it approaches the millennium. Crucial to guaranteeing a poverty-line income was a benefits system which covered basic human needs, together with the costs of housing. Beveridge's failure to deal fully with the issue of rent is commented upon by his biographer Josie Harris. On Beveridge's proposals for a flat-rate benefit which included a notional 10 shillings for weekly rent, Josie Harris observed that Beveridge

> thus allowed himself to be struck with the paradoxical position that benefits should be based on subsistence needs and yet should be uniform for all parts of the country. This paradox was acknowledged in the Beveridge Report; but it was nevertheless seized upon in Government circles as an excuse for rejecting the principle of subsistence. In future years it was to prove a continuing Achilles heel in Beveridge's scheme for the elimination of means-tests and the abolition of primary poverty. (Josie Harris, *William Beveridge*, Oxford, 1977, 399)

Making Welfare Work has a different perspective. It is not about how best to guarantee everyone an income above an arbitrarily defined poverty line. Rather it is to gain a comprehensive stakeholder's insurance cover which, together with individual effort, raises substantially the income of benefit households. So housing costs are important to our discussions for different reasons than those in the Beveridge framework. Means tests trap people on to low incomes. They also reward the worse side of human character—giving larger benefits to those who lie about their income or household circumstances. How do we begin a policy of disengagement from this means-test strategy which currently is growing like Topsy?

The dramatic growth in the cost of housing benefit was detailed earlier. A budget of £201m in 1976–7 (£730m in 1993–4 prices) soared to £8.7bn by 1994–5. And, even with some major restrictions being placed on the benefit claims in 1995, it is expected to grow further to a total of around £12bn by the end of the century.

Part of this increase has been due to the Government's pig-headed drive to push up council rents in order to persuade more tenants to buy their own homes. The increase is also due to the pushing up of housing association rents, again at the Government's behest. But these two moves take no account whatsoever of the partial deregulation of private sector rents and the impact of this on housing benefit expenditure. Partial deregulation has occurred in that tenancies subject to rent control and assessment become decontrolled with the death of the tenant or by the tenant ceasing to occupy the property. In the place of controlled rents there has been a mushrooming of short-hold tenancies, whereby security is offered on a six-month basis, and rents are thereby usually agreed outside the rent officer's purview.

A breakdown of the housing benefit budget shows that within a rapidly rising total, the most significant increase has been in the cost of the subsidy to tenants in the private sector—from £27m in 1976–7 to £3.8bn in 1993–4. Wirral, the region which includes the seat which I represent, is a microcosm of what is happening nationally. In a five-year period, from 1990 to 1994, average payments of housing benefit for council tenants increased by 36 per cent, while the benefits payments to private tenancies rose by almost a multiple of four. The total payments of housing benefits in respect of private landlord housing benefit cases rose over the same period by 228 per cent, compared to only a 38 per cent increase in the number of private tenants claiming benefit.

The biggest gainers from the housing benefit scheme are clearly the private landlords. They know only too well how to work the system. Local rents are quickly pushed up towards the unofficial ceiling which the local authority sets in an attempt to counter spiralling housing costs. Housing benefit claimants have no interest in attempting to modify their landlords' rapacious demands. Why should they? The taxpayer pays by courtesy of the housing benefit office. The local rent officers report that where a private tenant is not on housing benefit a bargaining process takes place, with tenants offering, and landlords often accepting, a lower rent than would be gained from tenants making successful claims for housing benefit.

The efforts of all tenants need to be mobilised to this end. Two reforms are urgent. A new radical government should make a clear distinction between the housing benefit monies paid to cover council rents and local housing association rents on the one hand, and rents from the private sector on the other. The budget for council and housing association tenants should be index-linked to the rate of inflation. The rent increases in this sector which, as we have seen, have been pushed up often at a rate of two or three times the rate of inflation over the recent past, will only be covered for housing benefit purposes up to the inflation ceiling. Local authorities pushing rents above this level will find themselves on the receiving end of a backlash from tenants whose rents would no longer be covered in full.

A similar technique of mobilising the power of the tenants against landlords must be applied in the private sector. For all new tenancies, housing benefit should only cover a rent level linked to the appropriate council tax band. This new procedure would operate as old tenancies expired and new ones were offered to private tenants. To ensure that landlords gain a fair return on their property, rather than the exorbitant one which many of them currently do, it will be necessary for the multiple of the council tax band to be set at a reasonable level. Over time two initiatives will initially see a major reduction in the size and scope of housing benefit, and then a greater proportion of tenants being in the position to meet their rent without resorting to housing benefit.

The last issue we need to consider is how to transform income support into a proactive welfare agency.

A Proactive Benefits Agency

The current income support system exemplifies some of the worst aspects of the old Poor Law. Benefit is paid only on condition that claimants remain idle. It acts as a great depository for low-income groups. It does nothing but pay out benefit and occasionally check on fraud. It is not very good at either task. The Comptroller and Auditor General has qualified his audit opinion on each account since income support was introduced. While the present Secretary of State places a greater emphasis on tackling fraud than his predecessors have demonstrated, the DSS's approach is all too reminiscent of the English cricket team's attitude to winning test matches. The revolution which the Department has to undergo affects both of these activities.

Income support is paid through the Benefits Agency and it is this body's terms of reference which need to be radicalised so that it becomes a proactive body with two equal duties. The first should be to promote the welfare of claimants (dropped by the Tories from the legal requirements placed on the income support scheme) and, for those below retirement age, of helping each individual to construct exits from means-test welfare dependency. Income support must be re-shaped into a body which acts as a life raft taking people back into work.

Two groups would particularly benefit from this change of direction—quite apart from the long-suffering taxpayers who have been called upon to underwrite the Government's detachment of concern in this area. Some tentative moves are being made in this direction through the introduction of the Job Seeker's Allowance. From April 1996 the already inadequate national insurance coverage for the unemployed will be reduced still further. Twelve months' entitlement to benefit will be halved. Moreover, any adult dependant's additions will be means tested from day one and the whole allowance for the unemployed person becomes means tested after six months. At this point the Restart interviews begin to take place.

These interviews of both unemployed claimants on Job Seeker's Allowance, or the vast majority of unemployed claimants on income support, should begin very shortly after the first registration of unemployment. The Government's proposal for the signing of Job Seeker's Agreements should be backed up with offers of work. The best way of achieving this end is for the Government to make it compulsory for employers to register all long-term appointments with Jobcentres. It is these Centres which would act as the hub of activity where officials and claimants will undertake to ensure a much quicker return to work. The introduction of job banks (Frank Field, Liam Halligan and Matthew Owen, 1994) linking all Jobcentres and other public bodies, such as post offices, into this national computer network recording all job vacancies, will help maximise claimants' chances of finding work whilst strengthening the hands of officials rooting out benefit fraud.

Merely to raise the issue of Jobcentres, however, puts on the agenda the need to redraw departmental boundaries so that the services are coherently delivered to claimants. Present departmental boundaries do not reflect the most effective means of pursuing public policy objectives. The responsibility for training and training budgets should be part of a revamped Education Department, giving this department a greater emphasis on the need for people to have skills to make them employable in a flexible labour market. The benefit functions of the Department of Employment should be part of a much reformed Department of Social Security. One outcome of such a change would be to remove one seat at an already over-crowded Cabinet table.

The Job Seeker's Allowance should be converted from what the Government clearly envisages it to be—yet another mechanical test of whether a claimant is actively seeking work—into a personalised programme of building skills, opening up job opportunities and the beginning of career prospects for today's claimants. Such a change cannot be ushered in overnight, not least because of the existing skills of the DSS's own staff, which themselves need to be radically developed for this new role.

A similar approach should be offered to single mothers. Each claimant should be required to draw up, with the help of their family and friends, together with departmental officials, an outline of their long-term job aspirations. The Department's response to this must be to ensure that relevant education and training courses are available for single mothers to join as soon as they wish. Mothers should not be left alone by the DSS until their children are approaching the age of 16, which is the current policy. Benefit entitlement for those mothers who seek to combine claiming benefit with undertaking education or skill courses would not be affected. Indeed the rules for disallowing claimants from gaining skills and educational qualifications while drawing benefit should be radically overhauled.

No claimants should be prevented from attending a further education course by threats of the loss of benefit. Indeed they should be encouraged to do so. Benefit entitlement would also remain for claimants who secure a place in higher education, provided they have been on benefit for two years or more. The two-year rule is important. The Filofax families would be quick to spot an opening. Young people leaving A-level courses at school or sixth-form colleges would quickly be put on benefit by their parents if the latter thought that such a move would result in their offspring automatically claiming income support for the duration of their university courses. But all other claimants who have been out of education for two or more years, and who are not disqualified from benefit (by leaving their last job without good cause, for example), should have the right to convert their benefit payments into educational maintenance allowances.

The thought of a university course is not something which many single mothers currently entertain. For many of them there is a need to gain the most basic skills in numeracy and literacy. It is here that a new proactive Benefits Agency would be concerned with raising the basic skills of children on income support, as well as of their parents. One or two experiments are already under way which bring parents, often the single mother, into school to help with their child's education. In so doing not only does the child benefit, but the mother herself also begins to acquire those skills which eluded her during 11 years of compulsory state education. The acquisition of these skills then opens up a new range of possibilities for poor parents on benefit, particularly single mothers.

Making Welfare Work means making work accessible. That means opening new routes back into education, training and employment. Pressure on resources means we have to put what is already available in the community to the fullest use. One of the cheapest and most effective strategies—and one which crosses the divide between social and educational policies—would be to put the resources and facilities of schools to better use. This is already beginning to happen. Many schools still offer a wide range of activities before and after school and in the holidays for children of all abilities. The 'added value' of organised after-school programmes is now being recognised and monitored for the first time by Education Extra, a new educational charity, which is also working with schools to develop a new generation of after-school programmes. The aim is, quite simply, to bring after-school activities within the reach of every child as part of a national strategy for raising achievement and enabling *families* to learn and earn. Universalising this policy will transform what can be expected from claimants in undertaking training courses and seeking work.

Schools have another vital role to play in helping families find and keep work. Alongside the need to provide pre-school childcare, children of school age also need care and supervision. As part of the Out of School Childcare Initiative (begun in April 1993), hundreds of new after-school clubs are now opening in primary (and some secondary) schools all over the country. But they are slow to grow simply because parents need proof that they are there to stay. That trust must be there before parents will contemplate taking a child away from a childminder, however inadequate, and before a mother will consider extending part-time work, taking up training or looking for work.

These childcare initiatives should be viewed in conjunction with the Child Support Agency's operation. The Agency is beginning to function and it will over time underwrite a reasonable part of the income support payments of a growing proportion of single mothers. The current public agitation over the Treasury gaining practically all of the enforced maintenance payments misses the point. The non-payment of such allowances has landed the taxpayer with a 4p in the pound income tax bill. The vast majority of maintenance payments cover only part of the taxpayers' bill for single parents on income support. But once the maintenance payments become regular, mothers will know that it is a secure income floor on to which they can add any income from work. With the education reforms advocated here, and the duty of single mothers to start training courses once there is the certainty of care for their older school children during working hours, a constructive attack on welfare dependency can begin in earnest.

Beating Fraud

The revamped Benefits Agency also needs to be much more proactive in its campaign against fraud. The chapter "Social Insecurity" detailed the main areas of claimant fraud: working on the side while claiming benefit, cohabiting, fictitious desertions as well as working full-time and claiming benefit. The different policy responses to each of these frauds have been detailed earlier. A strategy also needs to be developed to counter the fraud committed by officers of the DSS who fake claims for benefit and protect their fraud from the flimsy audit to which the Department currently subjects claims for benefit. Similarly, the attack on the DSS by organised gangs of criminals, not merely stealing whole tranches of order books, but creating identities for long-term benefit claims for whole groups of people who do not exist, needs to be met effectively by the Department. There needs to be an SAS-type core of officers countering fraud.

In addition the Benefits Agency should have the prime responsibility of co-ordinating central government and local authority anti-fraud campaigns as well as the very important fraud of housing benefit organised by landlords or their agents. An effective anti-fraud drive, employing highly-qualified, highly intelligent and highly paid staff, would bring a bonus to taxpayers of not merely hundreds of millions of pounds as at present, but of literally billions of pounds in saved benefit.

New Demands

The last task which would be allotted to a proactive Benefits Agency is the duty of reporting on the emergence of new trends of dependency. The growth of single mothers went undetected and therefore unreported for far too long. Even now political correctness in the media shields voters from being told how worrying the composition of single-parent families is. Similarly, the growing failure to seek and enforce maintenance orders for single parents on benefit was largely ignored by politicians and the media alike. As we have seen, the result of this silence led to a near-collapse of maintenance payments for single mothers on benefit and an escalating bill for taxpayers. For politicians to have been regularly reminded by the Income Support Agency of this new trend could have resulted in counter-action which would have made the hasty and ill-thought-out introduction of the Child Support Agency unnecessary.

Taking the Debate to the Country

The Canadian Government has embarked upon a reconstruction of its country's social security system. A new department of Human Resources Development has been established and covers the remit of the Departments of Social Security, Employment and part of Education. It brings together other responsibilities for improving the long-term job prospects of Canadians. The Canadian Government's first ideas on how social security changes can underpin its jobs and growth strategy were contained in a detailed discussion paper.

At the same time as unveiling its outline proposals for reform the Canadian Government gave details of a three stage process of consultation. The original timetable was for the first stage to take place in Parliament. Here the Human Resources Development standing committee held public hearings on the social security and labour market issues affecting the reform. The second stage involved consultations and analyses of the issues involved, both by the committee in Parliament and by MPs in their constituencies. The third and final stage involved the development, lobbying and debates on the legislation itself.

The remit of *Making Welfare Work* is broader than that set by the Canadian Government. It is about a social security strategy which both responds to and underpins an increasingly flexible labour market, while at the same time recognising the need to enhance those altruistic aspects of welfare which have played an important part in developments in this country. Where *Making Welfare Work* does concur with the Canadian experiment is on the need for as open and wide a debate as possible. *Making Welfare Work* proposes a clear alternative for restructuring welfare over the foreseeable future and beyond the millennium.

Britain's present welfare system has the worst of both worlds; it is broken-backed yet its costs escalate. In its efforts to support it actually restrains the citizen, offering disincentives rather than incentives, and educating people only about the need to exploit the system. *Making Welfare Work* proposes a restructuring which brings into a central drive position the role of self-interest and self-improvement. Its aim is to help individuals create freer and more fulfilled lives. Fifty years after the efforts of the Coalition and post-war Labour Governments it is crucial for Britain to recommence the massive task of welfare's reconstruction.

Bibliography

Averting the Old Age Crisis (World Bank, 1994)

Balls, Edward, *Work and Welfare: Tackling the Jobs Deficit* (IPPR, 1993)

Beveridge, William, *Social Insurance and Allied Services* (Cmd 6404, HMSO, 1942)

    The Problem of Pensions (Beveridge papers, 1942)

    Full Employment in a Free Society (Allen & Unwin, 1994)

    Basic Problems of Social Security with Heads of the Scheme (Beveridge papers, 1942)

    Voluntary Action (Allen & Unwin, 1948)

    Power and Influence (Hodder & Stoughton, 1953)

Booth, Charles, 'The inhabitants of the Tower Hamlet School Board Division', *Journal of the Royal Statistical Society*, vol. L, 1887

Bowley, A L, *The Nature and Purpose of the Measurement of Social Phenomena* (P & S King, 1923)

Bradshaw, Jonathan, and Lynes, Tony, *Benefit Upratings: Policy and Living Standards* (SPRU, 1995)

Braithwaite, William J, *Lloyd George's Ambulance Wagon* (Methuen, 1957)

Briggs, Asa, *Seebohm Rowntree* (Longmans, Green, 1961)

Brown, Joan, *A Policy Vacuum* (Joseph Rowntree Foundation, 1992)

Bullock, Alan, *Bevin*, vol. 2 (Heinemann, 1967)

Collini, Stephan, 'The idea of "character" in Victorian thought', *Transactions of the Royal Historical Society*, 35, 1985

Deacon, Alan, 'An end to the means-test?', *Journal of Social Policy*, 1982

    Re-reading Titmuss: Moralism, Work and Welfare, (University of Leeds Review, vol. 36, 1993–4)

DSS, *Households Below Average Income: A Statistical Analysis 1979–1991/2* (HMSO, 1994)

Employment Policy (White Paper, Cmd 6527, HMSO, 1944)

Field, Frank, *Poverty and Politics* (Heinemann, 1982)

    What Price a Child? (Policy Studies Institute, 1985)

    'Moore gives the trade unions a chance to steal the ball', *Sunday Times*, 16 October 1988

    'Employment Audits' in *The Full Employment Seminar* (Prudential, 1995)

    and Owen, Matthew, *Private Pensions for All* (Fabian Society, 1993)

    and Owen, Matthew, *National Pensions Savings Plan* (Fabian Society, 1994)

    and Matthew Owen, *Beyond Punishment: Hard Choices on the Road to Full Employability* (Institute of Community Studies, 1994)

    and Owen, Matthew/Halligan, Liam, *Europe Isn't Working* (ICS, 1994)

    and Gregg, Paul, *Who Gets What, How, and For How Long?* (Mimeograph, 1994)

Gilbert, Bentley, *The Evolution of National Insurance in Great Britain* (Michael Joseph, 1966)

Goodman, Alissa, and Webb, Steve, *For Richer For Poorer* (Institute of Fiscal Studies, 1994)

Green, David G, *Reinventing Civil Society* (IEA, 1992)

Gregg, Paul, 'Share and Share Alike', *New Economy*, Spring 1994 (IPPR)

Harris, Josie, *William Beveridge* (Oxford, 1977)
   'The Social Thought of William Beveridge', paper given at University of Edinburgh, 1982
   'The Webbs, the COS and the Ratan Tata Foundation' in *The Goals of Social Policy*, ed. M Bulmer, J Lewes and D Piachaud (Unwin Hyman, 1989)
   'Victorian values', *Proceedings of the British Academy*, 1992

Hasky, John, 'Estimated numbers of one-parent families and their prevalence in Great Britain in 1991', *Population Trends*, 78 (1994)

Hennock, E P, 'Poverty and social thought in England', *Social History*, January 1976
   British Social Reform and German precedence (Oxford, 1987)
   'Concepts of poverty in the British social surveys from Charles Booth to Arthur Bowley', in *The Social Survey in Historical Perspective 1880–1940*, ed. M Bulmer, K Bayles and C Cishklar (CUP, 1991)

Holman, Bob, *A New Deal for Social Welfare* (Lion, 1993)

Improvements in National Assistance (Cmnd 782, HMSO, 1959)

Lynes, Tony, *National Assistance and National Prosperity* (Codicote Press, 1962)
   'Making of the Unemployment Assistance Scale' in *Low Incomes*, Supplementary Benefit Administration Paper 6 (HMSO, 1977)

Maclagen, Ianthe, *Four Years Serve Hardship* (Youthaid and Barnardos, 1993)

Marshall, T H, *Citizenship and Class* (Pluto Press, 1992)

Marwick, A, *Britain in the Century of Total War* (Bodley Head, 1968)

McBriar, A M, *An Edwardian Mixed Doubles* (Oxford, 1987)

Muirhead, J H, *By What Authority?* (P S King & Son, 1909)
   Reflections by a Journeyman in Philosophy (Allen & Unwin, 1942)

One Parent Families, Report by Commission on (Cmnd 5629, HMSO, 1974)

Pilkington, Peter, 'Morality in a society without an agreed system of values', *Seek Ye First the Gospel* (St Mary's Bourne Street, 1992)

Rose, Richard, and Davies, Phillip L, *Inheritance in Public Policy* (Yale University Press, 1994)

Rowntree, B S, *Poverty: The Study of Town Life* (Macmillan, 1902)

Simey, T S and M B, *Charles Booth* (Oxford, 1960)

Social Insurance (White Paper, Cmd 6550, HMSO, 1944)

Social Security Select Committee, *Low Income Statistics*, House of Commons Paper 359 (HMSO, 1992)
   Low Income Statistics and Low Income Families 1989–92, House of Commons Paper 254 (HMSO, 1995)

Titmuss, R M, *The Gift Relationship* (Allen & Unwin, 1970)

Townsend, Peter, and Abel Smith, Brian, *The Poor and the Poorest* (Bell & Co., 1965)

Veit Wilson, John, 'Paradigms of poverty: a rehabilition of B S Rowntree', *Journal of Social Policy*, 1986
   'Condemned to deprivation' in *Beveridge and Social Security*, ed. J Hills, J Ditch and H Glennerster (Oxford, 1994)

Wann, Mai, *Building Society Capital* (IPPR, 1995)

Webb, Beatrice, *My Apprenticeship* (Longmans, Green, 1942)

Webb, Sidney, 'Lord Rosebery's Escape from Houndsditch', *The Nineteenth Century*, (September 1901)

Wright, Andrew, and Plant, Raymond, *Philosophy, Politics and Citizenship* (Blackwell, 1984)

Young, G M, *Portrait of an Age* (Oxford, 1977)

Index